TRANSFORMATIONAL JOURNEYS: AN ETHNOLOGIST'S MEMOIR

TRANSFORMATIONAL JOURNEYS: AN ETHNOLOGIST'S MEMOIR

Victoria R. Bricker

American Philosophical Society Press
Philadelphia • 2017

Transactions of the
American Philosophical Society
Held at Philadelphia
For Promoting Useful Knowledge
Volume 106, Part 5

Library of Congress Cataloging-in-Publication Data

Names: Bricker, Victoria Reifler, 1940- author.
Title: Transformational journeys : an ethnologist's memoir / Victoria R.
    Bricker.
Description: Philadelphia, PA : American Philosophical Press, 2017. |
Includes bibliographical references and index. |
Identifiers: LCCN 2017008925 (print) | LCCN 2017011718 (ebook) |
    ISBN 9781606180679 (ebook) | ISBN 9781606180655 (alk. paper)
Subjects: LCSH: Bricker, Victoria Reifler, 1940- | Ethnologists—United
    States—Biography. | Mayas.
Classification: LCC GN21.B66 (ebook) | LCC GN21.B66 T73 2017
    (print) | DDC 305.80092 [B] —dc23
LC record available at https://lccn.loc.gov/2017008925

For Susan Milbrath and Consuela Reifler,
who thought there was a tale to be told.

And for Harvey M. Bricker, who shared many
of the journeys that broadened the scope of our scholarly
lives.

CONTENTS

Preface   xiii

1. Hong Kong: Where It All Began   1
2. Shanghai: Life Under Japanese Occupation   11
3. Seattle: Becoming an American   31
4. Stanford and Germany: My First Encounter with Anthropology   45
5. Harvard and France: Becoming an Ethnologist   79
6. Chiapas: Exploring Maya Humor   111
7. Tulane: Seeking the Antecedents of Maya Myth and Ritual   139
8. Elut: Teaching and Preserving the Maya Language   159
9. Yucatan: Relating the Maya Present to Its Past   183
10. Colonial Documents: The Past Speaks in Maya   223
11. Moving Back in Time: Reading Maya Hieroglyphs   237
12. Historical Astronomy: Maya Records of the Sky   249
13. Katrina: Aftermath of a Disaster   273
14. Retirement: No, It Was Not the End of the World   291
15. Looking Back   309

Index   315

ILLUSTRATIONS

1.1. The Brown family in London. *Back, left to right*: Lilly, Mendel, Annie, Henrietta. *Front*: Millicent.

1.2. "The Three Graces." *Left to right*: Lilly, Millicent, Henrietta.

1.3. The Reifler family in Vienna. *Left to right*: Joschia, Erwin, Viktoria, Bernhard, Dorothy.

1.4. In front of my grandparents' shop in Vienna: Bernhard is in the center, and Erwin is on the right.

1.5. My parents' engagement portrait.

2.1. The form filled out by my mother upon entering the "Civil Assembly Centre" on Yu Yuen Road with Victoria and Frank on March 25, 1943.

2.2. Copy of the document authorizing my father to visit my mother, brother, and me in the "Civil Assembly Centre" on Yu Yuen Road on August 23, 1943.

2.3. The letter documenting our release from the "Civil Assembly Centre" on Yu Yuen Road on June 24, 1944.

2.4. Victoria with "Boy" after the Second World War (1945). Photo by Erwin Reifler.

4.1. Fasching in Rottweil in February 1960. Photo by Victoria R. Bricker.

4.2. Beside a dancing bear in Salonika. *Left to right*: Ann Cilley, Suzan Behrman, Victoria.

4.3. May Day in Berlin. *Left to right*: Erika Bauer, Ann Cilley, Victoria, Günther (an East Berliner), Suzan Behrman.

5.1. Our wedding portrait.

5.2. Our home on the Bouyssou farm in Lespinasse.
Photo by Harvey M. Bricker.

5.3. At dinner on the SS *United States* on our way to Europe in August 1968.

6.1. The Harvard Jeep returns from Merida over the Pichucalco road.
Photo by Harvey M. Bricker.

6.2. A house in the hamlet of Nabenchauc like the one belonging to the parents of the Second Regidor.
Photo by Victoria R. Bricker.

7.1. The sinkhole outside Carrillo Puerto where the Talking Cross first appeared.
Photo by Harvey M. Bricker.

7.2. The open chapel near the sinkhole outside Carrillo Puerto.
Photo by Harvey M. Bricker.

7.3. The church in Carrillo Puerto built for the Talking Cross in 1858.
Photo by Harvey M. Bricker.

8.1. Elut walking down Freret Street near Tulane in New Orleans.

8.2. Elut and Ofelia collecting plants on the outskirts of Hocaba.
Photo by Anne Bradburn.

8.3. A botanical specimen identified by Ofelia and classified by Anne Bradburn.

8.4. Elut and Ofelia conversing with a shopkeeper in Hocaba.
Photo by Anne Bradburn.

8.5. At the recognition ceremony for the Maya dictionary in January 1999. *Left to right*: Alba Isela Aguilar de Marrufo, Elut, Victoria, Valerio Canché Yah.
Photo by Harvey M. Bricker.

8.6. Elut's obituary in a Merida newspaper.

9.1. The church in Ebtun.
      Photo by Harvey M. Bricker.
9.2. Entrance crosses on the outskirts of Ebtun.
      Photo by Victoria R. Bricker.
9.3. A map of Ebtun. Drawing by Harvey M. Bricker.
11.1. Arranging glyphs on an illustration.
11.2. "Bigfoot" cartoon.
11.3. Offering glyphs in the rain-making almanac on pages 29b–30b
      of the Dresden Codex.
      After the second edition of *Códices mayas*, by J. Antonio Vil-
      lacorta C. and Carlos A. Villacorta, pages 68, 70. Guatemala,
      Tipografía Nacional. 1976.
12.1. The initial series and calendar round on Stela M at Copan,
      Honduras.
      After *Archaeology Biologia Centrali-Americana*, by A. P. Maud-
      slay, Vol. 1, Plate 74. London. 1889–1902.
12.2. Animals representing constellations in the zodiacal almanac on
      pages 23 and 24 of the Paris Codex.
12.3. Summer solstice pictures in the Venus table and almanac in
      the Dresden Codex. a. D.46a. b. D.32c.
      After the second edition of *Códices mayas*, by J. Antonio Vil-
      lacorta C. and Carlos A. Villacorta, pages 76, 102. Guatemala,
      Tipografía Nacional. 1976.
12.4. The hieroglyphic text on the façade of the Governor's Palace at
      Uxmal, Yucatan, Mexico.
      Drawing by Harvey M. Bricker.
13.1. Refrigerator graffiti.
      Photos by Harvey M. Bricker.
13.2. A house in the Lower Ninth Ward that had floated off its foun-
      dations and come to rest on an overturned truck.
      Photo taken by Harvey M. Bricker in January 2006, three
      months after the storm.

Cover: The Dance of the Pig's Head on June 13, 1979, in Ebtun,
with the *ramillete* in the background.

PREFACE

It is only because of the unusual circumstances of my earliest years in a scholarly family in China during the Second World War and the impact they had, directly or indirectly, on my intellectual odyssey that I have decided to write a memoir of my life. In it, I have emphasized how and why I became the kind of ethnologist I am. An ethnologist is an anthropologist who has an inclusive, multifaceted view of human behavior, encompassing the past as well as the present and the language as well as the culture in his or her purview. The past can be documented in oral traditions, written historical documents, or, in some cases, with archaeological data. The present is usually documented with fieldwork, employing the method known as *participant-observation*, with the ethnologist taking part in the life of the community and in that way achieving a deeper understanding of the culture and the nuances of the language. Participant-observation is often supplemented by informal, or open-ended oral interviewing, a technique I have also employed in my efforts to understand the cultures and languages of the people among whom I have lived and worked over the course of my life.

This memoir documents how I moved from an interest in humor to a focus on linguistics, on the one hand, and on ethnohistory, on the other, which led in turn to an interest in Maya hieroglyphs, followed by a thirty-year preoccupation with ancient astronomy. It chronicles the journeys, both physical and intellectual, that have given meaning and direction to my life.

I kept no diaries during my formative years, and the only journals I produced covered the six months I spent in Germany during my sophomore year in college and the two months in an internship program in a mental hospital in California during the summer after I graduated from college. Therefore, a memoir is a strange undertaking for me. I have written it at the insistence of a friend and one of my sisters that I had a tale that should be told.

Ethnologists are expected to keep field notes in which they describe the culture and language of the people they study. It took me some time to learn how to take useful field notes, and for this reason, my early field notes from Chiapas were dry, technical accounts of material culture. By the late 1970s, my field notes had become more informative, and those from then on are more appropriate for a memoir.

When I began learning about Mayan hieroglyphs, the ideas came so thick and fast that recording them on loose sheets of paper became unwieldy, and I decided to keep an intellectual journal in which I recorded what I was thinking about on a daily or weekly basis. Even then, I found myself writing up the same ideas weeks or months later, having forgotten that I had already trodden on the same paths. Eventually, as my ideas crystallized or as some were abandoned, I stopped keeping such a journal, but spent my time developing the better ideas into articles.

Thus, my memoir is largely based on sources other than diaries and journals, including letters to and from friends and members of my family, photo logs that provide a chronology of my travels, visas and dates stamped in passports, the prefaces of my books, transcriptions of tapes recorded in the field, official documents, my curriculum vitae and annual reports at Tulane, family records and photographs, and, of course, my memories of events that made the greatest impression on me. I also benefited from discussing with my husband, Harvey, the many experiences we have shared during the past fifty-two years. His keen eye for geographic details has been invaluable for situating events accurately in space.

This memoir has also benefited from the input of several other people. First of all, I am grateful to my brother, Frank Reifler, for reading the chapters on our experiences in China and commenting on the accuracy of my description of our lives there. Second, I appreciate the willingness of my good friend and colleague, the botanist Anne Bradburn, to read the chapter concerning our ethnobotanical research in Yucatan, as well as other chapters on that region, and her helpful suggestions for improving the quality of my prose. Third, I am deeply indebted to my good friend and mentor, Anthony Aveni, to whom I turned for advice on the best way to focus my memoir. It was he who guided me in what to expand and what to condense, so that the narrative would flow more smoothly. And fourth, I am grateful to my good friend and colleague, Susan Milbrath, for urging me to write this memoir and later suggesting ways of fine-tuning it so that it would be a more interesting and more coherent read.

Finally, I would like to acknowledge the assistance of Pamela Lankas in shepherding me through the editorial and technical aspects of transforming my manuscript into a published book. In particular, I appreciate her willingness to adjust her normal procedures to accommodate my skills in working with digital files. It was a real pleasure to work with such a competent and cooperative editor.

1

HONG KONG: WHERE IT ALL BEGAN

I was born in the Matilda Hospital on the Peak in Hong Kong on June 15, 1940, the day after Paris fell to the Germans during World War II. The news of the fall of Paris came as such a shock to my mother, an Englishwoman from London, that she went into labor and delivered me the next day, a month before the predicted date of my birth.

I was named "Victoria" after my paternal grandmother, Viktoria Zentner Reifler, who had died three years before, and also because my parents hoped that this name would presage victory for the Allied forces that were locked in mortal combat with the German army in Europe.

In those days, the lying-in period for women and their newborns in hospitals was two weeks. During that period, the Japanese army had reached the outskirts of Canton, and the Hong Kong authorities wanted all women and children to leave the island before the Japanese arrived. Accordingly, when my mother and I left the hospital, we went directly to a ship in the harbor, where we were joined by my grandmother, who had come down from Shanghai after my birth, and my father's sister, who was also living in Hong Kong. The ship took us to Shanghai, where my mother's parents were living. My father joined us there a few months later. My mother never returned to her home in Hong Kong.

How did my parents come to live in Hong Kong? My mother, Henrietta Brown Reifler, was born in London in 1917 (Figure 1.1). Her father, the Reverend Mendel Brown, was a Jewish pastoral minister catering to the needs of his congregation, rather than a rabbinical scholar, because he was ordained in a Jewish seminary, rather than in a Yeshiva (a rabbinic school). Such graduates were known as *ministers of religion* in England.[1]

Among my grandfather's pastoral duties was serving as the guardian of Jewish boys from Iraq, India, and Singapore, whose parents had sent them to England for their education. Apparently, these boys spoke well of my grandfather when they returned to their home countries. Word of him reached the ears of members of the Sephardi community in Shanghai, many of whom had originally come from Iraq, and he was invited to come to Shanghai to serve as their rabbi. He accepted this invitation and left London for Shanghai in 1932. My grandmother joined

FIGURE 1.1   The Brown family in London. *Back, left to right*: Lilly, Mendel, Annie, Henrietta. *Front*: Millicent.

him one year later, leaving my mother and her two younger sisters behind in London with relatives to continue with their education.

When my mother graduated from high school in 1935 at the age of 18, she decided that she and her sisters should join their parents in Shanghai because her youngest sister was not faring well without their mother (Figure 1.2). Thus began one of the great adventures of my mother's life. After crossing the English Channel in the company of two of their aunts, they traveled overland as far as Venice, where their aunts bade them goodbye after seeing them board a ship. At Port Said, they were met by their father's brother, who came down from Jerusalem by train to spend four hours with them, before returning to his job in the British administration of Palestine. Then the ship took them through the Suez Canal and around India. In Bombay, Singapore, and Hong Kong, before arriving in Shanghai, they were met and entertained by friends of their father.

FIGURE 1.2 "The Three Graces." *Left to right*: Lilly, Millicent, Henrietta.

My father, Erwin Reifler, was born in Vienna in 1903 (Figure 1.3). His father, Joschia Reifler, was a soldier in the Austro-Hungarian army, rising to the rank of corporal before being honorably discharged from military service. After driving a streetcar in Vienna for a while, he established a business selling and repairing bicycles, sewing machines, and gramophones. The family lived in a two-room apartment over the shop (Figure 1.4).

My father was a good student and attended a *Gymnasium*, the Austrian equivalent of high school, and later the University of Vienna. In a letter to a cousin, written in 1939, he explained how he became interested in the Japanese and Chinese languages, which eventually led to his presence in China:

> [I]f I had not been romantic, I would never have thought of studying Chinese and Japanese, and I would never have got to the Far East. As a boy some nineteen or twenty years ago a girl friend of my sister lent her a book by

FIGURE 1.3   The Reifler family in Vienna. *Left to right*: Joschia, Erwin, Viktoria, Bernhard, Dorothy.

Bernhard Kellermann entitled "Japanische Tänze" (Japanese dances), which I also read after her. It caused in me a romantic storm and on the following day I was the lucky possessor of a Japanese and a Chinese Grammar, which I had purchased from my pocket money. The following time I used to sit in my study in Vienna and day-dream of far-off countries, nations and languages. I decided that one day I was to go to Japan and China. Two or three years later having graduated from high-school, I entered Vienna University, where I found a young countryman of mine who for 12 years had been studying Japanese, and for one year I worked with him. At the end of this year I was convinced, that I had to study Chinese first, if I ever wanted to master Japanese, because the Japanese use the same Chinese characters, and their whole old Literature is Chinese. About this time the former Austrian Minister to China, the Baron a. v. Rosthorn, having returned to Austria in 1917 on account of the declaration of war by China against the Middle-European countries, was made Professor of Chinese at the University, and I registered for his lectures from the very first day. Soon I became his best student and he started to teach me privately. Later I was for three years Librarian in his Chinese Library. I then met many Chinese students and became a honorary member of the Chinese Student's Club. Before I had finished my studies at Vienna University I was invited to Berlin and became

FIGURE 1.4 In front of my grandparents' shop in Vienna: Bernhard is in the center, and Erwin is on the right.

editor of the Chinese News Agency for Europe there, member of several Chinese Government travelling Committees for the study of organization and administration. Three years later I returned to Vienna and graduated as a Doctor of Political Science. Then I went to China at long last, where I first became an assistant to the foreigner advisor of the Municipality of Greater Shanghai, and three months later was appointed Professor at Chiaotung-University.[2]

My father received his doctoral degree in 1931 and went to China in 1932, the same year that my mother's father arrived in Shanghai.

By the time my mother and her sisters arrived in Shanghai in 1935, my father was offering a class in Chinese for foreigners, in addition to his courses at Chiaotung University. His class provided an opportunity for my mother and the older of her two sisters to learn the language of the country in which they had recently taken up residence. My mother was fascinated by his skill as a teacher. According to her, "he had developed a mnemonical approach to coping with Chinese characters, breaking them into their elements and telling stories about them." This was the context that brought them together in Shanghai.

By 1936, it had become apparent to my father that Hitler would soon be invading Austria, and he persuaded his mother and his sister, Dorothy, to join him in Shanghai (his father having died earlier the same year). His mother died a few months after her arrival in Shanghai. According to my mother,

> when in August 1937 the Sino–Japanese War broke out, he and Dorothy were on a Blue Funnel cruise to Japan. On their return to Shanghai, they found themselves in the middle of a shooting match on the river so that the boat could not dock and proceeded on to Hong Kong. Once there, he decided not to return to Shanghai. He found there was great interest in his ideas on the development of the Chinese writing system. A number of government officials, including the police chief, enrolled in his classes.

After my father moved to Hong Kong, he kept in touch with my mother through correspondence. In August 1939, he came up to Shanghai and asked her to marry him (Figure 1.5). Their wedding took place the following month in Shanghai, after which my mother moved

FIGURE 1.5   My parents' engagement portrait.

with him to Hong Kong, where they lived together until the evacuation ordered by the British authorities the following June.

And that is how I came to be born a British subject in the Crown colony of Hong Kong.

NOTES

1. Writing about her own background, my mother explained her father's education as follows: "my father, at age 23, was graduated from the University of London and was ordained at Jews College to be a minister of religion."
2. Letter from Erwin Reifler to Ruth Segall, July 8, 1939.

2

SHANGHAI:
LIFE UNDER JAPANESE OCCUPATION

SHANGHAI: LIFE UNDER JAPANESE OCCUPATION

After returning to Shanghai in the fall of 1940, my father obtained a position teaching Latin and modern languages to medical and pharmacy students at the Medical College. In addition, he offered Chinese language courses for the American Chamber of Commerce until the United States entered the Pacific War in December 1941.

During the first two and a half years that I lived in Shanghai, I shared a room with my parents in my grandparents' house at 188/1 Avenue du Roi Albert (now Shaanxi Road) in the French Concession of the city.[1] Also living in that house were my grandparents, my mother's sisters, Lilly and Millicent (whose nickname was "Peter"), and my father's sister, Dorothy.

In those days, tuberculosis was rampant in Shanghai, and my mother's youngest sister, whom I knew as "Auntie Peter," contracted this disease after a bout of typhoid in 1939. Her condition worsened as time went on, and, in desperation, my grandparents decided to send her on the first repatriation boat that left Shanghai in August 1942 as far as South Africa, where they had relatives in Johannesburg, hoping that her health would improve in that location. Her sister Lilly accompanied her on this voyage. My earliest memory is of standing beside my mother, waving goodbye to them as the white ambulance pulled away from our house. Lilly and Peter went ashore at Cape Town in South Africa, where Lilly contacted a friend who made arrangements for them to take a train to Johannesburg to join other members of their extended family. Peter died a few days after arriving in Johannesburg. In the meantime, Lilly herself came down with TB, but was successfully treated for it in a sanatorium outside Johannesburg and lived for many years afterward. Almost 50 years would pass before I saw her again.[2]

The Japanese had invaded Shanghai in 1937 and occupied the Chinese parts of the city, but they had left the international sectors—the International Settlement controlled by the British and the American and French Concessions—alone until December 8, 1941, the day after the Japanese attacked Pearl Harbor, when America declared war against Japan. Many homes and businesses belonging to Europeans in those parts of the city were taken over by the Japanese after that date. Before then, my grandfather had quietly transferred the lease on our house to the name of my father, who, because he was born in Austria (a province of Germany after the *Anschluss* [March 1938]), was not regarded as an enemy by the Japanese authorities in Shanghai. For this reason, we were able to continue living in our house throughout the war.

My brother, Frank, was born during the first part of January in 1943. Not long afterward, the Japanese authorities ordered all British and American citizens in Shanghai to report to the euphemistically named "Civil Assembly Centres" in the city, which were established in retaliation for the relocation of people of Japanese descent from the West Coast of the United States into the interior, following President Roosevelt's executive order in February 1942. My grandparents were exempted from this decree at that time because of their age, and my father was not affected by it because of his birth in Vienna, even though, by then, he had renounced his Austrian citizenship and was technically stateless. So, also, was my brother, because he was born in Shanghai and, as a Caucasian, did not qualify for Chinese citizenship. Therefore, only my mother and I had to be interned. Nevertheless, Frank (only two months old at the time) came with us so that my mother could continue nursing him and caring for him in other ways.

We entered the "Civil Assembly Centre" at 404 Yu Yuen Road on March 25, 1943 (Figure 2.1).[3, 4] It was located in a compound that had once contained municipal schools and their grounds[5] and army huts once used by the British army adjoined the school grounds.[6] According to my mother, we lived in two different huts during the fifteen months we were in the camp. She preferred the second hut, even though it was smaller, because it faced a large green, at the end of which was an apartment building in which a friend had an apartment that overlooked the campgrounds. My father came every Sunday morning to stand at the window for a while. My mother placed Frank's buggy in sight of the window every day of the week so that no one would suspect that my father was watching us on Sunday mornings. Once we moved to the second hut, it was natural for me to be outside playing on the green

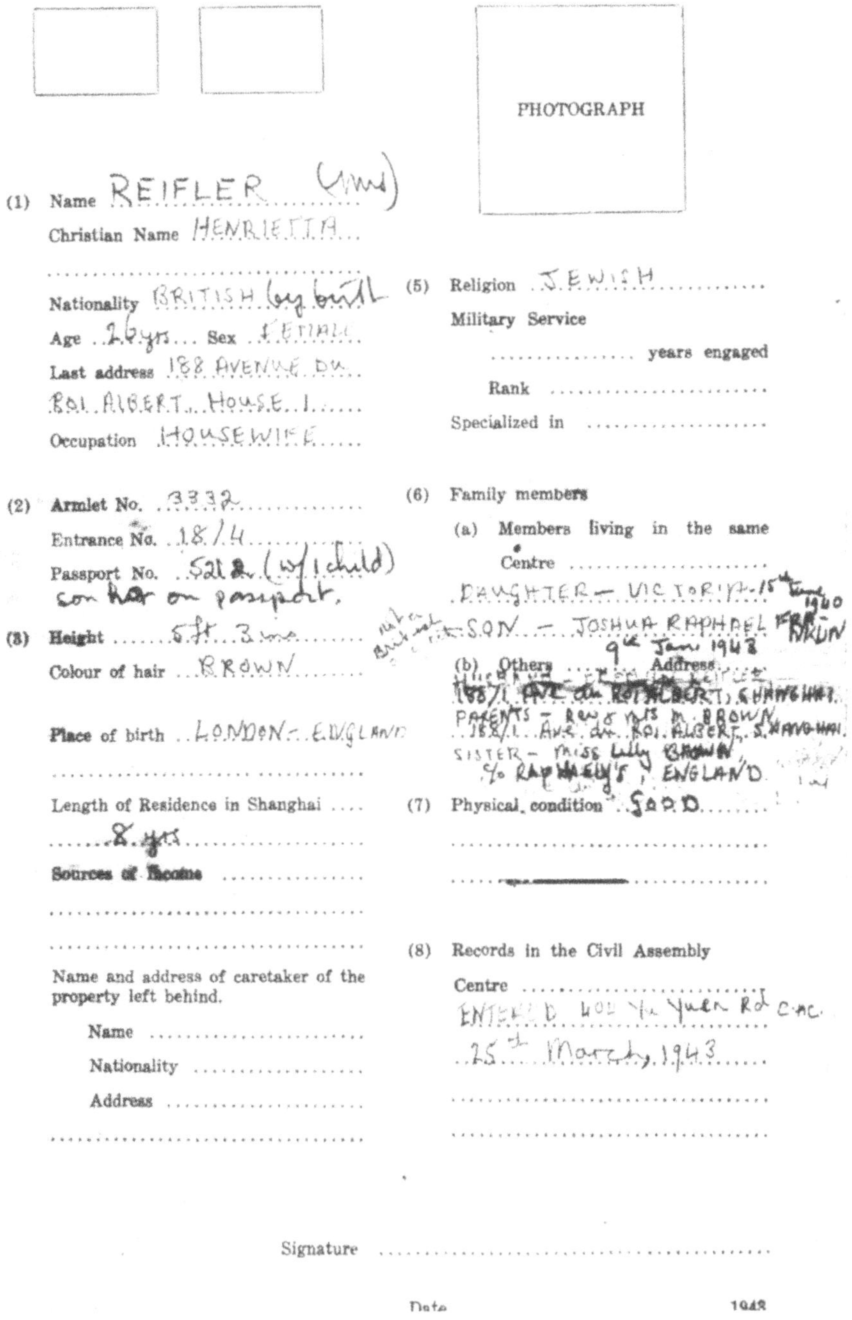

PHOTOGRAPH

(1) Name REIFLER (Mrs)

Christian Name HENRIETTA

Nationality BRITISH by birth

Age 28 yrs. Sex FEMALE

Last address 188 AVENUE DU BOI ALBERT. HOUSE 1

Occupation HOUSEWIFE

(2) Armlet No. 3332

Entrance No. 18/4

Passport No. 522 (w/ 1 child) son her on passport.

(3) Height 5 ft 3 ins

Colour of hair BROWN

Place of birth LONDON - ENGLAND

Length of Residence in Shanghai

8 yrs

Sources of Income

Name and address of caretaker of the property left behind.

Name

Nationality

Address

(5) Religion JEWISH

Military Service

years engaged

Rank

Specialized in

(6) Family members

(a) Members living in the same Centre

DAUGHTER - VICTORIA - 15 June 1960

SON - JOSHUA RAPHAEL FRA BRUN 9th Jan 1943

(b) Others Address

188/1 AVE DU ROI ALBERT, SHANGHAI.

PARENTS - REV & MRS M BROWN 188/1 AVE DU ROI ALBERT. S. SHANGHAI.

SISTER - MISS LILY BROWN c/o RAPHAEL'S ENGLAND

(7) Physical condition GOOD

(8) Records in the Civil Assembly Centre

ENTERED 404 Yu Yuen Rd C.A.C.

25th March, 1943

Signature

Date 1943

FIGURE 2.1. The form filled out by my mother upon entering the "Civil Assembly Centre" on Yu Yuen Road with Victoria and Frank on March 25, 1943.

next to Frank's buggy. I remember only the second hut. I can still picture the arrangement of furniture in that room and the small canteen at one of the far corners of the green.

In coping with the exigencies of camp life, my mother showed ingenuity in other ways as well. Each inmate, adult and child alike, was allowed to send one letter a month from the camp on forms provided by the Red Cross. My mother received three such forms a month, one for her, one for me, and one for Frank. Neither Frank nor I could read or write, so she ghosted letters in our names. Some of them went to my father, others to my grandparents, and still others to my Aunt Dorothy. In the letters she wrote for us, she used vocabulary characteristic of a child, as in the following letter to my grandparents attributed to me:

9th May, 1943
Miss V. Reifler, 18/5
Civil Assembly Centre,
404 Yu Yuen Rd.
Room T44

Dear Grandpa and Grandma,

I am always talking about you, Daddy, Auntie Thea, Auntie Lilly and Auntie Peter. Mummy has some photos of you all and I can still remember you.

I am very brown from playing in the sun and baby brother is growing into a big boy. He looks at me and smiles very nicely. Sometimes he laughs and coos, but he can cry very hard when he is hungry.

I try to help Mummy, but she says I give twice as much work, especially when I upset her soapflakes or give her clean washing with my dirty hands. . . . I will now close my letter for this month. Don't forget to answer me soon. You are allowed to do so.

Please give my love to all, including Aunt Sopher.[7]

Your loving grand-daughter

Victoria

In both London and Shanghai, my mother was accustomed to having servants who did the cleaning and laundry, and, in Shanghai,

```
                                        CIVIL ASSEMBLY CENTRE
                                          404 YU YUEN ROAD
                                              SHANGHAI.

                                         August 19th, 1943.

To      Mr. Erwin Reifler,
          188, Avenue Du Roi Albert,
            House No. 1,
              SHANGHAI.

        THE COMMANDANT OF THIS ASSEMBLY CENTRE WILL BE PLEASED

TO ALLOW:               MR. ERWIN REIFLER

TO VISIT THIS ASSEMBLY CENTRE BETWEEN 3 P.M. and 4 P.M.

ON MONDAY, AUGUST 23rd, 1943 FOR THE PURPOSE OF INTERVIEWING:-

                     MRS. H. REIFLER    &
                     HER TWO CHILDREN

NOTE:-    Only the persons whose names appear in this letter
          will be permitted to enter this Centre.
          No letters or articles of any description will be
          allowed and visitors are particularly warned that
          any violation of this order will prohibit them
          from further interviews.

          VISITORS MUST BE IN POSSESSION OF THIS LETTER WITHOUT
          WHICH ENTRANCE WILL BE REFUSED.
```

FIGURE 2.2.   Copy of the document authorizing my father to visit my mother, brother, and me in the "Civil Assembly Centre" on Yu Yuen Road on August 23, 1943.

we had a cook. In the camp, there was no one to help her with such tasks. With two children less than three years old, she had to do laundry every day. There was a roofed washroom without walls containing tubs and scrubbing boards. I remember running around that washroom, playing hide-and-seek with my friend, Wendy Barnes-Cooke, while my mother washed our clothes and diapers and bedding each day.

After we had been in the camp for five months, my father received a letter from the commandant, authorizing him to visit us for one hour on August 23rd, 1943 (Figure 2.2). I do not remember that visit, but my memory of him must have faded to some degree by then (in spite of the photos we had in our hut), because, in a letter sent to me several weeks later, my Aunt Dorothy said: "I am sorry to hear that you were shy when your daddy came to see you."[8]

This was the only visit from my father during the fifteen months we remained in the camp. However, we were allowed to make one visit to our home in the city after my grandfather had suffered a mild heart attack. I remember talking to my grandmother across a bed and receiving a nougat candy from her on that occasion.

There was a hot plate in our hut where my mother prepared some food for us. But I also remember eating in a common dining room, with the smell of cooked carrots wafting up from large platters as we descended into the room where the communal dining took place. To this day, I loathe the smell of boiled carrots, which I still associate with the months I spent in camp. Of course, I was too young to realize that we were lucky to have carrots to eat because they were nutritious and good for our health.

I remember being sick with the measles while I was in the camp. Amazingly enough, the Emperor of Japan had a policy of providing an egg a day for one week for any child who was ill in one of the Japanese internment camps. I don't remember eating them though. My mother may have eaten some of them herself.

Near the end of our stay in the camp, my mother had to go into the sick bay for six weeks, after spilling boiling water on her left leg and ankle. A neighbor took care of Frank and me during that time. I remember standing by the door of the sick bay with Frank and peering into the room at my mother lying in bed.

While she was in the sick bay, my mother ghosted a letter to my grandparents in my name in which "I" described the condition of her leg and how we were being cared for:

> Mummy still in sick bay. Burn in some places second degree, so taking some time to heal. No infection and doctor pleased. . . . Friends are caring for us and have thoroughly spring-cleaned hut, cleaned cereals and done many jobs that Mummy has no time to do.[9]

My grandfather responded to "my" letter as follows:

> My dear Victoria. We were delighted to receive your letter and glad to learn that Mummy's legs are gradually healing and that you and Franklin are being so nicely cared for by kind people.[10]

We were released from the camp on June 24, 1944 (Figure 2.3), much earlier than the other internees, because my father's nonenemy alien status had kept him from being interned.[11] The very next day, my grandparents went into another internment camp elsewhere in the city, the exemption for elderly enemy aliens having been rescinded by then.[12]

Although we were not evicted from our home as many other Europeans were, parts of the house were used for billeting Japanese personnel, both civilian and military, who had come along to assist in the war effort.[13] The two bedrooms and bathroom on the top floor of our house were taken over by the Japanese gendarmerie and assigned to two women, one Japanese and the other Korean, and a Japanese soldier was placed on the ground floor. I remember that the soldier constructed a shack made of boards and metal bars next to the staircase leading from the ground floor to the first floor. The women were nicer than the man, and Mrs. Satayoshi, who worked for the Yokohama Specie Bank in Shanghai, was apparently trusted enough by my parents to take my brother and me to a nearby park from time to time.

After we left the internment camp, my mother placed Frank and me with an amah, who dealt with our needs on a daily basis, except on her day off each week, when our mother spent the whole day with us. It may have been then that she taught me how to read, because I could already read by the time I went to school. Our amah was also the one who took me to and from school, and Frank went along with us. He and I were together when I was not in school or visiting my friend, Betty Palmer, who lived across the street from our house. We shared a bedroom that had an engraving of the statue of Peter Pan in Kensington Gardens hanging at the foot of his bed. I remember my mother reading to us about Peter Pan and Wendy and Tinker Bell on our amah's day off.

The cook was the servant in our household whom I liked best. I knew him only as "Boy." I sometimes heard my father calling down to him through the dumbwaiter in the upstairs kitchen, addressing him as "Dasavu," an honorific that means "Big Chef" in Chinese. I would creep down to his kitchen on the ground floor and stand beside his chopping block, watching as he cut blocks of dried bean curd into

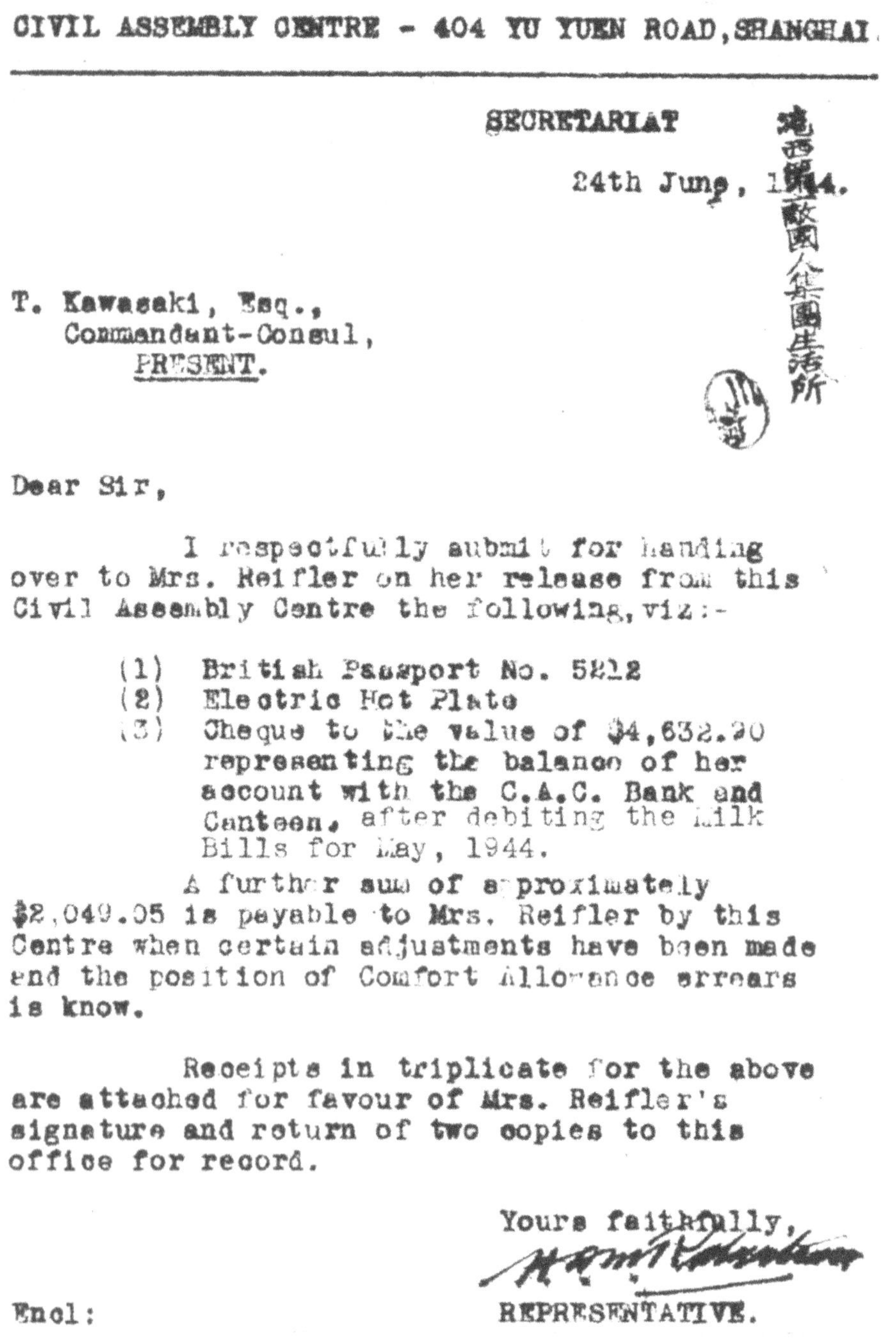

CIVIL ASSEMBLY CENTRE - 404 YU YUEN ROAD, SHANGHAI

SECRETARIAT

24th June, 1944.

T. Kawasaki, Esq.,
     Commandant-Consul,
          PRESENT.

Dear Sir,

        I respectfully submit for handing
over to Mrs. Reifler on her release from this
Civil Assembly Centre the following, viz:-

        (1)   British Passport No. 5212
        (2)   Electric Hot Plate
        (3)   Cheque to the value of $4,632.90
              representing the balance of her
              account with the C.A.C. Bank and
              Canteen, after debiting the Milk
              Bills for May, 1944.
        A further sum of approximately
$2,049.05 is payable to Mrs. Reifler by this
Centre when certain adjustments have been made
and the position of Comfort Allowance arrears
is know.

        Receipts in triplicate for the above
are attached for favour of Mrs. Reifler's
signature and return of two copies to this
office for record.

                            Yours faithfully,

Encl: REPRESENTATIVE.

FIGURE 2.3.   The letter documenting our release from the "Civil Assembly Centre"
on Yu Yuen Road on June 24, 1944.

FIGURE 2.4. Victoria with "Boy" after the Second World War (1945).
Photo by Erwin Reifler.

narrow strips or chopped vegetables for soup. He could speak some English, so we were able to converse with each other. He must have liked me too, because I am pictured in several photos in our family album being carried by him or standing by his side (e.g., Figure 2.4), and he gave me a going-away present of a rice bowl with a matching Chinese spoon, when the time came for us to leave Shanghai.

The infrastructure of the city was neglected under Japanese rule, and there were periodic floods when the river that ran through Shanghai overflowed after heavy rains because it was no longer being dredged. I remember looking out of an upstairs window over the street and seeing boys rowing small boats past our house.[14] The front door of our house was wide enough for a rickshaw to enter, and, during one flood, I saw a male visitor crawling over the banister of the staircase leading up to the first floor and dropping into a rickshaw below, whose owner then pulled it out of the house and into the street.

By the time my grandmother went into the internment camp, she was suffering from TB that she contracted while taking care of Peter before the latter's departure on the repatriation ship. In December of 1944, she was moved to a hospital in Shanghai because of her deteriorating health, where she died on February 13, 1945. My grandfather was released from the camp under Japanese guard to attend her funeral. I remember him stopping by our house for lunch on his way back from the funeral, with Japanese guards standing around him. He returned to the camp, where he remained until the end of the war.

By the end of 1944, the American forces under General Douglas MacArthur had retaken the Philippines from the Japanese, and shortly thereafter had initiated daily bombing raids over Shanghai. I remember those raids well. The planes arrived about noon each day while we were eating lunch. We would retreat to the kitchen on the ground floor and sit there trembling in fear, listening to the sound of bombs falling on the city. Sometimes, when the air-raid siren gave us enough warning, we were able to leave the house in advance of the bombing to take shelter in the basement of a large apartment building nearby, where friends of my parents lived. On one memorable day, the planes arrived early, while our amah was bringing Frank and me back from the park, and we scurried home amid the sound of bombs seeming to crash around us. To this day, I do not like being around firework displays on the Fourth of July or New Year's Eve. They bring back too many memories of the last year of the war in Shanghai.

It was not until many years later that I actually met someone who was responsible for dropping these bombs on Shanghai. In my junior year of high school, I took the required course in American history taught by Mr. Rasmussen. One day during the spring of 1957, Mr. Rasmussen showed up for class dressed in his airman uniform, carrying the diary he had kept during the war. In order to give us an idea of what it had been like to be an American soldier at the end of the war, he read the entire entry in his diary describing one of his bombing raids over Shanghai, taking off in the Philippines in the morning and returning to his base later in the day, having dropped the bombs from his plane over Shanghai at noon. After the class ended, I went up to him and said: "Mr. Rasmussen, you were bombing *me* that day!"[15]

Not long after the bombings began, the Japanese living in our neighborhood built a large slit-trench bomb shelter for their use at the foot of the garden behind our house. Because that part of Shanghai had originally been a marsh, water always welled up into that structure. The Japanese women in our neighborhood were ordered to bail it out on a regular basis. However, Mrs. Satayoshi refused, saying that she would rather die in the house than drown in a bomb shelter!

On the day of Japan's surrender in August 1945, the Japanese residents in our house, who by then included Mrs. Satayoshi's husband, who had been wounded in the war, asked permission to listen to our radio,[16] because the Emperor was going to make an important announcement, namely, his call to Japanese soldiers, wherever they were, to lay down their arms. My mother told me many years later that the Satayoshis sat there with bowed heads, drawing in their breath sharply multiple times as they listened, and the next day, they were gone.

The end of the war brought numerous changes, including some in my family. My sister Anne was born some weeks later at the end of September. My grandfather was released from his internment camp on the day after the surrender. He stayed in Shanghai for a few months before returning to London, leaving the house on the Avenue du Roi Albert in the hands of my parents.

I remember the jubilation in the streets that followed the end of the war. The children went about singing: "We won the war in nineteen forty-four!" This was not strictly true, but "forty-four" rhymed better with "war" than "forty-five."

And suddenly the city was filled with American GIs, driving around in jeeps, offering rides and handing out Wrigley's spearmint chewing gum to the children (including me). I loved it! On a less pleasant note, I also remember observing the soldiers pestering some of the European women on the streets, a sight I had never witnessed before.

My family remained in Shanghai for another two years after the war. My father continued offering courses in Chinese at Aurora University, a French Jesuit institution, where he had been employed since 1943. I began my formal education at the Shanghai Jewish School, where my grandfather had been the principal before he was interned in the "Civil Assembly Centre" on Lincoln Avenue. Also during that time, my father let a Chinese family move into what had once been our drawing room on the ground floor of our house, where my mother had read Peter Pan to Frank and me. There were two children in the Chen family, both boys, whose names were Doong-doong and Na-na. Doong-doong and I were the same age, and we played together so much that I began to learn Chinese from him and his parents.[17] Unfortunately, Doong-doong was diagnosed with TB during my last year in Shanghai and was sent away. I never saw him again.

In the meantime, civil war had erupted in China, pitting the Nationalists led by Chiang Kai-shek against the Communists led by Mao Zedong. There were frequent parades and demonstrations in the streets. I remember one such demonstration with only Chinese women as participants, preventing us from crossing the street.

As the Communists consolidated their gains, it became apparent that it would not be long before they reached Shanghai, and when that happened, Europeans would no longer be welcome. The question was: Where could we go? My grandfather discouraged my parents from going to England, because the bombing during the war had created a severe housing shortage there.

After the war, some of my father's former pupils at the American Chamber of Commerce had returned to Shanghai. They suggested that he look for a university position in the United States. They offered to help him with the transportation expenses, and he decided to accept their offer after receiving an invitation to give a talk at the annual meetings of the American Oriental Society in April 1947, in Washington DC. With their help, and the help of his cousins in California and New Jersey, he was able to spend six months in the United States after the professional meetings in Washington were over. During those months, he criss-crossed the country by train from coast to coast following employment leads. My mother taught his beginning classes in Chinese at Aurora University during his absence, providing the necessary income for our household in Shanghai.

With the war over and subsequent political developments in China receiving international attention, several universities in the United States were beginning to expand their course offerings in Chinese. After visiting a number of universities, including Harvard, Yale, Princeton, the University of Michigan, the University of Washington, and Stanford, my father received an offer for a one-year position as a Visiting Associate Professor of Chinese in the Far Eastern Department of the University of Washington in Seattle, with the possibility of renewal after that. After accepting that offer, he flew back to Shanghai to pack up for the move to Seattle, a task that took less than a month. When we were ready, we boarded the *Canadian Mail*, a cargo ship with a few staterooms for passengers, and left Shanghai for good. A vivid memory of this trip is seeing Mount Fuji in the distance as we passed by Japan, the land that had determined my family's fortunes for so long.

The sea voyage across the Pacific lasted for twelve days. We arrived in Portland, Oregon, with the intention of taking the train to Seattle. But my father's sister, Dorothy, who came with us, did not have the necessary papers to enter the country. She was suffering from multiple sclerosis, and as a sister, rather than the wife or a child of my father, she did not qualify for the same immigration status as the rest of us. My father telephoned George Taylor, the chairman of the Far Eastern Department in Seattle, who was able to persuade Immigration to let my aunt accompany us to Seattle, where an effort would be made to regularize her status, and my father's cousins in New Jersey posted a large bond on her behalf. Nevertheless, Immigration treated my mother as a hostage, because they wanted her to accompany my aunt back to Shanghai, and we traveled on the train to Seattle under police guard that night.

NOTES

1. Pan Ling, *In Search of Old Shanghai* (Hongkong: Joint Publishing Co., 1982), 80.
2. We met again in Johannesburg in 1989 and 1994, where my husband and I celebrated our 25th and 30th wedding anniversaries with Lilly and other members of her family.
3. During a visit to Honolulu in April 2013, I attended an exhibition honoring the contribution of Japanese American soldiers to the American war effort in Europe that brought an end to that part of the Second World War. At the entrance to the exhibition, I noticed a sign concerning the opening of the Honouliuli Internment Camp north of Honolulu on March 1, 1943, a few weeks before we entered the internment camp on Yu Yuen Road in Shanghai. The temporal proximity of the opening of these two camps, the one in Hawaii closely followed by the one in Shanghai, underscored for me the retaliatory nature of the action taken by the Japanese against American and British civilians in China.
4. While participating in a grant-review panel in Washington, DC, in 1980, I met a Japanese American sociologist who was born in Seattle during the war and had spent time in a Japanese relocation camp in California with his parents. He was amazed when I told him that I had spent fifteen months in a similar camp established by the Japanese in Shanghai in retaliation for the internment of his people on the West Coast of the United States. On one of the evenings in Washington, the members of the panel had dinner together at a Japanese restaurant. The sociologist sat next to me and offered me choice tidbits from the serving bowl in the middle

of the table. After watching me eat with chopsticks for a few minutes, he exclaimed: "You eat children style!" It was only then that I realized that my use of chopsticks was unusual. Having left China when I was seven years old, I had never learned to use them like an adult.

Perhaps because of this conversation, I was anxious to visit the site of one of the Japanese relocation centers in California. That opportunity came during the summer of 2000, after we had visited friends in the Owens Valley. On the west side of the road between the towns of Lone Pine and Independence was the camp known as *Manzanar* ("apple orchard" in Spanish). The site was dry and dusty, and there were no fruit trees in sight. Only one structure was still standing: the theater building. The rest of the site was covered with the foundations of buildings that had once housed the detainees. In the cemetery, we saw the grave of a child that was still being tended, with small toys on the surface.

We visited Manzanar again five years later during the summer of 2005. The theater had been renovated and converted into a Visitors' Center. A graphic on one wall inside the building listed the names of more than 10,000 Japanese Americans, who spent all or part of World War II at Manzanar. An old man stood in front of the wall with a small boy on his shoulders, who may have been his grandson, quietly reading off some names, obviously recounting some of his experiences there. Other exhibits consisted of photographs of the internment center and its inhabitants, some shown being herded there from other places, including urban areas. I was struck by some pictures of women who had obviously assimilated to American culture, wearing high heels and stylish dresses of the period. They lent perspective to what my mother, brother, and I were experiencing at the same time on the other side of the world.

5. Ironically, the Public School for Girls of the Shanghai Municipal Council, where my mother had prepared girls for the English matriculation exams during the fall of 1941, was one of the buildings

in that part of the "Civil Assembly Centre," although it was not the building in which she would later be interned with my brother and me.

6. The first hut we lived in was Number T44, and the second was Number T51.

7. Auntie Thea was my Aunt Dorothy, whose full name was Dorothea ("Thea" was her nickname). The Sophers were friends of our family in Shanghai. At that time I called all women except my mother and grandmother "Auntie," all men except my father and grandfather "Uncle." "18/5" was my internee number. Letter from Victoria Reifler to Reverend Mendel and Annie Brown, May 9, 1943.

8. Letter from Dorothy Reifler to Victoria Reifler, September 6, 1943.

9. The reference to "cleaned cereals" could be an allusion to the removal of weevils from the infested grain provided to camp inmates. Letter from Victoria Reifler to Reverend and Mrs. M. Brown, May 14, 1944.

10. Letter from Reverend Mendel Brown to Victoria Reifler, May 21, 1944.

11. Reparations to the Japanese Americans from the West Coast who were relocated in internment camps in the interior were slow in coming after the war, and it was not until 1992 that they were completed. A few years later, the British government transferred funds to the War Pension Agency in Blackpool, England, to be distributed to "Ex-Far East Prisoners of War, Merchant Seamen imprisoned by the Japanese or Civilian Internees." A friend of my mother's notified her about this program and urged her to apply for these funds, and she informed me about it as well. I suggested that she submit her application first, because she had the stronger claim, having been born in London, and, if she was successful, I would submit my own claim. Both of our claims were accepted, and we received our payments promptly. I shared mine with my brother, Frank, who, not being British by birth, was not eligible for this program, but had undergone the same deprivations in camp that I did. No such reparations were made by Japan to British and American civilians who had been held in camps in the Far East.

12. That camp was located on Lincoln Avenue in a former housing compound of the Bank of China that was set up for elderly and ill internees like my grandparents (letter from Greg P. Leck to Henrietta Reifler, April 17, 2004). See also Greg Leck, *Captives of Empire: The Japanese Internment of Allied Civilians in China, 1941–1945* (Bangor, PA: Shandy Press, 2006), 456–59. Our camp on Yu Yuen Road is described on pages 512–17 of this book.

13. Many years later, the Japanese anthropologist who translated my first book into Japanese told me that she was born in Shanghai in 1942. Her parents were there because her father was a travel agent who arranged periodic furloughs back to Japan for Japanese soldiers stationed in China.

14. I saw a similar sight one day many years later in front of the Anthropology Building at Tulane on Audubon Street in New Orleans, where some fraternity boys had obtained a small boat and were poling it down the street after a storm had inundated our part of town. Like Shanghai, much of New Orleans was built on what had once been marshy ground near a river, but in New Orleans the high levees maintained by the Army Corps of Engineers protected us from river flooding, but not from flash floods produced by violent storms.

15. My sister Consuela informed me recently that he did not repeat his account of the raid over Shanghai when she was in his American history class ten years later.

16. My parents' possession of a radio was illegal under Japanese rule. Evidently, the Japanese living in our house were aware that we had a radio, but did not betray us to the Japanese authorities.

17. My parents had wanted our amah to speak to me and Frank in Chinese, so that we could learn to speak the language from her, but she insisted on speaking only pidgin English with us.

3

SEATTLE:
BECOMING AN AMERICAN

W e arrived in Seattle early in the morning of October 9, 1947. My Aunt Dorothy was taken by ambulance to St. Vincent's Home for the Aged in West Seattle. Before returning to Shanghai to pack up and bring us to America, my father had arranged with the Mother Superior for her to stay there. The rest of us were invited for breakfast at the home of Professor George Taylor and his wife, Roberta. We then moved into a furnished one-story duplex apartment in Union Bay Circle, where the University provided temporary housing for new faculty for one year.

As soon as we were settled in our house, my mother took me to Laurelhurst Elementary School, where I entered the second grade, in a room that accommodated both first- and second-grade students. Our teacher alternated her instruction between the two groups of students, who sat on different sides of the room. When she was occupied with teaching the first graders, the second graders worked on whatever she had assigned them to do at their desks, and vice versa.

I was two years ahead of my class in arithmetic and was also more advanced in reading than the other students in second grade. My teacher, whose name I do not remember, was understanding; she told me that when I finished my assignments, I could get a book from the closet in the classroom to read at my desk. Although I learned very little at school that year, I benefited from the less demanding atmosphere in the classroom, because it freed me to focus on the adjustments I had to make in my new life in America.

The major challenge for me was to replace the British accent I had acquired from my mother and her parents and sisters with an American one, namely, the accent characteristic of the Pacific Northwest. What, in an older child or an adult, might have been regarded as an asset by peers, was a cause for derision in a seven-year-old. I set for myself the task of identifying and stripping from my speech all traces of a British accent and vocabulary, which I had accomplished by the end of my first year in Seattle.

During that year, my father received an invitation to give a lecture on "The Chinese Language in the Light of Comparative Semantics—A

New Approach to Historical Linguistics" at the spring 1948 meeting of the American Philosophical Society in Philadelphia. My mother went with him, leaving their three children in the care of a live-in baby sitter for two weeks. It was not a happy time for me and my siblings, so recently uprooted from our home in Shanghai. My parents enjoyed their travels by train to the East Coast, with visits to Cambridge, New Haven, and New York City after the meeting in Philadelphia had ended.

Because we were limited to a single year of housing in Union Bay Circle, my parents began looking for a more permanent home for us before the end of that academic year. They bought the two-story house at 1909 Naomi Place, two blocks north of Ravenna Park, which was close enough to the University for my father to commute back and forth on his bicycle.

I entered the third grade at Ravenna Elementary School in September 1948. I coasted academically that year as well. My teacher was Mrs. Liston. I became friends with two girls in that class, Cece Tenney and Mary Jane Stilo; those friendships continued throughout my time at Ravenna, until we moved on to different junior high schools after sixth grade.

A strange custom that I first encountered in third grade was "bank day," when an hour or so was set aside one morning each week for the students to deposit money in savings accounts that the school had arranged with a local bank. Apparently, this was regarded as an opportunity to teach thrift to public school students. One of the students served as the teller, and, one by one, the students who wanted to make deposits went up to the front of the classroom with his or her money to place it in their account. For this purpose, the minimum deposit was five cents, and there was no minimum balance. My mother refused to let me engage in this activity, claiming that it did not make sense for me to deposit her money in an account because I had no money of my own. I recognized the logic of her explanation, but I later learned that, for some families, these were the only savings accounts they had.

The high point of third grade for me was a unit on Mexico, which was my first exposure to the culture of that fascinating country, where I later spent much of my career. As part of that unit, our class put on a play called *The Painted Pig*, which was based on a book of the same name by Elizabeth Morrow. The play was performed at night, and I served as the narrator.[1]

The pace of my education picked up in fourth grade because the material that was taught that year was new to me. My homeroom teacher was Mary Fullington, whose specialty was art. My language arts teacher was Florence Ludlow, whose large classroom also served as the school library, with many books on floor-to-ceiling bookshelves around the room. She was my homeroom teacher in fifth grade, and I remember being assigned to check out books to other students, a task that I enjoyed.

Miss Ludlow was a wonderful teacher, who taught social studies as well as language arts. Under her tutelage, I learned to write essays, several of which I have kept to this day. In her class, we were encouraged to write fan letters to our favorite authors. I chose Laura Ingalls Wilder, and I still have her brief reply to my letter. Miss Ludlow liked to travel during the summers, and I still have in my possession the postcard she sent me from Portugal one summer. Miss Fullington's art classes were also enjoyable because she gave us interesting projects to work on, whether or not we had any artistic talent (as I did not). They were my favorite teachers in grade school.

It was during the summer of 1950, just before I entered fifth grade, that my sister Consuela was born. I was ten years old at the time, and after she entered my life, I lost interest in dolls, finding caring for a real baby much more interesting and fun.

During that fall, the Far Eastern Department held a weekend retreat at a hotel called Alderbrook Inn on Hood Canal, which both of my parents attended. They took me along to look after Consuela. The other children stayed at home with a baby sitter. I did not mind staying with Consuela while my mother took part in some of the activities. It was so peaceful being away from the rest of the family. On one of the evenings, my mother remained with Consuela so that I could attend the Japanese Sukiyaki dinner with my father. That was the first time I ate raw oysters in a cocktail sauce, which I enjoyed very much.

While I was in sixth grade, my mother was bedridden for some months with complications associated with her last pregnancy and my Aunt Dorothy died during the spring of that year (1952). After I came home from school, as well as on the weekends, many of the household chores and much of the care of Consuela fell on my shoulders. In June, my youngest sister, Michaela, was born prematurely and spent the first five weeks of her life in an incubator. It was a very hard year for everyone concerned.

I struggled to keep up in school that year. The one bright spot for me was the opportunity to stand behind the counter serving food to other students in the school lunchroom for one month. What appealed to me was not the work itself, but the fact that it was, in effect, my first "paying job," because I received a free lunch, worth twenty-five cents, in return for this work. My parents could not afford the school lunches for me, so I usually brought a lunch with me to school, as did many of the other students. As a special treat, my mother did give me money to buy my lunch at school during Thanksgiving week, when delicious slices of roast turkey were served with all the trimmings.

Near the end of that year, I and several other students in my class were chosen to take part in a special foreign language program in junior high school the following year. The language that was being offered was Spanish. My parents would have preferred for me to learn French, but that was not offered before ninth grade. They reasoned that the opportunity to learn a foreign language in seventh grade was more important than which language it would be, so they agreed. This was a fateful decision on their part, because it set me on a course that would have a significant impact on my adult life.

In order to make room for that Spanish course each semester, the number of required courses in art, music, and home economics (for the girls) or shop (for the boys) was reduced. As a result, I took only one course each in cooking and sewing and art and music while I was in junior high school. I made up for the missing home economics courses in high school, with courses in tailoring and foods and nutrition, and sewing lessons at Singer's during the summer. I made up for the missing music course by taking piano lessons for five years and by playing in the junior orchestra before school started in the morning in eighth grade (described in the text that follows). Having no talent whatsoever in art, I made no effort to supplement my deficiency in that subject.

The Spanish courses taught by David Osuna at John Marshall Junior High School were delightful. He had grown up in Texas near the Mexican border and clearly had great enthusiasm for teaching. The emphasis was on conversation, rather than writing. To this end, we elected class officers and began each day with minutes concerning what had taken place in class the day before, recited in Spanish by me as class secretary. Mr. Osuna also encouraged us to perform skits, which gave us additional practice in speaking Spanish. I was fortunate to have him as my Spanish teacher during seventh and eighth grade. Our ninth-grade teacher was Mr. Young, who was less charismatic than Mr. Osuna. The whole year was spent reviewing what we had learned during our first two years of Spanish, instead of learning anything new.

The most interesting course I took while in junior high school was in printing, the only "shop" open to both girls and boys. (The other shops or "industrial arts" were mechanical drawing, wood, and metal). Our teacher, Mr. Jahnke, had obtained for the school two cast-off, but still functional, treadle-operated printing presses that were used for putting out the school newspaper. In the course, I learned how to set type with a "composing stick," after memorizing the distribution of letters of metal type in a "job case," in which the letter "e" occupied the largest compartment in the lower right-hand corner, because of its high frequency in the English language. Em- and en-spacers were used for separating words, and strips of metal of different thickness called *leadings* were used for separating lines of type. If type was dropped and mixed up, it was said to be "pied." Although I did not know it at the time, what I learned in this course would be useful to me years later, when I served as the editor of two journals and a series of books.

I participated in several kinds of extracurricular activities during junior high school. In eighth grade, I spent the hour before classes began in the morning in the percussion section of the junior orchestra, playing the base drum, cymbals, and triangle. I was not talented enough in music to qualify for the senior orchestra in ninth grade. Instead, I worked as a volunteer in the school library during the same period in the mornings. Although I was certainly no athlete, I participated in after-school sports in the afternoons and ice-skating in the downtown arena on Saturday mornings, often walking home from there beside the Aurora highway with my friend, Carol Uitti.

I assumed that I would continue studying Spanish in high school, but when I learned that the next course in the sequence would be using the same textbook as in the previous year, I changed my mind. I could not see the point of reviewing the grammar I had learned in the seventh and eighth grades once more. So, I dropped the course and took two years of Latin instead. As a result, I never did learn when it was appropriate to use the Spanish subjunctive.

The focus of my education changed in other ways as well during the three years that I attended Roosevelt High School. In the effort to catch up with and even surpass the technological achievements of the Soviet Union in the post-Sputnik era, the public schools in Seattle were involved in upgrading what are today referred to as STEM courses (science—technology—engineering—mathematics), and my high school was no exception. Its location in the same part of town as the University of Washington meant that many of its students came from the well-educated families of the professors and other employees of the university. It was therefore possible to offer challenging courses in mathematics and the sciences (chemistry and physics, as well as biology) to that student body.

One such course was accelerated geometry, in which I enrolled during my sophomore year. It covered the same topics as the traditional geometry course more rapidly, leaving time in the second semester for learning solid geometry as well. Although I did not find geometry as interesting as algebra, I enjoyed being with other academically minded students in that course.

I took the full three-course sequences in both chemistry and physics while I was in high school. I found physics especially interesting. During Physics II and Physics III, the Boeing Airplane Factory south of the city sent one of its employees to give us workshops on how the early mainframe computers were used in industry. Each workshop ended with a field trip to the Boeing plant, where we watched how plug boards in the direct analogue computer were wired to model the amount of stress a bridge could tolerate before failing.

I was the only girl enrolled in Physics III during my last semester in high school. All the students were expected to demonstrate self-designed projects involving principles of physics to the rest of the class. Unlike other students in the class, I lacked the technical expertise to design and execute such a project. Anticipating my plight, David Scott, our teacher, handed me an issue of *Popular Mechanics* and pointed out an article for me to read on how to demonstrate the components of colors. He said that after I had read it, he would lend me a small motor to use in my demonstration to the class.

The project involved the preparation of three cardboard discs, each painted with one of the three basic colors. A hole in the center of each disc permitted it to be mounted on a small rod protruding from the motor, and a slit on each disc extending from the hole in its center to its perimeter made it possible to overlap the discs so that the amount of each disc that was visible could be easily changed. When the overlapping disks were rotated rapidly on the motor, intermediate hues were produced, depending on how much of each disk was visible. If equal amounts of the three basic colors were exposed, the resulting color was white.[2]

I postponed taking Algebra III until the first semester of my senior year. Another girl and I were the only seniors in the class. The rest of the students were sophomores, who had already taken geometry in junior high school and were expecting to take a recently introduced course in "pre-calculus" the following year. Halfway through the algebra course, I asked the teacher, Philip Stucky, whether I should take trigonometry during the spring semester. He advised me not to, saying that I would never need it. However, he thought better of his advice at the end of the semester, when he saw that I and the other senior girl in the class had earned the highest grades on the final exam in the course. He had the grace to tell me that he had made a mistake in advising me not to take trigonometry the following semester, but by then, my sched-ule for the rest of the year had been set, and I completed my education at Roosevelt High School without trigonometry.

In addition to the required courses in language arts, U.S. history, world history, contemporary problems, health education, and physical education, there were electives in home economics (tailoring and cook-ing), typing, creative writing, and photography, with which I rounded out my curriculum. I contemplated a career in food technology, combin-ing my interests in science and home economics, but because the college I attended did not have such a major for undergraduates, I did not pursue it.

One day, early in my junior year of high school, a friend asked me to accompany her while she went looking for jobs. Although I had no intention of looking for a job for myself, I went along with her. One of the jobs she applied for was at the Roosevelt branch of the public library, and on a whim, I applied for it too. Where the application asked for a reference, I wrote the name of the teacher who had supervised my work as a volunteer in the library of my junior high school before classes began in the morning. I got the job.

The job entailed shelving books after school for two hours on two afternoons a week and preparing display copies of magazines for three hours on two evenings a week. Occasionally, I was asked to substitute for one of the librarians on Saturdays as well. The pay was 90 cents per hour. I saved most of the money I earned in that job for college.

I applied to a number of colleges during my senior year. After the acceptance letters came in, I narrowed down my alternatives to Stanford University and Reed College. I had visited the Stanford campus on a trip to California with my parents in 1954, but knew little about Reed. My mother suggested that she and I take the train to Portland to visit the Reed campus to help me make up my mind. We did so, as a result of which I chose Stanford. I was accustomed to the large size of my high school (there were 630 students in my senior class). Reed had only a few hundred students in all. I thought I would be happier at a larger institution, where the students had more diverse backgrounds and interests and where there would be a greater variety of programs and courses for undergraduates. Stanford fit that description better than Reed. My parents made no effort to influence my decision. Only after I had chosen Stanford did they tell me that it was what they had hoped I would do.

There was one piece of unfinished business that had to be taken care of before I left for college in the fall. Stanford's General Education requirements permitted entering students to choose between a language and a mathematics track. The language track required six quarters of a foreign language, whereas the math track could be completed in only four quarters of calculus, with courses meeting five times a week during the first year (in six quarters, with courses meeting three times a week). I was anxious to fulfill the General Education courses as quickly as possible, so I chose the mathematics track, even though I had more aptitude for foreign languages. However, both Algebra III and one semester of trigonometry were prerequisites for entering beginning calculus. If I chose the mathematics track, I would have to take trigonometry during my first quarter in college for no credit or pass a placement exam in this subject before classes began in the fall.

What to do? My brother, Frank, two and one-half years younger than I, came to my rescue. He was a gifted mathematician (as I was not), having taught himself calculus when he was only eleven years old. I asked him whether he would teach me trigonometry during the summer so that I could pass the placement exam in the fall. He agreed and suggested that I request a list of the topics that would be covered in the exam. The irony is that, with his help, I learned what I needed to know for passing the exam in only half the time that I would have spent in a semester-long course in high school.[3]

Although I have emphasized the role of school and school-related extracurricular activities in my life during the eleven years that I spent in Seattle, other experiences I had during those years also had a profound influence on the person I became. Equally important was the fact that my departure from Shanghai did not completely sever the emotional ties I had with that part of the world. My father's teaching position in the Far Eastern Department at the University of Washington meant that our most frequent social contacts were with his Chinese, Japanese, and Korean colleagues and their families, as well as other professors who were experts in East Asian affairs. The annual all-day picnics at the Mercer Island home of one of the professors always had a delicious assortment of food from that region. The wife of one of the professors offered a course in Chinese cooking through the University's evening division, which she invited me to attend after she learned of my interest in cooking. I still have the dittoed copies of the recipes she demonstrated during those evening sessions. These contacts, as well as the ornately carved wooden chests, the beautiful hanging scroll and other Asian paintings, and the Chinese carpets that came with us from Shanghai and decorated our living room, kept my link with that part of the world alive in me during the remaining years of my childhood and instilled in me an appreciation for other customs that had a significant influence on what I would eventually choose as my life's work.

A more subtle influence was my father's interest in languages, not only ancient and modern Chinese, but also the ancient and modern European languages (Latin and Greek, French and Italian, Russian, as well as the German he grew up speaking and the English that we spoke at home), ancient Hebrew and Aramaic, and Japanese. So, also, was his work with machine translation, of which he was one of the pioneers. This was during the Cold War, and the grammatical algorithms he developed for this purpose were intended for decoding Russian texts. Although I did not share his interest in the Chinese language, having forgotten it during my first year in Seattle when I was trying to replace my British accent with an American one, his support for language learning in general, as shown by his willingness for me to learn Spanish in junior high school, certainly made a positive impression on me. His enthusiasm for languages and his prowess in speaking them were infectious, and all five of us know multiple languages, ranging from ancient and modern Hebrew (Frank and Michaela) to Chinese and Thai (Anne) to Latin, French, Spanish, and Portuguese (Consuela), to Spanish, German, French, Tzotzil, and ancient and modern Yucatecan Maya (me).

NOTES

1. At a recent annual meeting of the American Philosophical Society, I spotted a copy of *The Painted Pig* among the remaindered books for sale to members. I could not resist buying it, even though it was intended for very young children, because of the memories of the play it brought to mind. I realize now that it was set in Central Mexico, because the surnames of the principal characters were Chimalpopoca and Tlaxochimaco, which come from the Nahuatl language that is still spoken in that region.

2. I was reminded of this project many years later, when I carried out a comparative study of color terms in several Mayan languages. The approach used in my physics project would not have been meaningful in those languages, because their color terms are more concerned with discriminations based on variables other than hue (see Chapter 8).

3. I considered the possibility of placing out of more than one quarter of Spanish in the placement exam for that language that was also offered at the beginning of the school year, but that result seemed unlikely because I had not studied Spanish during my three years in high school. I did take the placement exam in Spanish anyway, but did not perform well enough to place out of more than one quarter of that language.

4

STANFORD AND GERMANY: MY FIRST ENCOUNTER WITH ANTHROPOLOGY

One afternoon in the middle of September in 1958 (now age 18), I boarded the train to San Francisco. After sitting up all night, I left the train in Oakland, where I was met by Ruth, the wife of my father's cousin Alfred Feldhammer. The next day, she drove me down to Stanford to begin my first year of college.

That journey represented a major watershed in my life. This was the first time I had left home and my family. It marked my transition to adulthood and life on my own.

After moving into my dormitory (Branner Hall) and meeting my roommates (Barbara Blair and Arley Timm), I was swept up in orientation activities, including a campus tour, a "mixer," and an afternoon gathering with a few other students at the campus home of a professor and his wife. Orientation lasted for a full week, and at the end of it I felt sufficiently at home for classes to begin.

All students were required to take a sequence of three courses in a science during their freshman year, followed by one quarter of a different science during a later year. If the student had not studied biology in high school, as was my case, then the full-year course in a science had to be freshman biology. My other required courses that first year were English composition, history of Western civilization, and, of course, the calculus sequence.

Not surprising in light of my strong science training in high school, I found the biology course most interesting. The two lecture sections each week had 350 students; Professor Regnery was a dynamic lecturer who incorporated the details of his ongoing research in his presentations in a way that I found fascinating, in spite of the large class. I was less enamored of the three-hour lab that I attended each week. I liked the labs that were devoted to a discussion of problem sets during the unit on genetics, but not the ones involving dissection and measuring small changes in the composition of liquids. I lacked the manual dexterity necessary for dissection and the patience for detecting small changes in quantities. I concluded from that experience that I was temperamentally not suited for a career as a "bench scientist," and after completing the science requirement with a course in noncalculus physics during the fall quarter of my junior year, I decided to focus on the humanities, with a major in philosophy.

Early in the fall quarter of my freshman year, I became aware that Stanford had an overseas program for sophomores in Germany. Because of my religious heritage, I was, at first, reluctant to contemplate spending time in Germany so soon after the Second World War. Several of my father's relatives, including his older brother, had perished during the Holocaust, and my father himself had renounced his Austrian citizenship and stopped speaking German after the Anschluss. However, the idea of going to Germany was something I could consider, in part because the war did not mean quite the same thing to me and my family as it did to some of my American friends. Although both of my parents were European and Jewish, the fact is that they and their children did not spend the war years in Europe. They understood the mortal danger of Nazi Germany (and my father had taken care to get his mother and sister out of Austria before the Anschluss), but for us the war with the greatest reality was the war in China. At that time, the greatest immediate threat to our continued existence was posed, not by the Germans, but by the Japanese. So I was able, with some misgivings, to contemplate spending part of my college years in Germany.

Several friends in my corridor at Branner Hall—Ann Cilley, Suzie Behrman, and Janie Breeden—were applying for that program, and I eventually overcame my misgivings and applied as well. We were all accepted for the fourth group of Stanford-in-Germany, the one that would begin with the winter quarter of our sophomore year (1960).

I had chosen the math track over the language track in order to fulfill that requirement as quickly as possible. Now, however, I would have to complete two quarters of German in order to be eligible for the study-abroad program. This would be possible only if I learned enough German during the intervening summer to place out of the first quarter of the course, in order to be qualified to take the second quarter of the language during the fall.

There was also the question of how my parents would react to the prospect of my spending six months of my sophomore year in Germany. In essence, they responded in the same way as they had to the possibility of my learning Spanish seven years before. They would have preferred that I spend the two quarters abroad in France, but the Stanford-in-France program would not come into being for another two years. On the other hand, my parents were both of European origin, but they could not afford to send me to Europe themselves, whereas Stanford would cover all my expenses, except for my trip back to the United States. Furthermore, being in Germany would give me the opportunity to become acquainted with my father's relatives who were still living in Germany and Greece and the members of my mother's extended family in England. This was too good an opportunity for me to miss. So my enlightened parents swallowed hard and gave me permission to go.

In addition, my father agreed to teach me German during the summer before my sophomore year (1959). He told me to get a copy of the textbook that was used in the course and to find out how much of it was normally covered during the first quarter. I would study the language on my own during the day, and he would converse with me in German on walks we would take during the evening.[1]

When summer came, and our work together began, my father told me that he had discovered that the best way to learn a foreign language was by memorizing texts. If one memorized lots of texts, the grammatical rules of the language would be internalized automatically, and it would not be necessary to learn them explicitly. My father was a polyglot who had learned at least thirteen languages during his life. Therefore, I assumed that he knew what he was talking about and decided to try his approach.

I found that it was a time-consuming, but effective, approach. Not only did I perform well enough on the placement exam to register for the second quarter of German in the fall, but I also discovered that, when I arrived in Germany, I was able to respond automatically and usually appropriately to questions addressed to me, contrasting in this respect, with some of my fellow students, who did not feel comfortable speaking German for some weeks after we arrived. According to my roommates, I sometimes spoke German in my sleep!

My journey to Germany began in Seattle, where I was visiting my family at the end of the fall quarter of my sophomore year (1959). I took the night train to San Francisco on December 27, where I joined

other members of the Stanford-in-Germany group the next day, before
setting off for Europe on the following day.

Our flight from San Francisco to New York was on one of the
first commercial jets operated by United Airlines. It was also my first
experience on a plane. That leg of our journey took five hours. In New
York, we changed to a chartered, propeller-driven plane provided by
Sabena Airlines, which took seventeen hours to cross the Atlantic, with
a refueling stop in Gander, Labrador, in the middle of the night. I have
vivid memories of my first sight of Europe and flying over the English
countryside and London, the distinctive high-pitched red-tiled roofs
on the houses in France and Belgium, before landing in Brussels in late
morning on December 30. From there, we flew to Stuttgart, landing at
1:00 p.m. After a bus tour of Stuttgart, we were bussed to Beutelsbach,
an agricultural village of 3,000 inhabitants in the Remstal Valley, twelve
kilometers further south. From there, we were taken to the Stanford
campus on a ridge overlooking the valley.

Stanford had leased an estate called *Landgutburg* for its overseas
campus in Germany. The manor house, known as *Grosses Haus*, was a
beautiful three-story building, with the kitchen, dining room, and living
room on the first floor and dormitory space on the two floors above.
Most of the girls in our group were housed in this building. Janie
Breeden, Patty Cline, and I shared a room at the head of the stairs on
the second floor. Six other girls (including my close friends, Ann Cilley
and Suzie Behrman) were housed in three rooms in the basement of
Kleines Haus; a small apartment on the first floor was occupied by one
of the professors and his wife. The German director of the program
and his wife (a former Stanford-in-Germany student) lived in another
small house on the property.

Stanford had constructed two buildings, one called *Stanford Haus*
that served as the boys' dormitory and the "Library," which contained
a large classroom on the first floor and a "Ratskeller" in the basement,
as well as an apartment for another professor and his wife on the second
floor. These buildings and the three original buildings on the estate

represented our home away from home during the six months we spent
in Germany.

The next morning, after a good night's sleep, we walked down to
Beutelsbach in small groups in order to get acquainted with the town
and its surroundings. The steep hillside was covered with tiny vineyards
and the valley with narrow plots of land, both the result of a system
of partible inheritance that divided landholdings among all the children
in the family. Each child received a small piece of each kind of land,
so that the plots of land owned by a family were not contiguous but
were widely dispersed over the hillsides and the valley. As we later
learned, this system was already on its last legs. The plots of land that
were owned by a family were so small that their tractors could not be
used efficiently in them, but served primarily as transportation from
one small field to another over a wide area.

In town, we wandered the streets staring at the novel sight of
multistory farm houses in town, rather than on the land, with livestock
occupying the ground floor, marked by a pile of manure beside the
double doors leading into the barn, and the family's living quarters on
the floors above. Although we never saw them outside, there were cows
in the barns (we occasionally heard them mooing). The fields were too
small for them to be used as draft animals. Their function was to provide
milk, and their body heat warmed the upper floors of the houses during
the winter.

In the evening, many of us returned to Beutelsbach for the New
Year's Eve festivities in the local hotels. They gave us an opportunity
to drink the local wine and become acquainted with some of the townspeople. We saw the New Year of 1960 in with mulled wine and songs
and then returned to the "Burg" (our name for the Stanford campus)
to sleep off the effects of the celebration.

The next afternoon, Dr. Boerner, the director of our program,
introduced me to two members of a Beutelsbach family who had been
alerted to my arrival by a fellow student who had been a member of a
previous Stanford-in-Germany group the year before. The student in

question had lived across the hall from me during the fall semester. This family, composed of two sisters and their brother, their spouses, and small children, became fast friends of Ann, Suzie, and me.

Classes began a few days later. They were held four days a week. The three days without classes gave us time to travel on the weekends. Professor George Spindler, who lived with his wife in the apartment above the Library, taught us an introductory course on cultural anthropology. Unlike such courses on the main campus in California, the emphasis of this course was on fieldwork conducted by the students in the class. Our first task was to become acquainted with a family in Beutelsbach or another nearby town and write an essay on child-rearing practices and interpersonal relationships. Our second assignment was to write a longer paper on some aspect of the culture of one of the towns in the region, either alone or in collaboration with another student. "My" family was the family that had already been introduced to me. For the other assignment, I conducted a study of law enforcement and crime in Beutelsbach with another student. There was only one policeman in the town; he welcomed us as guests in his home and for interviews because we were not permanent residents of the town. He and his wife came from northern Germany and were not allowed to fraternize with the local townspeople. We, being outsiders, were fair game.

Mr. Nanney offered a course in music appreciation that took advantage of our presence near Stuttgart and our trip to Rome later that quarter to introduce us to live operas and symphonies in those venues. We went to Stuttgart frequently in the evenings to attend musical events in the Liedershalle and the opera house there. We were expected to become familiar with every movement of Beethoven's Fifth Symphony and Verdi's operas, *La Forza del Destino* and *Don Giovanni*. It was rich fare, and I loved it.

We also took two language courses, one focused on German literature and grammar and the other on conversation. Our teacher was Fräulein Doerfel, a charming woman who got us all up to speed in conversation.

It was also possible to earn an activity credit that quarter by participating in the chorus. This was the only time in my life that I was
welcomed into a choral group. I learned to sing many German songs,
including some in Schwäbisch, the local dialect.

A few days after arriving in Germany, I received a letter from my
father's cousin Herbert Hoesch, inviting me to visit him and his wife
for a few days in their home in Bischofsheim, Bavaria. Several weekends
later, I took the train from Beutelsbach to Stuttgart, where I caught
another train for Würtzburg. There I was met by the Hoesches' chauffeur,
who drove me to Bischofsheim.

I spent three wonderful days with Uncle Herbert and Aunt Kordi
(as they asked me to call them) in their beautiful home. In one of our
conversations, Uncle Herbert mentioned that he had been in Berlin
with my father, when he was working for the Chinese News Agency.
The Chinese-American actress Anna May Wong, was performing in
Berlin at that time, and he said that my handsome father was often
seen with her then.[2] In this way and others, he fleshed out the stories
my father had told me about his youth.

During the weeks that followed, Ann and Suzie and I frequently
visited the three families whose menfolk had introduced themselves to
me on New Year's Day. The women in the families often spent time
together during the day, and, in their company, we soon established a
close relationship, using first names and the German second-person-
singular familiar pronoun "du" with each other. They became the focal
point of our experience, the context in which we came to understand
the local culture, improve our fluency in the language, and even learn
the local dialect, Schwäbisch. It was that experience more than any
other that year that led to my decision to become an ethnologist.

At the end of January, all the students in our group, except for
two who were very ill with the grippe, set out on a week-long field
trip to Rome. There we benefitted from walking tours of Renaissance
and Baroque art and architecture led by a student at the American
Academy of Fine Arts. Other tours focused on the landmarks of
ancient Rome.

On the day that we visited the Vatican museum, we attended a general audience with Pope John XXIII. The Catholic students in our group had brought along crosses for him to bless, including one for a student who was too ill to make the journey to Rome.

For me, one of the high points of our stay in Rome was the opportunity to attend performances of Verdi's *La Forza del Destino* and *Don Giovanni* in the city's magnificent opera house. Apparently knowing in advance that these two operas would be performed during our stay in Rome, Mr. Nanney had briefed us on them in great detail during our music appreciation course the previous month, and I had spent hours listening to them on the record player in the Library before coming to Rome. *La Forza del Destino* was my favorite opera from then on.

The other high point of my time in Rome was a bicycle trip to the Tivoli Fountains—35 kilometers outside Rome—that I made with another student. On our way out of the city, as well as upon our return, it was necessary to ride past the Coliseum, which was a hair-raising experience as he and I wended our way through the traffic, hoping that the cars would dodge us as they whizzed by. It was a beautiful day, and the mountains were lovely, although riding over cobblestones was not very comfortable. We stopped at Hadrian's Villa on the way back, walking over the ruins. Everything was crumbling, and sheep grazed over the once majestic floors. Mosaics in the ground crumbled and separated as we walked over them. We got back to Rome just in time to return our rented bikes and head for the train station. Completely exhausted after our long ride, I slept well on the train all the way back to Stuttgart.

The next big event on our schedule was *Rosenmontag*, or "Rose Monday," during Fasching, the period of merriment and release leading up to Ash Wednesday and the beginning of Lent. Most of the students in our group went to large cities like Munich and Cologne to take part in the celebrations. A few of us, including Ann, Suzie, and me, were intrigued by Professor Spindler's characterization of the Rosenmontag parade in the small town of Rottweil and decided to witness the celebration there. He told us that Rottweil had preserved ancient pre-Christian rites of spring in their yearly Rosenmontag festivities. We had to rise at 4:15 a.m., in order to catch the train to Rottweil, arriving at 7:45 a.m., in time to see the parade.

And what an amazing parade it was! It began with costumed riders on horseback with bugles carrying a banner as in the old days, coming through the town gate. Then came a swarm of children tickling adults with feathers and cows' tails because it was just before Lent, and they could be as bad as they wanted to be. They were mostly dressed as clowns.

Then came the most unbelievable horde of nightmarish creatures in traditional masks and costumes. Their garments were white with brightly colored scenes painted on them, with vines and flowers to beg the spring to come quickly. Some costumes were of flannel with feathers all over. The headpieces included beautiful lifelike masks, which seemed to change expression. A bunch of feathers was worn on top of the head, and ornaments, mirrors, and false hair surrounded the masks. Foxtails hung behind.

The men in these costumes wore braces of enormous bells over their shoulders and around their waists, which jingled when they jumped (Figure 4.1); some of them meant a burden of ninety pounds for the wearer. Little boys were dressed exactly like their fathers, whose hands they held. It was like an invasion.

The parade went through town twice, and then there was nothing to do because everyone either went home to meals with the family or to family dinners in hotels. The costumed men went around telling jokes and fortunes to groups and passing out candy. We followed the band, and there was dancing in the streets.

It was not at all commercial—there were few tourists. It seemed to be a family holiday, and we felt left out. So we went home.

Nevertheless, this festival in Rottweil made a great impression on me, one that I would remember in the years to come, because of its

FIGURE 4.1.   Fasching in Rottweil in February 1960.
Photo by Victoria R. Bricker.

resemblance to the festival of Saint Sebastian in Zinacantan in Mexico, where I carried out my first anthropological fieldwork, and to Mardi Gras in New Orleans, where I lived for many years.

After winter quarter ended, with final exams during the second week of March, we had a three-week vacation, which gave me an opportunity to visit my father's cousin Anna Koufas, known in our

family as "Anna of Greece." She lived in Salonika (originally Thessalon-
iki) in northern Greece with her husband, Dino. Ann and Suzie came
with me on this journey. We traveled from Stuttgart to Salonika through
Yugoslavia on the "Yugoslavian Express," a train with shoddily built
second-class cars jammed with passengers and an almost empty, but
luxuriously equipped first-class car. The poverty we saw as we passed
through the Yugoslavian Alps shocked us. Both the people on the train
and those standing next to the tracks in the train stations were shabbily
dressed. The men's pants were covered with patches, and they had no
jackets or coats. There were no cars in sight on the street in Belgrade,
only trams and bicycles and carts drawn by animals. The contrast with
Germany was striking.

On the other hand, the scenery as we traveled through the mountains was breathtakingly beautiful in the moonlight. Ann and I stood
for most for the night looking out the open window in the hallway,
letting Suzie stretch out across our seats for a good night's sleep.

In Salonika the next morning, the tourist police helped us change
money and call the Koufas home on the telephone. Anna's son, Nagi,
came for us and took us to their home. Anna did not know that I had
brought two friends with me, but she rallied to the occasion by arranging
for them to stay in the clinic attached to the office of her husband,
who was a doctor. Anna and Dino had met in Vienna, where Dino was
in medical school and Anna in dental school, while my father was
studying Chinese at the University of Vienna during the 1920s.

The arrival of Ann and Suzie in the clinic caused quite a sensation.
All the patients hopped out of bed to see the strangers. The three of
us slept for the rest of the day, I in Anna and Dino's guest bedroom,
Ann and Suzie in the clinic.

The next morning, Ann and Suzie came over after breakfast, and
Nagi briefed us on the history of Salonika. After lunch, Dino and Anna
took us on a tour of the city. On the way to visit a prison on top of a
hill, we passed a gypsy with a dancing bear, so we got out of the car
and had our picture taken with the bear (Figure 4.2). The bear's owner

FIGURE 4.2.   Beside a dancing bear in Salonika. *Left to right*: Ann Cilley, Suzan Behrman, Victoria.

refused to let an American journalist take a picture of the dancing bear, because she was unwilling to pay for the privilege, saying that if she had to pay for every picture, she would not be able to make a living.

The prisons on the hill were part of the old wall and were used as a military fortress. Dino got permission for us to go upstairs, and he gave the soldiers permission to help us upstairs because we had heels on, and the steps were rough-hewn. The soldiers were very gentle with us, and Dino said that Greek girls would never allow soldiers to help them and that the soldiers felt this a special privilege.

We then went to an old monastery, where Dino and Anna had been married and where the sign of the fish was visible in the floor. There were also ancient mosaics there. The atmosphere was so different from the churches we had seen in Germany and Italy because of the many candles and the ikons in the monastery.

In the evening, Nagi took us to a restaurant for dessert and then to a dance place on the beach.

The next day, Nagi served as our tour guide. He took us to several churches and to White Tower, where he obtained permission for us to climb to the top. From there, we could see the gulf, with Mount Olympus apparently suspended in the air.

We spent the evening at Dino and Anna's home, just sitting around talking. They showed us slides of Nagi and his sister, Calliope, when they were children. Nagi recommended several inexpensive hotels in Athens where we could stay and restaurants where we could have a good meal.

We arose early the next morning in order to catch the train to Athens. On long train trips like this one, I usually brought along some knitting to pass the time. I soon discovered that such a project had an added benefit when rolling through countries whose languages I did not speak. Invariably, a local woman seated in the same compartment with me would watch me for a while and then signal that she would like to add a row or two to the sweater I was knitting. I would hand over my knitting and watch her as she added a few rows to my work. It was a form of communication without words, and it never failed to elicit a smile and, I hoped, a sense that we had something in common, even though we obviously came from different cultures. It was a great icebreaker.

And that is exactly what happened while we were on the train between Salonika and Athens. A lady knitted on my sweater for a few minutes and then offered us some chewing gum from the Isle of Korfu. It consisted of a greenish sap and was quite tasty.

After arriving in Athens, we went to the Youth Hostel, where we had planned to spend the night. We were appalled at the low level of sanitation there, so after dinner, we looked into one of the hotels that Nagi had suggested to us: the Banghion on Omonia Square in the center of Athens. The hotel let us have cheap rates—three for the price of two—110 drachmas per night. We decided to move in the next day.

From there, we took day trips, first tours within the city that included a visit to the Parthenon and several museums and then to places like Corinth, Mycenae, Delphi, and Epidaurus. These places were familiar to me because of the humanities course in ancient literature I had taken during the fall quarter before coming to Europe.

After thirteen days in Greece, we decided to move on to Vienna by train on March 26. I sent a telegram to Anna, informing her that we were coming back and at what time we would arrive in Salonika. After boarding the train, we found seats in a car whose ultimate destination was Paris. A Greek lady helped me knit and wind yarn, and we spent a pleasant night, with five in our compartment.

Anna and Nagi met our train in Salonika at 6:30 the next morning. They came on the train, and we talked, Nagi filling gaps in the conversation and making us laugh, with remarks on Greece as an "underdeveloped" country. They had brought us a bag of food and some cognac for Aunt Kordi, whom I would be seeing again in a few weeks. It was sad to wave goodbye to them—never to see them again.

We arrived in Vienna two days later at 10:00 in the evening. The man at the information desk made a reservation for us at the Pension Carina, and we took a taxi there. It took a while for someone to open the door for us. As we went upstairs to our room, the lights suddenly went out. This was our first experience with what the French call a *minuterie*, a light that lasts for only one minute, giving the user time to reach another timer switch further along. But our room was very nice, with three wooden beds and hot water.

Vienna is a beautiful city, with magnificent architecture, but spring had not yet arrived at the end of March while we were there. It seemed cold and dark, compared with the bright sunshine and blue skies we had enjoyed in Salonika, Athens, and the archaeological sites we had visited in other parts of Greece. Nevertheless, it was exciting to be in the city where my father was born and raised before leaving for China.

We visited the palace at Schönbrunn and the Hofburg, where we watched the Spanish Riding Academy practice for a performance, but the highlight of our stay in Vienna was the opportunity to attend several operas: *Carmen* and *Aïda* at the Stadtsoper and *Die Lustige Witwe* ("The Merry Widow") at the Volksoper. Carmen was sold out, but students could attend it, if they were willing to stand at the back of the opera house and watch the performance from there. We began standing in line for this privilege at 3:30 in the afternoon. We were let into the place at 4:00 to sit waiting until 6:00, after which we had to stand until the end of the performance. In our standing position, we were able to see and hear the opera very well. It was performed in French and was well worth the discomfort of standing. For *Aïda*, which we attended on our last day in Vienna, we had both tickets and seats. The performance was wonderful, serving as an appropriate climax to our stay in this beautiful city and our three-week vacation.

The courses offered during the spring quarter were economics, taught by Lorie Tarshis, medieval world literature, taught by Virgil Whittaker, and, of course, intensive German and conversational German, taught by Fräulein Doerfel. The non-German language courses that quarter did not have the same relevance to our location in the heart of a traditional agricultural region as did the cultural anthropology and music courses offered during the winter quarter.

The next journey we made was to Berlin. We did not go by train this time, because to do so would have meant crossing East Germany, which was not recognized by either West Germany or the United States. Instead, we flew from Stuttgart to the Tempelhof airport in West Berlin. From there, we went to the *Haus der Zukunft* ("House of the Future"), a hostel maintained by the West German government on the western edge of the city near the border separating West Berlin from East Germany.

After breakfast the next morning, the man in charge of our hostel briefed us at length on the situation in Berlin. He told us that, for transportation in the city, we could take the U-bahn (the underground train) or the S-bahn (the above-ground train), but when taking the S-bahn, we had to watch for our stop carefully, because the S-bahn did not stop at the zone border, and, if we got into Potsdam in the East Zone, we were likely to be thrown in jail.[3] The American government could not help us in that situation, because it did not have diplomatic relations with East Germany. In case we were detained in the east sector, we should insist on seeing the American Commandant, and if not he, then the Russian Commandant. The situation in Berlin was such that the Americans regarded themselves as occupation forces and Russia as that also; therefore, any communication with East Germany must come through the Russian Commandant. However, East Germany wanted to be recognized, and Russia wanted it to be recognized. All Russia had to do was to withdraw her occupation forces, as it was then fifteen years after the war, and it was ridiculous that Berlin was still occupied. This would have forced the United States to recognize the East German government, admitting that a part of Germany must remain Communist. Clearly, Russia was calling the plays.

With these sobering thoughts on our minds, we moved about West Berlin, making sure that we got off the S-bahn at the station before the border with East Germany. Within the city, we noticed great differences between the two Berlins. In West Berlin, much of the rubble had been cleared away and replaced by modern shops and architecturally striking high-rise buildings so that the city could serve as a model of economic prosperity in the free world, whereas in East Berlin, near the boundary with West Berlin, the Russians had left the rubble as a reminder of

Germany's defeat in the war. One evening, several of us decided to attend a performance of the ballet *Swan Lake* in the east sector. After crossing into East Berlin, we had to pick our way in the dark over the rubble to the small Stadtsoper, where the ballet was performed. The Kurfürstendamm, the principal shopping street in West Berlin, resembled Fifth Avenue in New York in the elegant styling of its buildings with plate-glass windows and the opulence of its merchandise. The economic differences between the two Berlins could not have been starker.

All this was not lost on the East Berliners and the people in the city's hinterland in East Germany. They were fleeing to the West in droves during the months I spent in Germany. Six thousand refugees came into West Berlin in four days during the Easter weekend. These refugees, who were called *Flüchtlinge* or *Vertriebene*, were brought to refugee camps, called *Flüchtlingslager*. We visited one refugee camp—the Marienfelderlager—during our week in Berlin and attended four hearings with refugees in which they explained why they had left the East Zone. The principal reason seemed to be economic, the difficulty in making a living under the Communist regime. Many of the refugees were resettled in West Germany, as was the case in Beutelsbach and other towns in the region. Because they were landless, they did not adopt the culture of their new neighbors. Instead, they established businesses in the towns, thereby diversifying the economy and the culture of the region.

The German counterpart of the American Labor Day was celebrated on the first of May in both East and West Berlin (Figure 4.3). Most of the students in our group decided to observe the festivities in East Berlin. We took the train as far as Checkpoint Charlie and then walked across the border into the eastern part of the city.[4]

We joined people watching a parade, but the crowd was so large, that it was not possible to see anything. Some of us decided to join the parade behind the marching soldiers, mounted guns, and tanks and eventually found ourselves walking through Marx–Engels Platz in front of the dignitaries in the stands. No one noticed us there, walking along

FIGURE 4.3.   May Day in Berlin. *Left to right*: Erika Bauer, Ann Cilley, Victoria, Günther (an East Berliner), Suzan Behrman.

taking pictures and eating peanuts. We continued walking in the parade for some time until we realized that we were back in Marx–Engels Platz! The parade was being recycled, giving the false impression that the soldiers and weapons were more numerous than they actually were.

We flew back to Stuttgart late the next day. The Tempelhof airport was crowded because one thousand refugees were scheduled to be flown to West Germany that night to make room for a like number that had come into West Berlin the day before. I saw people with a nervous excitement waiting for the adventure of going into a new land, not knowing what awaited them there. I saw farmers who would never again be able to farm because there was not enough land in West Germany for them to follow their traditional way of life.

That experience in Berlin, more than any other, made me realize that deep changes were under way in West Germany. The resettling of so many people from the East Zone in the West explained all the new construction I had seen on the outskirts of Beutelsbach. The new housing in high-rise apartment buildings contrasted markedly with the traditional single-family farmhouses in the rest of the town. As I learned some years later, what I witnessed in Beutelsbach in 1960 was a community on the threshhold of profound changes that would ultimately sweep away the traditional peasant way of life forever.[5]

The seeds for such changes were already in place while I was living at the Burg, but I was not aware of their significance. There were two plantations below the Burg, where an experiment in cooperative farming was underway, which was breaking up the picturesque, but tiny vineyards on the hillside and consolidating them. One of my friends in Beutelsbach was farsighted enough to realize that change was inevitable. He was Herr Koch, the head of one of the three families with whom Ann and Suzie and I had a close friendship. I remember him telling me that his way of life was doomed, but I was too naive to believe him then.

Of the three families we came to know well, only two were engaged in farming full time. The head of the third, Herr Romaersch, worked in a utility company in Waiblingen, not far from Beutelsbach. His family lived in a newly built, modern house on the outskirts of town. He and his wife did some farming, especially in the vineyards on the hillsides, but it was no longer their principal means of subsistence, as it was for the other two families.[6]

Shortly before the end of spring quarter, Ann and Suzie and I decided to explore the possibility of staying on for another month with the three families and helping them in their fields. Their response was both positive and enthusiastic, and it was arranged that I would live with the Kochs, Ann with the Staibs, and Suzie with the Romaerschs. We learned how to cut grass for hay on the scattered long and narrow fields in the valley, stack it to protect it from rain while it was drying, and bring it to the barns on wagons pulled by tractors. We also learned how to tie grapevines to the stakes in the families' widely separated vineyards on the hillside and picked strawberries and cherries in the small fields in the valley. It was a highly rewarding experience to share the daily activities of these kind and hospitable people.[7]

Near the end of June, Suzie's boyfriend and future husband, Jim Stewart, came with a friend of his to take her with them on a tour of Europe for some weeks. Ann and I traveled together by train to London, where she would visit a friend whose father had a position in Lambeth Palace, the administrative headquarters and residence of the Archbishop of Canterbury, and I would spend the next five weeks visiting my mother's English relatives. On the way to London, we spent a few days sightseeing in Paris and its environs, including a visit to the Louvre Museum, where we enjoyed seeing Leonardo da Vinci's portrait of Mona Lisa, and the palace at Versailles. Then we took the boat train to Le Havre and crossed the English Channel on a ferry. Ann was met by someone at the train station, who took her to Lambeth Palace. I had not made contact with any relatives of mine before Ann left. She asked me to call her later to let her know that I had succeeded in meeting up with my relatives.[8]

Three of my mother's relatives had come to Waterloo Station to meet me: her Aunts Esther and Queenie, who were her father's sisters, and my mother's stepmother, whom we knew as Aunt Anne. My grandfather had married her after returning to England from Shanghai after the war (and after the death of my grandmother before that).

They took me in a taxi to Aunt Esther's flat in northwest London, where I stayed for much of the time I was in England. A day or so later, there was a party at which I met many members of my mother's family. Her aunts and uncles and cousins were anxious to meet a daughter of the woman they had last seen in 1935, twenty-five years before I showed up in London.

I was royally treated by my mother's relatives, who took me sightseeing both in London and places outside the city. With them, I visited the Roman wall outside Winchester and the seaside in Bournemouth and Brighton. In Brighton, I sampled the candy called *Brighton Rock*, which was the title of a novel by Graham Greene that I had read during a course in Masterpieces of British Literature in the fall of 1959. While I was staying with Aunt Esther, I also explored London on my own by foot or on public transportation.

My experiences in London helped me to understand what my mother's childhood must have been like in the bosom of a large extended family so unlike my own childhood in Shanghai and Seattle, where our social contacts were limited to people who were not related to us. My mother thought of the years of her childhood as some of the happiest years of her life, and she corresponded with her relatives in England frequently in handwritten letters and later e-mails until the last year of her life, when she could no longer use a computer. Meeting her relatives and seeing how close they were to each other made me realize how difficult it must have been for her to live in a place without such bonds. I, for my part, was just as glad that such a large and ever-present family was not a part of my childhood.

Soon after arriving in London, I decided to write a letter to my father in German, while the language was still fresh in my mind. He responded with a letter, also in German, in which he commented that this was the first time that he had written to one of his children in German![9] It was also the last.

He went on to address a concern I had expressed in my letter, namely, my uncertainty about what I might do in the future:

> Your concern about the future, especially the choice of a profession, is completely natural and reminds me of my own University days in Vienna. We can discuss that in detail after your return [to Seattle]. The final decision lies entirely with you. It does not matter what it is, as long as it is something that corresponds to your talents and interests you greatly, so that whatever you choose is something that you can accomplish.[10]

I was deeply moved by his response, which was, of course, in character, reflecting his own adventurous spirit when he was my age and later. Neither of my parents dictated the path I or my siblings should follow, encouraging us to pursue our own interests, as spelled out in this letter.

When it came time for me to leave London, I took the train to Southampton on August 5th, where I boarded a French boat, the *Flandre*, for my journey to New York. Suzie and Jim met me in Southampton, and we traveled together on the *Flandre* back to America. Suzie and I shared a cabin with two girls from New York.

Suzie's father met our boat in New York on August 11th. He had arranged for Suzie and me to stay in the apartment of his sister, who was away at the time. He took us sightseeing in New York and to a Broadway play. I had a wonderful time getting to know a city I had heard so much about.

One day while I was in New York, I traveled to Passaic, New Jersey, to meet my father's cousins, who had been so helpful to him during the months in 1947, when he was looking for the job that brought us to the United States. This family had emigrated from Vienna to this country early in the twentieth century while my father was a boy.

From New York, I flew to Detroit to meet other cousins of my father. They also saw to it that I had a good time during the few days I was there.

My entire family was at the airport in Seattle to welcome their "world traveler" home. I was the first child in my nuclear family to travel abroad, beginning a pattern that was followed by Frank and Anne when they became older. It was the three oldest children who were born in China who continued this tradition. It is as though having been born in an exotic land, we had been destined for travel. Consuela's and Michaela's travel has been limited to places in the United States and Canada.

My mother was hungry for news about her relatives, what they were like, and what I thought about each one. We spent hours talking about them after I got home. My father had met them on one of his trips to Europe after coming to Seattle, but Mother had too many responsibilities at home for her to go with him then.[11]

After a few weeks at home, I took the train to Stanford to begin my junior year. I returned to Lagunita, the dorm where I had lived during the fall quarter of my sophomore year, joining Arley Timm, my roommate from freshman year and also the first quarter of my sophomore year. Janie and Patty had stayed on in Germany for six months to work in a hospital, and Ann and Suzie moved into another dorm.

Although the members of our Stanford-in-Germany group were now scattered in different dormitories across campus, we enjoyed many social occasions together. The Spindlers and Tarshises sponsored reunions in their homes several times during my junior and senior years. When our friends Bob Harden and Jesse Kalin rented a house in Palo Alto, it became the locus of impromptu get-togethers for some of us. I remember attending potluck dinners at Thanksgiving in their home both years. They and other students who had been in Germany with me became my reference group for the rest of my time at Stanford.[12]

Once back at Stanford, I plunged into my philosophy and humanities courses, which were both interesting and challenging. I liked the tutorial system for students majoring in philosophy, in which I and five other students met for several hours once a week with a professor to discuss the work of a single philosopher. During the first half of our junior year, we could choose either Aristotle or Plato for this purpose. I chose Aristotle, and in our weekly meetings we discussed a few pages of his *Posterior Analytics*, a dense work that required much concentration to master.[13] For the other half of the year, the choice was between Hume and Kant. I chose Kant, and our tutor for his work was an advanced graduate student, Jane Burton. From these tutors, I learned how to dissect the writings of philosophers in order to identify their basic principles and assess the validity of their arguments.

The students majoring in philosophy met alone with their tutors during their senior year. I had benefited greatly from Jane Burton's efforts to improve my writing in the essays I wrote on Kant, encouraging me to streamline my prose by reducing it to the essential components of my argument. Therefore, I was happy that she was willing and able to serve as my tutor during my senior year as well. In that capacity, she also directed my honors thesis on a topic in the philosophy of language.

For my minor in the Humanities Honors Program, I wrote a "senior essay" on the folklore of the Kwakiutl Indians of the Pacific Northwest, the region of North America where I had lived before coming to Stanford. For this purpose, I considered the myths collected and published by George Hunt and Franz Boas.[14] The focus of my essay was the Kwakiutl worldview, specifically their attitude to life and death, as revealed in two objects that were mentioned in a number of the myths, called the *death-bringer* and the *water of life*. These were magical objects. When used as instructed, the "death-bringer" had the power to kill animals for food during times of scarcity, and the "water of life" had the power to restore life to dead people under certain conditions. My analysis of the role played by these objects in Kwakiutl myths concluded that the people who believed in them did not regard death as inevitable or final. This was my first serious encounter with oral tradition as a topic for investigation, to which I would return years later, after I had received professional training as an ethnologist (see Chapter 7).

At that time, all students at Stanford were required to take two senior colloquia during their last year of college. For me, one of them had to be the colloquium offered by the Humanities Honors Program. It was taught by Virgil Whittaker, the great expert on Shakespeare, who had been one of my professors in Germany. We met at his home once a week in the evening to discuss literary works of his choosing, sweetened by servings of strawberry ice.

For the other colloquium, I chose the one offered by Duane Metzger, a professor in the Anthropology Department, who was carrying out ethnographic research in Chiapas, Mexico. This choice was influenced by a medical student I was dating at the time, who spent his summers on a project investigating genetic differences in blood types among different communities in highland Chiapas. He had suggested that I might carry out some fieldwork in Chiapas that summer, while he would be working there. Taking a course from a professor who had an ongoing field project in Chiapas might be a way of exploring such a possibility.

With the help of Duane Metzger, I did apply for grants for that summer, without success. Nevertheless, once the idea of working in Mexico entered my head, I pursued it because I already had some knowledge of the national language of the country (Spanish). Therefore, when applying to graduate schools, I mentioned my interest in specializing in the anthropology of Mexico. I was admitted to the graduate programs in anthropology at Harvard, Cornell, and the University of Chicago. I chose Harvard because it was the only university that offered me financial aid.

My entire family drove down to Stanford for my commencement on June 17, 1962. After Commencement, I remained in California for most of the summer in order to participate in a ten-week program sponsored by the Western Interstate Commission on Higher Education (WICHE) to recruit college students into the mental health professions. The program began with a one-week intensive course in the sociology of mental health at the College of the Pacific in Stockton, followed by eight weeks of paid employment as a psychiatric technician in one of the mental hospitals in the state, and ended with a one-week wrap-up of the course back at the College of the Pacific. My internship and those of several other students took place in Stockton State Mental Hospital. Other students in the program were assigned to mental hospitals in other cities, such as Agnew near Stanford, Merced, and Sonoma State, which was a facility for mentally handicapped patients. For comparative purposes, visits to the other hospitals were arranged from time to time, to which we traveled in state cars.

During the eight weeks I spent at Stockton State Hospital, I rotated through the acute, chronic, medical, and geriatric wards, one week at a time. In addition, each week I "shadowed" a different specialist on his or her rounds: a psychologist, a psychiatrist, a social worker, a medical doctor, and a nurse.

On the acute ward, I was expected to attend "therapeutic community" meetings with groups of patients and staff, converse with individual patients, and assist in holding down patients who were undergoing electroshock therapy. I found the forced participation in electroshock therapy distasteful, but I could see that it was an effective (if brutal) treatment for catatonia, because after some days, the patient recovered the ability to communicate with others.

I remember that a catatonic patient with whose treatment I assisted came up to me some days later and thanked me for helping her, indicating that she had been aware of what was going on around her, even though she was unable to speak or show emotion while she was in her catatonic state.

Anticipating that, in a few months, I would begin my graduate training in anthropology, I was especially interested in a recently committed Mexican patient and a Native American member of a tribe in northern California, who was a patient on the chronic ward. The Mexican patient came to my attention when I attended a set of commitment hearings in the hospital's courtroom. I was disturbed by the fact that he did not speak or understand English, that only the interpreter understood or spoke Spanish, and I thought that the interpreter misrepresented the patient's answers to the questions that were directed to him. I mentioned my suspicion that he had been wrongly committed to the psychologist I was "shadowing" that week. The psychologist arranged for me to talk to the patient in Spanish in his presence. I later learned that this patient had been released. He had been committed only because his brother had a grudge against him. In any case, I wondered how Mexican patients could be helped by a therapeutic community when these patients could neither speak nor understand English well enough to communicate with the staff or other patients.

I learned about the Native American patient from the doctor I "shadowed" some weeks later. Knowing of my interest in anthropology, the doctor told me that he had a patient whose hallucinations included images of falling water, and he arranged for me to talk to him. I later realized that this patient's descriptions of water had a shamanistic quality, and I wondered whether the definition of mental illness might vary from culture to culture.

In my work on the different wards, I was impressed with the way that patients tried to help each other—how they rallied around those among them who became despondent and regressed and by the need-relationships that developed between patients: the young man palling around with an older woman, providing her with a son and him with a mother; the teenager who was scolded and comforted by a sensible forty-year-old woman. It was clear that they were compensating for the loss of relationships resulting from being away from their families or friends or benefiting from the opportunity to form relationships that they did not have in the outside world. Their efforts to provide a community for each other seemed to me more therapeutic than the artificial "therapeutic community" imposed upon them by the staff.

As the weeks passed, I gradually realized that there is a narrow line between sanity and insanity, and I learned how to recognize conditions in a person's social or psychological environment that can push him or her across that line. I also came to the realization that people cannot be helped by advice, but can only be helped to help themselves. As I wrote in the summary of my summer experience:

> This is a line of thinking towards which I have been moving throughout my last year in college, and it has now crystallized for me. I am sure now that it isn't other people's acceptance which is most important to the individual but his own acceptance of himself as he is without any guilt for being what he is which is most important. And the inner strength to resist the attempts of others to destroy his self-confidence and sense of worth by innuendo and manipulation. And all this I can remember to consider when thinking of myself, of others, and of my relations with others.

During the weeks I spent learning about mental health in the internship program that summer, I returned to a matter to which I had given much thought while I was a student at Stanford. Like many college students, I wrestled with the question of whether there was any intrinsic meaning in life. Although I was raised in a religious faith, I did not find meaning there, and I did not practice my religion after I left home, nor did I affiliate with any other religious community. By the time I graduated from Stanford, I had concluded that meaning came from immersing myself in the lives of other people. Like my father, I identified with the university community of which I became part and the larger community of scholars that expanded through time. It was in my relationships with colleagues, students, family, friends, and the people among whom I worked in Mexico that I have found meaning in life.

NOTES

1. My father preferred to speak English for the rest of his life. However, German was the only language he had in common with some of his relatives, and his correspondence with them was always in German. In addition, I noticed that he used the German words for numbers when counting and engaging in arithmetical calculations out loud. His English was fluent but heavily accented. I once asked him why he had retained his German accent with English, but spoke Chinese without such an accent. He replied that it was probably because he cared more about speaking Chinese like a native.

2. My father had already met Anna May Wong in Vienna, before going to Berlin. Knowing of his great interest in the Chinese language and culture, it was she who suggested that he go out to China himself, thereby initiating the greatest adventure of his life. A picture of her in a family album from that period is inscribed "To Erwin."

3. Service on the U-bahn was provided by West Berlin, but service on the S-bahn was provided by East Berlin, which was affiliated with the East Zone.

4. Our visit to the two Berlins took place one year before the wall separating them went up. It was therefore possible to move freely

between the two parts of the city, as many refugees from the East Zone did. After the wall went up in 1961, the exodus from East Germany slowed to a trickle, giving the East German government greater control over its people. The next time I was in East Berlin was in July 1992, less than three years after the wall came down (see Chapter 10).

5. These changes are described at length in *Burgbach: Urbanization and Identity in a German Village*, by George Spindler and "Student Collaborators," of whom I was one. In the early 1970s, in a program called *Flurbereinigung* "land consolidation," the fields in the valley and on the hillside were stripped of such cultural accretions as stone terraces and tool houses. All the soil was removed and mixed together and returned to the land. This was followed by an exchange of titles in which adjacent parcels of land were re-allocated to form larger, more efficient holdings, leaving many farmers without land. Nothing is left of the traditional peasant culture in the Remstal region of southern Germany. Beutelsbach is now a bedroom suburb of Stuttgart called *Weinstatt*, its new name but a faint reminder of the town's former emphasis on growing grapes for fine wine. Nothing is left of the town I remember from 1960, where I had my first anthropological experience.

6. Eight years later, when I returned to Beutelsbach with Harvey to visit these families, I discovered that Herr Koch had gone into industry in Waiblingen. His family lived in a new house on the edge of town, next door to his brother-in-law. Only the Staib family was still involved in agriculture full time, and they had to diversify their activities in order to make ends meet.

7. These were not the only people in Beutelsbach I came to know well. Early in the winter quarter, I had met a Beutelsbacher named Herr Bäcker on the train between Stuttgart and Beutelsbach. He told me that he had been a prisoner of war for two and one-half years in Florida, where he had worked as a farm laborer, thereby missing most of the action in Europe during the war. I visited him and his wife and daughter frequently and came to know them well.

I also visited the Lang family in the town of Endersbach near Beutelsbach, whose daughter, Rosemarie, was a good friend of Janie and Patty.

8. Aunt Esther was stunned when, upon my arrival in her home, I told her that I had to call my friend in Lambeth Palace to let her know that I had found my relatives in the train station, and she was even more surprised when I succeeded in reaching her there. The notion of a member of our very religious family having the audacity to make a call to the seat of the Anglican church in England was astounding and served as the major topic of conversation at the family get-together that took place shortly afterward.

9. "Dies ist das erste Mal, dass ich einem meiner Kinder auf Deutsch geschrieben habe!" Letter from Erwin Reifler to Victoria Reifler, July 31, 1960.

10. "Deine Zukunftssorgen, besonders was die Berufwahl anlangt, sind vollkommen natuerlich und erinnern mich an mein Universitaets-zeit in Wien. Wir koennen das nach Deiner Rueckkehr in allen Einzelheiten besprechen. Die letzte Entscheidung liegt natuerlich bei Dir. Es ist gans gleichgueltig, was es ist, solange es etwas ist, das Deinen natuerlichen Anlagen entspricht und Dich sehr interessiert, sodass Du auf dem Gebiete Deiner Wahl etwas leisten kannst." Letter from Erwin Reifler to Victoria Reifler, July 31, 1960.

11. I spent the summer between my junior and senior years at home in Seattle, carrying out temporary clerical tasks in various offices of the University of Washington. Upon learning that my father would be traveling in Europe for some weeks that summer, I offered to look after the household so that my mother could go with him to England to see her relatives again. Her sister flew to London from Johannesburg, and they were reunited for the first time in nineteen years.

12. For years after we graduated from Stanford, various members of our group would arrange reunions, usually at five-year anniversaries of the time we spent in Germany in 1960, but also in conjunction with the general five-year reunions of our graduating class. In the

early years, they were not held at Stanford, but in the city where the organizer(s) lived. I remember that one reunion was in Washington, DC. More recently, those reunions have taken place on the Stanford campus. I attended three such reunions at Stanford: in 1995, 2000, and 2005. My husband, Harvey, accompanied me the last two times. There was another reunion at Stanford in 2015 we were not able to attend.

13. This work was so hard to make sense of that I was not able to take notes on it in preparation for our weekly discussion sessions. I turned for help to Professor Jeffrey Smith, who was teaching the humanities seminar on biography that semester. He told me that he had had the same problem when he was a graduate student at Oxford and that his mentor, Professor Collingwood, had suggested that he rewrite each paragraph of Aristotle's work in his own words. I followed this advice, with good results.

14. George Hunt and Franz Boas, *Kwakiutl Texts*, Memoirs of the American Museum of Natural History, Volume 5 (New York: 1902).

5

HARVARD AND FRANCE: BECOMING AN ETHNOLOGIST

I began to feel at home at Harvard and in Cambridge very soon after my arrival at the end of September in 1962, after a three-day journey by train from Seattle. I enjoyed the more urban campus and the greater formality of New Englanders, compared to the casual social atmosphere I was familiar with on the West Coast. The housemother in my dorm was a third-year graduate student in anthropology. She took me under her wing and guided me during the first weeks of the semester, helping me select courses and acquainting me with the academic culture of the Peabody Museum on Divinity Avenue, where the Department of Anthropology was housed. However, she did not tell me that I had a mailbox in the library; therefore, I did not receive the invitation to the tea for new graduate students nor the request to meet with the chairman of the department, who would have assigned me an adviser. Instead, I went directly to classes on the first day of the semester.

I signed up for the course in South American Indians because it was taught by Professor Evon Z. Vogt, who I knew had a field site in Mexico. At the end of the first meeting of the class, I went up to him, introduced myself, and asked him to be my adviser. He looked surprised and suggested that I make an appointment to see him in his office at 9 Bow Street, which I did. I later realized that he was accustomed to choosing his own students. Nevertheless, our meeting went well, and he agreed to be my adviser. He was a wonderful mentor and friend and a strong supporter of my academic career from then on.

A few weeks after the beginning of the semester, the department secretary notified me that the Chairman, Professor William Howells, wanted to see me. I wondered why. It turned out that because I had not checked in with him when I arrived on campus, there was no official record of my matriculation in the graduate program. Fortunately, my seeming independence was not taken amiss and, in light of the prevailing attitude toward women students in the department (of which, see more in the text that follows), it may have been perceived as a positive trait.

My other courses that first semester were anthropological linguistics, taught by Richard Diebold, one on the cultural anthropology of

India, taught by Cora Du Bois, and an evening proseminar in social and cultural anthropology required of all first-year graduate students, co-taught by Douglas Oliver and the other sociocultural anthropologists in the department. I found them intellectually less difficult than the philosophy courses I had taken at Stanford. What I did find challenging was the need to consider empirical data in term papers. Having been taught to write essays based entirely on logical reasoning without resort to concrete examples, I now had to engage in analysis and argumentation in which empirical data were primary. I made that transition by the end of my first semester at Harvard and have remained a dyed-in-the-wool empiricist throughout my subsequent academic career.

There were twelve students in our entering class, nine men and three women. One of the women dropped out before the end of the first month, and one of the men dropped out at the end of the first year. The rest of us formed a cohesive community. There was a clear sense that we were all in it together, in spite of our different research interests, and it fostered a kind of camaraderie and concern for each other's welfare, providing a noncompetitive environment in which we could flourish. It was the first time in my life that I felt that I belonged.

We would gather for lunch in the smoking room in the basement of the museum, which was the only place in the building where smoking was permitted. Other smokers in the building, both faculty and research staff, would join us in that room. Although I have never smoked, I enjoyed socializing with other students in that room.

It was also in the smoking room that I first came to know Tatiana Proskouriakoff, who had joined the research staff at Peabody Museum after a career at the Carnegie Institution of Washington. She was one of the great pioneers of Maya epigraphy, the one who proved that the content of the hieroglyphic texts on stone monuments at Classic Maya sites concerned the lives and exploits of the ruling families in those cities and were therefore not limited to religious matters and astronomy as scholars had previously thought. My own interest in this field of research came many years later, long after I had left Harvard, where I focused on the cultures of the living Maya, not of their Precolumbian ancestors. Nevertheless, she took an interest in me while I was still a student and one day invited me to visit her office, where she showed me what she was doing with the jades recovered from the large sinkhole at the site of Chichen Itza.[1]

I also enjoyed the experience of attending classes in a museum. There was a large totem pole at the end of the hall that led from the front door to the collections on the first floor. The department office was reached by turning right at the totem pole. Whenever I wanted to take a break from studying in the library, I would wander through the exhibits on the first and second floors.

My parents visited me in Cambridge after classes ended in December, and I traveled with them to Baltimore, where my father attended meetings and Mother and I went sightseeing. We took the train up to Washington, DC, and toured the city one day.

Several Stanford-in-Germany students besides me had moved on to graduate school at Harvard. One of them was my former roommate, Janie Breeden, who was studying medicine at the Medical School. Another was Lorene Yap, who was in the graduate program in economics. I spent the second half of the Christmas vacation in Lorene's apartment because my dorm was closed for the holidays. Janie was staying with Lorene for the same reason.

Still another was Louise Lamphere, who was a member of the Stanford-in-Germany group after ours and was Lorene's roommate at Harvard. Because she was concentrating in social anthropology in the Department of Social Relations, she was a fellow student in several of my courses, whom I came to know well.

Harvey Bricker was one of the students in our cohort. We began dating in the middle of the fall semester, and by the middle of the spring semester, we realized that we cared enough about each other and had enough goals in common to spend the rest of our lives together. Shortly after having made that decision, Harvey's professor, Hallam Movius, invited him to spend the next year in France, including the summers of 1963 and 1964, for a total of sixteen months. We decided to postpone our marriage until after he came back from France.

My father visited me in Cambridge again during the second week of April 1963 after attending a professional meeting in Washington, DC. This was an opportunity for him to meet Harvey, whom he liked right away. He recognized Harvey as a serious, scholarly person, and, in a letter, he told my mother that seeing us together reminded him of the days in Shanghai when he was courting her.

The week after my father's visit was spring vacation. Harvey took me to Lancaster, Pennsylvania, where I met his parents and other members of his family who lived nearby.

I spent the summer of 1963 in Mexico, learning to speak Tzotzil, the language of the Zinacantec Indians, who live in the highlands of the state of Chiapas, near the city of San Cristobal las Casas. My experiences during that summer and the summer of 1964, as well as the fieldwork I carried out there in 1965–1966 and 1968–1969, are described in detail in the next chapter.

At the end of that first summer in Mexico, I returned to Harvard via Seattle, where I visited my family for two weeks. My father was most interested in the tape recordings I had made of the Tzotzil language and insisted that I meet with his colleague, the eminent linguist, Dr. Li Fang-kuei, at the University of Washington, and play them for him. Dr. Li listened intently to one of the tapes and then showed me one of his field notebooks containing sentences in the Athapascan language that had been the subject of his dissertation at the University of Chicago.

The courses I chose during my second year at Harvard were, for the most part, intended to prepare me for the oral exams, called *Generals*, which were normally taken at the end of the third year of residency in the PhD program. In those days, the graduate students were required to demonstrate proficiency in two geographic regions, one in the Old World and the other in the New World. My New World area was, of course, Mesoamerica. And to deepen my knowledge of that region, I took Gordon Willey's seminar in Mesoamerican archaeology during the fall semester, thereby complementing the course on Mesoamerican ethnology I had taken the previous spring. I chose Southeast Asia as my second area of concentration, and to that end, signed up for a two-semester course on that region taught by Cora Du Bois. In order to have some knowledge of physical anthropology, I took human genetics from William Howells, and I audited his undergraduate course in primate evolution. And, in order to broaden my knowledge of sociocultural anthropology, I took John Pelzel's course on the Far East and audited Douglas Oliver's course on Oceania. I rounded out my knowledge of archaeology by enrolling in Stephen Williams's course on Eastern North American archaeology, the sequel to his course on Western North American archaeology I had taken the year before.

My studies that year were interrupted only by the trip I made to France to visit Harvey during the Christmas break and reading period. A brief visit from my father in the spring provided a welcome distraction from my heavy academic schedule.

After a very productive summer in Mexico collecting texts in the Tzotzil language for my dissertation (as explained in the next chapter), followed by a visit to Seattle, I flew to Philadelphia, where Harvey, who had finally returned from France, met me and drove me to Lancaster. After a few days there, we drove up to Cambridge for his second year of courses and my year of preparing for the General exams and serving as a teaching fellow in a large lecture course on evolution for undergraduate students.

Before leaving Cambridge for Mexico in June, I had leased an apartment for the next academic year, where Harvey lived alone during the fall semester, and had rented a room in a friend's apartment in the same building, where I lived temporarily until we were married.

Our wedding took place in my parent's home in Seattle during the Christmas break and reading period in December 1964 (Figure 5.1). We took a low-cost charter flight from Boston to Seattle that had been arranged by the Harvard Student Agencies on a propeller plane that lasted for many hours, with an unscheduled last-minute stop in Idaho for refueling, before arriving at the Seattle–Tacoma airport in the wee hours of the morning.

Our honeymoon included visits to Snoqualmie Pass in the Cascade Mountains, Alderbrook Inn on Hood Canal, and a drive up the east

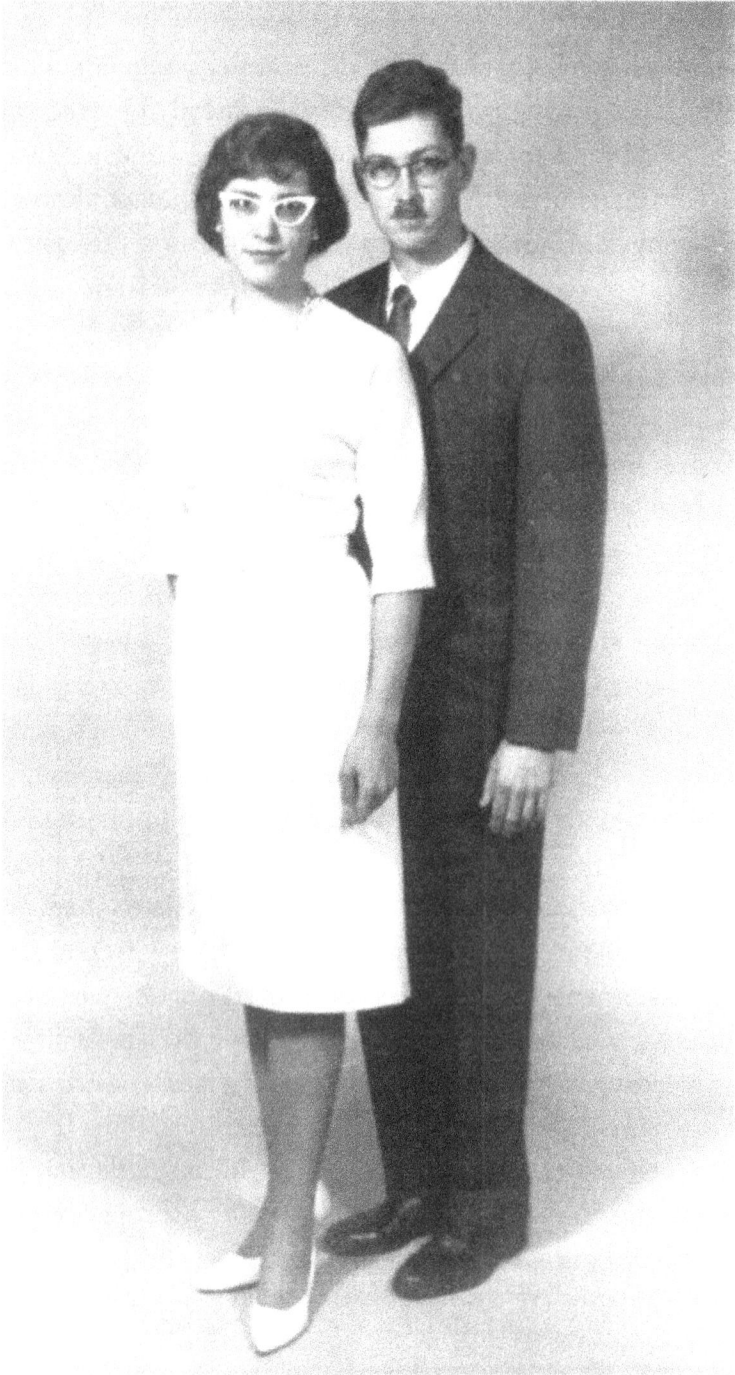

FIGURE 5.1.   Our wedding portrait.

side of the Olympic Peninsula to Port Angeles, where we boarded a ferry that took us to Victoria, British Columbia. In Victoria, we spent much of a day at the Burke Provincial Museum, where we saw wonderful exhibits of Northwest Coast art and culture. On our return to Seattle, a ferry brought us through the scenic San Juan Islands as far as Everett, Washington, where we landed and drove the rest of the way.

I took no courses for credit that year, but, at the suggestion of George Collier, a fellow graduate student whom I had come to know well during my summers in Chiapas, I audited a course on computers that he was taking for credit. I was intrigued by the possibility of learning how computers actually worked and decided to attend it. The course was taught by Arthur Couch, a clinical psychoanalyst, and covered subjects like binary coding and the underlying structure of machine language. I remember learning how to wire a plugboard and actually wired one for a machine that produced printed output from punched cards.

During that year, I met the well-known Finnish folklorist Elli Köngas and her husband, Pierre Maranda. Pierre was a fellow graduate student in anthropology, who was conducting research on the mythology of the Gê people of Brazil. Knowing that I was putting together a large corpus of texts on humor, he suggested that I consider having them analyzed by a computer and told me about the set of programs called the *General Inquirer* being developed by the psychologist Philip Stone. I was interested in this possible tool for my research and included it in the grant proposal I was preparing for my dissertation research the following year.[2]

But my principal responsibility that year was to prepare for the oral exams at the end of May, and I did so with some trepidation. There were very few women in the Harvard graduate school when I entered the anthropology program in the fall of 1962, and I sensed a certain wariness in the professors in the Anthropology Department whenever I hove into view. The only female professor in the department was the psychological anthropologist Cora Du Bois, who taught courses on India and Southeast Asia, and she was in the department only by virtue of the fact that she occupied the Radcliffe Chair for Women Professors that had been endowed by the Zemurray Foundation. I soon realized that, in order to succeed, women students had to outperform the men, especially in terms of toughness and stoicism. Any signs of weakness in a woman elicited a hostile response and, if they continued, efforts to remove the offender from the program. Men could have physical or psychological problems, whereas women could not.

The general exams that were taken at the end of the third year of residency in the program were the greatest hurdle that all graduate students had to face. They were oral exams, usually involving five faculty examiners. Beginning several years before I arrived, all the women who took the exams had failed, and this pattern continued during the two years while I was taking courses. In one case a woman had failed because the members of the examination committee complained that "she knew too much."

One day early in the fall of my second year at Harvard, Cora Du Bois spotted me in the hallway and flagged me down. She offered to coach me for my orals, which were scheduled for the end of my third academic year. Of course, I said yes, but I was flabbergasted at this offer, because, although I had taken one course from her during the previous year and was taking another course from her during that semester, I was not one of her students. On the other hand, I had learned through the grapevine that she had given her colleagues a tongue-lashing the previous year, saying, "How can you flunk someone for knowing too much?" Because I was the next woman to come up for orals, she must have selected me as the guinea pig for breaking this pattern of failure.

That coaching began in a sporadic way during the first half of her course on the Peoples and Cultures of Southeast Asia in which I was enrolled that semester. Whenever I asked her for advice on the term paper I was working on for her, she gave it freely, but also challenged me with questions that she expected me to respond to on the spot and debate with her. She was clearly trying to bolster my self-confidence in responding to the kinds of questions I might be asked on my oral exams. This activity was formalized during the second semester as a reading course, during which she assigned reading on diverse theoretical and methodological topics in North American and Mesoamerican ethnology. On one occasion, she counseled me that it was not enough to regurgitate the ideas of the scholars whose writings I had absorbed; I also had to be prepared to evaluate the validity of their ideas and suggest my own alternatives.

I was surprised at how much she knew about Mesoamerican anthropology and the advice she gave me of how I should study for that part of the oral exams. She suggested that I read the annual reports in the yearbooks of the Carnegie Institution of Washington to get a sense of what had been going on in the archaeology, cultural anthropology, and physical anthropology of the region. One day she took me into an empty classroom and asked me to draw a map of Mesoamerica on the blackboard, on which she told me to place all the Native American languages, listed in order from north to south (a task that I was asked to perform during my orals the following year).

But the most useful advice she gave me concerned how I should comport myself during the exam. She told me that I should frame my answers to questions in such a way as to influence what the next question would be. In that way, I could steer the examination toward topics that I knew well and away from other topics in which I had less expertise.

On the day of the exam at the end of May in 1965, I sat at one end of the large table in the smoking room in the basement of the Peabody Museum, with the five examiners seated around the rest of the table. They included Evon Vogt (my adviser and mentor), Cora Du Bois, Gordon Willey, Stephen Williams, and William Howells. Professor Du Bois was the first person to ask me a question, which was: "Your second area is India, isn't it?" I had had a premonition that she might throw me a curve on the exam, so I was prepared for that question, answering: "No, it isn't. My second area is Southeast Asia. But I have also boned up on India, so feel free to ask me questions about that region as well." I saw her relax in response to my answer, and she limited her questions to facts about Southeast Asia. I suspected that she had deliberately set me up with that question to help me gain psychological control of the situation.

The custom among the graduate students was to hold a vigil on the front steps of the Peabody Museum while an oral exam was in progress. There was usually a break for tea after the first hour or so of the exam, when the participants could use the rest rooms, and the janitors lurking in the basement of the museum tried to assess how the exam was going by reading the expressions on the faces of the examiners. If they were scowling, it meant that the exam was not going well and that it was likely to be a long, drawn-out affair, as the student was probed for evidence that he or she knew anything at all. If, on the other hand, there were smiles on the faces of the examiners, then it was likely that the exam was going well and would not last long after the tea break ended and the participants returned to the smoking room. This information was relayed by one of the janitors to the other students standing vigil on the steps of the museum. The janitor's report on my performance is, unfortunately, not part of the historical record. But I passed!

I have realized increasingly in light of hindsight how important Cora Du Bois was in my graduate education. Her informal methods of "testing" me and then expecting me to defend my ideas gave me the courage to rise to the occasion on my general exams.[3] In so doing, she also provided lessons on how to conduct myself in an academic setting after I graduated and how to navigate in other university contexts. I know that they were equally important in my later professional career.[4]

My joy over passing these exams was tempered by the fact that my father had died the month before. At the beginning of April, I received a telephone call from my mother, informing me that he had had a heart attack. He was in the hospital for three weeks and seemed to be recovering, but died suddenly on April 23 in his sixty-first year. I flew out to Seattle for a week to attend his funeral and to spend a few days with my family after that. I realized then that my wedding at the end of the previous December was the last time my family was together.

My father's death left my mother with four children at home to support on her own and dashed her hopes of completing her education with a doctorate in English literature. She had earned her BA at the University of Washington while I was in junior and senior high schools and began work on her MA degree during my first year of college. In addition, she had worked as a teacher of English at St. Nicholas School for Girls, where she was responsible for choosing and directing the senior play each year. She subsequently taught English composition at Everett Junior College, and at the time of my father's death, she was teaching in the Freshman English program at the University of Washington, which entailed long hours in the evenings grading essays.

It was time for her to make a career change. In order to make up for the loss of my father's income, she needed a more dependable and better paid form of employment than teaching English composition. A career as a reference librarian looked promising because the training for it could be accomplished in two years. After receiving her MLS degree in library science, she left Seattle for a position as a reference librarian in the Humanities Library of Washington State University in Pullman. By then, Anne and Consuela had married and Frank was in graduate school in mathematics and financially independent, with teaching fellowships at the University of Washington. Michaela completed her last year of high school during my mother's first year in Pullman while boarding with the family of a classmate in Seattle.[5]

I mention all this because my mother's constant and ultimately unsuccessful efforts to complete her education served as an object lesson to me. It was the reason why I resisted the temptation to interrupt my education after college and completed my PhD degree five and one half years after entering Harvard.

At the end of the semester, Harvey and I drove down to Lancaster to visit his parents, who hosted a large get-together for their extended family to meet me. Relatives came from all over Pennsylvania, enabling me to get acquainted with aunts and uncles and cousins whom I had not met earlier.

All too soon, it was time for Harvey to leave for France, where he would spend the summer. I stayed behind with his parents for some days and then took the train back to Boston and Cambridge, where I had unfinished business to take care of before leaving for Mexico.

Although I had previously taken a few lessons from a driving school in Seattle on an automatic shift car, I had not had time to practice driving sufficiently to pass a driving test. Now that it was time for me to carry out my long period of fieldwork in Mexico, I would be using the Harvard Jeep, and for that I would need to have a license for driving a vehicle with a manual gearshift. Therefore, upon returning to Cambridge, I began taking lessons from a driving school. Although I flunked the first and second tests, I passed the third! As a result, my departure for Mexico was delayed for almost two months, until the middle of August in 1965.

In the meantime, I closed up our apartment and put our belongings in storage, after which I shared an apartment with a friend in Somerville for a few weeks and then with my former roommate, who was living in Jamaica Plain at that time. And when I wasn't practicing driving, I was preparing Tzotzil texts for analysis by the General Inquirer and working with the computer technician who would be processing them while I was in Mexico. When Harvey visited me in Mexico during the Christmas vacation later that year, he brought along printouts of seventy-nine Tzotzil texts and an analysis of the frequency of the humorous themes in them.

I remained in Mexico until the end of April, carrying out the fieldwork for my dissertation. My experiences in Chiapas during those months are described at length in the next chapter.

I saw Harvey twice during those months, first in November at the annual meetings of the American Anthropological Association in Denver, Colorado, and then one month later, when he joined me in Mexico for the Christmas vacation. He spent the rest of that academic year preparing for his oral exams, which he took and passed shortly before I returned to the States in April 1966.

Harvey and I left for France less than one month later, where we would be spending the next sixteen months, while Harvey collected material for his dissertation and I wrote up the data I had obtained in Chiapas during the previous eight months for mine. We arrived in Les Eyzies (Dordogne) on one of the nights of the annual fête (May 20th). We stayed at the Hotel du Centre in the middle of town that night. The fête was in full swing outside our window on the town square for much of the night and kept us awake for hours.

The next day, we moved into the cottage on the Bouyssou farm in the hamlet of Lespinasse that would be our home while we were in France. Lespinasse was about eight kilometers from Les Eyzies and belonged to the Commune of Tursac. Our cottage was at one end of a series of barns across the courtyard from the large farmhouse where the owners, Gabriel and Paulette Bouyssou, lived with their daughter and son-in-law. The large main room and kitchen of our cottage had been the home of Madame Bouyssou's parents before they died. The Bouyssous had renovated those rooms and the adjoining shed into a comfortable two-bedroom apartment for us.

I have always thought of that cottage as our first real home because it was not part of an apartment complex and was entered directly from the courtyard (Figure 5.2). Next to it was Madame Boyssou's large flower and vegetable garden. Behind it was a grassy valley, where cows grazed, and in the valley bottom was a spring, which served as the source of our water and later supplied water to the entire commune. It was a beautiful place, and I have fond memories of living there.

A few weeks after we had moved into our new home on the Bouyssou farm, we went by train to Rome to attend an international symposium on "Mathematical and Computational Methods in the Social Sciences," where I had been invited to present a paper on my use of the General Inquirer for analyzing the seventy-nine Tzotzil texts that Harvey had brought to me in Mexico the previous December. The title of my talk was "The Pattern of Interaction Between the Computer and the Ethnographer in the Field." In it, I described how the computer analysis of that first group of texts had guided my subsequent fieldwork in Chiapas. Today, of course, with the easy access to the Internet,

FIGURE 5.2.   Our home on the Bouyssou farm in Lespinasse.
Photo by Harvey M. Bricker.

even in remote corners of the world, such an interaction between the ethnographer and a computer is commonplace and virtually instantaneous, but it wasn't then!

The symposium began on July 4th and lasted through July 8th. Harvey and I visited the Roman forum and the Vatican while we were there. We spent a day in Nice on our way back to Les Eyzies, where we visited the Roman archaeological site of Cimiez and walked along the beach.

A few days after we returned to France, my sister Anne and her husband, Teck, came to stay with us for a week during their honeymoon in Europe. After they left, I settled down to work on my dissertation.

I decided to begin with the topic on which I had the richest data, namely, the ritual humor that I had tape-recorded at the two major fiestas I had attended during the previous year. I spent about six weeks translating the texts on those tapes and another six weeks writing the chapters based on them. I followed the same schedule for the rest of my dissertation: six weeks working up and analyzing the data for a topically related group of chapters, followed by a similar amount of time on the actual writing.

My greatest challenge that year came not from the task of writing my dissertation, but from learning how to speak French. I had been exposed to the language in a limited way as a child because my parents used French in private conversations that they did not want to be overheard by their children. But ever alert, I soon learned to recognize some key words in their French conversations that indicated that they were talking about us. One such word was *enfant*, which I heard as "ongfong." Other than the few days I had spent in Paris on my way to London in the summer of 1960 and during my brief visit with Harvey in southern France in late December 1963 and early January 1964, I had never been around French-speaking people, nor had I received any instruction in the language. I hit that language "cold," so to speak, which was a first for me as an adult, having had at least some preparation in the other languages I had learned (Spanish, German, and Tzotzil) before having to speak them.

At the beginning of the summer, Madame Bouyssou had exclaimed in my presence: "When are you going to be able to *talk* to me?' I replied through Harvey: "In September." Well, when September came, I was still unable to participate in a French conversation, and Madame Bouyssou decided to take matters into her own hands. She began by inviting me to bring my knitting over to her house in the afternoons and to sit in the kitchen with her daughter and listen to their conversations while the three of us knitted. After several weeks of listening to them talking French in the afternoons, I began to join their conversations.

The venue for our conversations changed after her daughter's baby was born, and her doctor insisted that the infant needed to breathe outside air for at least an hour a day. This meant going on walks with the baby in her buggy, and I was invited to accompany them on their walks in the countryside and participate in their conversations. It was an idyllic way to learn a language, and I will always be grateful to those two women for facilitating my learning of French by involving me in their lives.

For a long time, there was a disconnect between speaking and reading French. When I spoke French, I generated sentences that were apparently grammatical, but I did not know how the words in them were spelled, and when I read French, I knew what the words meant, but not how they were pronounced. As a result of numerous "aha!" moments, I gradually combined the two skills, but to this day, I cannot verbalize the grammatical rules of French.

My daily conversations in French were interrupted for two weeks by a visit from my mother during the last week of August and the first week of September. At the beginning of the second week, we flew from Bordeaux to Frankfurt en route to visit my father's cousin and his wife in Bischofsheim, Germany, where I had last been in 1960. Uncle Herbert and Aunt Kordi were as hospitable as ever, and we enjoyed the days we spent with them in their beautiful home and on excursions into the countryside. After returning to Frankfurt, Mother went on to London via Paris to visit her relatives, and I returned to our home on the Bouyssou farm via Bordeaux. After my return from Germany, Harvey and I decided to convert the master bedroom in our cottage into a joint study and sleep in what had been the guest bedroom. We borrowed small tables from the Bouyssous to use as desks and constructed a bookcase of bricks and boards. Before leaving Cambridge, Harvey had purchased a second-hand rotary calculator that he had shipped to France in one of our trunks and had brought along a transformer so that it could be used with French current. However, the calculator interfered with the Bouyssous' television, which meant that he could use it only after they had gone to bed at night. In spite of this inconvenience, he was able to make progress on his dissertation research.

I welcomed the new arrangement in our home, which meant that I no longer had to work in the cramped space afforded by the much smaller guest bedroom. I continued working on my dissertation and finished writing drafts of the chapters on ritual humor by the end of October.

It was time for a change, and Harvey and I decided to take advantage of the lovely fall weather by making a trip to Romaneche-Thorins, where he would examine collections of artifacts from two sites, Vigne Brun and Saut de Perron, both of which were related to the Gravettian level at the Abri Pataud in Les Eyzies, which was the focus of his dissertation. The scenery in the Massif Central that lies between Les Eyzies and Romaneche-Thorins was breathtaking, and the local cheese made from goat's milk was delicious. After reaching our destination, I helped Harvey by recording the information he dictated to me as he was examining and measuring the artifacts. This was the first of several *voyages comparatifs* that we made during the sixteen months that we spent in France in 1966–1967, in the course of which Harvey collected comparative data for his dissertation and I became acquainted with a number of regions in that country.

The cold weather in November and December kept us indoors for much of the time, while we worked away on our dissertations. We took time out to stuff and roast a duck on Thanksgiving Day and to dine with the Bouyssous on Christmas Day, sharing a delicious, farm-raised roast turkey in their large kitchen, heated by a fireplace at one end. We settled back into our work routine the next day, and our second wedding anniversary the day after went unnoticed until two days later!

At the beginning of January (1967), Harvey received a letter from his friend Berle Clay, informing him that he was in Spain with his professor Walter Taylor and their wives and suggesting that we join them in Valencia on the Mediterranean coast for a few days. We welcomed the opportunity to take a vacation at that time and escape the unusually cold weather that had gripped southern France that winter.

We made the trip during the second half of January in our car, a functional, but minimally equipped vehicle called the *Deux Chevaux*, whose name can be translated as "Two-Horses," which aptly described its low horsepower. Therefore, we decided not to take the most direct route to Spain through the high Pyrénées, but drive through the foothills along the Mediterranean coast. Driving in northern Spain was difficult because of the torn-up roads. The country was in the midst of a great push for modernity, and instead of improving the roads section by section, all the sections were being worked on at once. The road had no shoulder, and the sheer drop-off on the right side made driving precarious. Spain was still under the thumb of the dictator General Franco, and the *Guardia Civil* was in evidence everywhere in their tricorn hats and capes. The few people we saw in the towns we passed through seemed dispirited and lacking the vitality we were accustomed to in the small towns in France. There was a thick smog in Barcelona and the traffic was in gridlock, a far cry from the beautiful city it has become in recent decades.

I hadn't realized how mountainous all of Spain is. As we drove along, I couldn't help thinking that the Spanish *conquistadores* must have felt right at home in northern Mexico, for the landscape is quite similar. I was surprised at the many dried-up rivers, and we thought it appropriate that one such river was called *Rio Seco* "Dry River." One of the most interesting parts of our trip was noticing the gradual transition from French to Spanish orthography in the road signs as we moved from north to south. The language of the region we were going through was Catalan, which had obvious similarities to both French and Spanish.

We arrived in Valencia during the height of the orange season. On the road, we had seen many trucks laden with crates of oranges to be sold in France. We brought back ten mammoth oranges as a gift to the Bouyssous, which pleased them greatly. We sampled various specialties of the region, enjoying most of all the *paella*, which is a saffron rice and shellfish baked dish, with the seafood served in the shell.

The Clays and the Taylors were staying at a government-sponsored resort hotel on the beach in the municipality of Gandia, south of Valencia, and we joined them there. They were on a reconnaissance mission, searching for a habitation site representing the Bell Beaker culture. Accompanying the group as interpreter and guide was an archaeology student from the University of Barcelona, whose first name was Luis.

Berle, like Harvey, was writing his dissertation on one of the levels of the Abri Pataud. They had first met during one of the summers when they were both excavating at the site. He, like his wife, Brenda, was a graduate student at the State University of Illinois in Carbondale. Walter

Taylor was a well-known archaeologist at the same institution who had excavated a cave site in northern Mexico and was famous because of his book, *A Study of Archaeology*, which served as a precursor to the "new archaeology" that was in vogue while we were in graduate school.

With Luis as our guide, we visited the site called *Cueva de la Recámara* in the mountains west of the coastal plain. However, I was more interested in what he could tell me about fiestas in Spanish villages and towns, of which he had considerable knowledge. In my conversations with him, I was able to test some of my ideas about the Iberian substrate of the fiestas I had seen in Zinacantan the previous year.

We returned to our home on the Bouyssou farm in France on January 26th and went back to work. Not long afterward, Berle Clay and Walter Taylor showed up in Les Eyzies, and we spent some time with them there. Berle stayed on for a few more days after Walter went back to Ilinois, so that he and Harvey could discuss their research on the Abri Pataud. While he was there, Harvey happened to mention that there was a matrix sorter in the lab at the Abri Pataud in Les Eyzies, and they decided to experiment with its usefulness for identifying clusters of attributes in Upper Palaeolithic tools. I noticed that it had possibilities for grouping themes in my humor data and included a matrix analysis in my dissertation. Because of all the time I spent in the company of archaeologists that year, the methodology I used in my dissertation included some archaeological techniques not normally employed by cultural anthropologists or sociologists.

Harvey and I spent one week in March in Bordeaux, where Harvey studied François Bordes's collection of artifacts from Corbiac in Bordes's lab at the University of Bordeaux, with me serving as his scribe. This was my first time in a French lab or office, and I was struck by the etiquette, the fact that every morning we went around to shake the hand of every person in the lab and say "Bonjour Monsieur!" or "Bonjour Madame"! Everybody else, including the members of the staff, did the same thing.

In May, Harvey and I drove to Lyon in eastern France so that he could study the artifacts from the site of La Colombière that his mentor, Hallam Movius, had excavated not long after the end of World War II.

From there we went on to Switzerland and were amazed at how well our underpowered car performed in crossing the Alps to Lake Geneva (in first gear, of course!). On the way back, we traveled through the beautiful region of Annecy.

At the beginning of June, Harvey's parents came to visit us before taking a Scandinavian tour. When we picked them up in Bordeaux, they looked askance at our car, never having seen such a minimalist passenger vehicle like that before, but they found it surprisingly comfortable, in spite of its barely upholstered seats and bouncing ride.

We took them sightseeing in the region, of course, but what had the most lasting impression on them was our life on the Bouyssou farm, which was like a trip down memory lane to their childhoods in small Pennsylvania towns. On a whim, Harvey's father decided to make sauerkraut. It was the height of cabbage season, and the farmers' market in Sarlat featured enormous cabbages that we purchased for this purpose. We borrowed a crock from Madame Bouyssou, and Harvey or his father whittled a plug for it from a piece of wood. Lacking a slaw knife, Harvey's father improvised with one of the knives we had at hand. He cut the cabbage into narrow strips, layered them in the crock, and covered each layer with salt. The plug rested on the top layer in the crock and was weighted down with a heavy stone. The crock was then set aside to "cure" for some weeks.

In late June, after Harvey's parents had left, we drove to the National Museum of Antiquities at St. Germain-en-Laye (the former royal palace of Napoleon III) near Paris, where the collections from the type site of La Gravette were housed. We stayed in an inexpensive hotel in Versailles not far from St. Germain, and when not working at the museum, we visited the royal palace of Louis XIV in Versailles.

On the way home, we suddenly realized that we had forgotten about the crock of sauerkraut that we had left to "cure" on the floor of our bathroom and were afraid that it had rotted during our absence. However, when we arrived, we discovered that, even though it had a strong odor, the fabrication process was a success. Madame Bouyssou declared that it had an excellent flavor, and we shared it with her family.

Early in January, Harvey had decided that he wanted to apply for jobs for the following year because, as he put it, he did not want to feed at the public trough any more, and therefore would not apply for a renewal of his National Science Foundation (NSF) grant. When informed of Harvey's decision, Hallam Movius said that he wanted Harvey to spend another year at Harvard working on his dissertation, and he arranged for him to have the position of Acting Head Tutor in the Department of Anthropology. Therefore, I decided to go ahead and apply for a one-semester renewal of my National Institute of Mental Health fellowship, which would allow me to complete my requirements for the PhD by the end of the fall semester, and Vogtie promised to work out some part-time employment for me during the spring semester of 1968. All of this came to pass, and I spent the last two months of our stay in France that year preparing a complete draft of my dissertation to present to the members of my committee in the fall.

Harvey and I returned to the States at the beginning of September in 1967. We went first to Lancaster to visit his parents and to retrieve the belongings that we had stored in their house the year before. Harvey's job as Acting Head Tutor began on September 18th. I settled down to study for the last set of oral exams, called *Specials*, that covered topics in cultural anthropology, sociology, and social psychology, which I passed in the late fall.

In the meantime, I had distributed copies of my dissertation to the other two members of my committee, who approved it with minor revisions. I spent almost the entire Christmas vacation at the typewriter in Harvey's parents' home in Lancaster producing the final version of the dissertation for submission to the Graduate School in January. It was accepted, and my PhD degree was awarded in March 1968, although I did not receive the diploma itself until commencement in June.

During the spring semester, I had several kinds of responsibilities for which I was compensated. To begin with, Vogtie's large monograph on Zinacantan had been accepted for publication by the Harvard University Press,[6] and he hired me to serve as his go-between with his editor at the Press, an assignment that continued into the following academic year. I, like several other present and former students of his, had read and commented on drafts of each chapter. Now I was given an opportunity to learn something about how manuscripts become published books.

This meant frequent meetings with the editor to discuss problems of nomenclature, spelling, and formatting. Later, after I was no longer living in Cambridge, I read the galleys and page proofs of the book and dealt with issues that arose in correspondence with Vogtie and the editor. This experience gave me a sense of how to communicate with authors and presses, one that proved invaluable in my later career.

Vogtie wanted me to produce the index for his book, but the editor balked at that suggestion, saying that it would require the work of a professional indexer. After indexing one of my own books some years later, I realized that it was a wise decision on her part.

My second job that semester was as the senior teaching assistant in Vogtie's primitive religion course, for which I gave two lectures of my own when he was out of town. However, my principal duties for that course were grading papers and exams and handling student complaints about the grades they received on those assignments.

My third job had two facets. The Department of Anthropology had received an NSF grant to place some of its undergraduate concentrators in the field during the upcoming summer. I was asked to coordinate the program and to conduct tutorials to prepare some of the students for their summer research in several parts of the world.

My fourth job was to teach the Tzotzil course to students who would be working in Chiapas during the summer, a course I had taught for the first time in 1965 (as explained in the next chapter).

With my dissertation completed and my Specials behind me, I welcomed this variety of assignments that kept me occupied through the spring semester and beyond. It was an exciting way to complete my last year in Cambridge.

Harvey's mother came up to Cambridge during the second week of June to attend the commencement ceremony on June 13, where I received my diploma for the PhD degree I had completed in March. For the first time in many years, it rained on Commencement Day, which meant that the ceremony had to be held in Memorial Hall, where there was not enough seating for the many graduates and their families. Priority was given to the students who had completed their four years of college and their families. I learned that only thirty-five graduate students would be able to march across the stage at Commencement. Tickets for them would be handed out on a first-come, first-served basis, beginning at seven o'clock on Commencement morning at one of the buildings on campus. I rose early that morning and trudged through the rain, arriving at the designated place shortly after six o'clock. I was the third person in line and received an envelope with three tickets: one for me, one for Harvey, and one for his mother. I was one of the few PhD graduates who had the opportunity to see the Shah of Iran receive an honorary degree and give his commencement address!

Also in June, I assisted John Haviland and Eric Vogt in preparing a field dictionary drawn from the typed version of Bob Laughlin's massive Tzotzil dictionary with the goal of persuading him of the feasibility of computerizing it. John wrote the computer program that was used in compiling the field dictionary. I chose the entries that would be included in the field dictionary and edited the result. And Eric coordinated the computer aspects of the project. At the end of the month, Eric took the field dictionary to the Smithsonian Institution in Washington, DC, and presented it to Bob. Our effort succeeded in persuading Bob that it would be worthwhile to computerize the larger version of his dictionary.

We moved out of our Cambridge apartment in August 1968, because we were returning to France for another twelve months, where Harvey would be assisting Hallam Movius in co-editing a series of monographs on the Abri Pataud, the site of his dissertation research. We packed our belongings in our car and a U-Haul trailer and drove them to Harvey's parents' home in Lancaster, Pennsylvania. Harvey's father had constructed storage space in the basement of their house for our books and other possessions, and they remained there during the time we were in France. Later in August, Harvey's father drove us to New York for our rendezvous with the SS *United States*, the ship on which we crossed the Atlantic to Europe (Figure 5.3). After five or six

FIGURE 5.3.   At dinner on the SS *United States* on our way to Europe in August 1968.

days at sea, we left the ship in Bremerhaven on the north coast of Germany and took the train to the Volkswagen factory in Wolfsburg, where we picked up the car that would provide us with transportation during our time in France and that we would bring back to the States at the end of our stay. We drove from Wolfsburg to Beutelsbach to visit the three German families that had befriended me in 1960.[7] From there, we drove to Mainz, where Harvey wanted to see the materials from a Palaeolithic site in the Mittelrheinisches Landesmuseum. My brother, Frank, met us there on his way home from spending a year in Israel and accompanied us to the Bouyssou farm in southwestern France, which would serve as our home base for the next twelve months. He stayed with us for ten days and then went on to London to visit our English relatives, before returning to the States.

Our lives in France that year were complicated by a series of currency crises, during which we could neither cash traveler's checks, nor transfer funds from our bank account in the States. Harvey's monthly salary was paid in dollars and deposited directly in our U.S. bank account, from which we transferred money into our account in the Société Générale in Périgueux. The officers of our French bank cooperated with us by permitting overdrafts during the currency crisis. Nevertheless, we were strapped for cash most of that year.

During the previous spring semester, Hallam Movius had approached me about working as his secretary one day a week while we were in France. What he had in mind was for me to help him with his correspondence by taking dictation and typing up the letters. Fortunately, I had agreed to his request, because he paid me in francs, which alleviated our currency problems to some degree. The eighty francs he paid me each week covered our groceries and enabled us to get through the three months I worked for him before leaving for Mexico at the beginning of December to augment the fieldwork I had already carried out for my dissertation before converting it into a book manuscript (see next chapter).

I had planned to stay in Mexico until the end of March in 1969, but my return to France was delayed by more than one month because I became ill with both typhoid and paratyphoid during my last field season in Chiapas. And when I was ready to leave Mexico, I could not travel directly to France because the water supply on the farm where we lived was directly downslope from the septic tank of our cottage. I was reluctant to return to France until it had been determined that I was not a carrier of such diseases. Knowing this, the Vogts invited me to come and live with them in Cambridge while I underwent tests for various microbes and parasites in the Harvard medical complex. Only when the tests showed that I was free of all infections would I go back to France.

I arrived in Boston on April 9, a few hours after students demanding that Harvard sever its ties with the Reserve Officers' Training Corps program took over University Hall and forced all administrators and staff to leave the building. That night, the president of the university called in the city and state police to remove the students from the building. This move precipitated a student boycott of classes that continued throughout the time I spent in Cambridge.

Having graduated the year before, I did not enter the fray, but paid close attention to what was going on in different parts of campus as events unfolded. I was amazed at the heightened level of interaction between students and faculty. Normally shy students felt emboldened to walk up to professors and engage them in conversation. Perhaps as a result, the number of students seeking psychiatric help dropped dramatically. It was as though the crisis had reduced everyone to a single level, thereby opening up avenues for communication that normally did not exist in a university community. There was fear, but also exhilaration in the openness that accompanied the turmoil of those weeks.

I stayed in Cambridge as the guest of the Vogts for almost a month until I received a clean bill of health and could return to France. In the meantime, however, political unrest had developed in Paris, and by the time I left Cambridge it had spread to other cities in France. Fearing that I might have difficulty with internal transportation after arriving in Paris, Harvey decided to meet me there. He came by train instead of by car because of the uncertain availability of gasoline en route. After meeting me in Paris, we took the night train back to Les Eyzies and drove from there to our home on the Bouyssou farm without incident.

By the third week of May, life had returned to normal in France, and Harvey and I decided to take a vacation in England in order to visit his good friends Paul and Anny Mellars at the University of Cambridge. This was my second visit to the "other" Cambridge.[8]

Refreshed by our vacation, we returned to France at the end of May, when I began to analyze and write up the data I had collected in Chiapas some months before for inclusion in a revision of my dissertation that I hoped to publish as a book in the near future. All went well until sometime in July, when Harvey's appendix ruptured, landing him in the hospital for a week. After the doctor in Les Eyzies had diagnosed his condition, he arranged for him to be hospitalized in the Clinique Francheville in Périgueux. I remained with Harvey at the Clinique during the night after his surgery and was there when he regained consciousness. I slept on a bed that pulled out from one wall of the room (similar to the drawers in a morgue!). From then on, I drove to Périgueux every day until Harvey was released from the hospital and could come home. Once he had recovered sufficiently, we went to the museum in Aurignac in the foothills of the Pyrénées so that Harvey could study some collections there.

Our year in France came to an end during the first week in September, when we drove up to Paris to turn our car over for shipment to Louisiana and then went on to Le Havre to board the SS *United States* once more for our return to the States. Our ultimate destination was New Orleans, where, as explained in the next chapter, we would be taking up teaching positions at Tulane University. We were woefully ignorant about the location of our new jobs. We did not realize that New Orleans was one of the largest ports in the country. Therefore, we told the shipping agent in Paris that we assumed that Shreveport was the nearest port to New Orleans. Of course, he quickly disabused us of that notion, and some weeks later, we recovered our car from one of the docks on the Mississippi River in New Orleans.

NOTES

1. Of course, she was one of the first people I wanted to talk to after I became interested in hieroglyphic decipherment myself. This opportunity came in 1980, when I was invited to give a talk at Harvard. I spent an afternoon with her at her home, where she showed me what she was working on at that time: a history of the Maya based on hieroglyphic texts, which was published in 1993, eight years after her death in 1985.

2. Among the programs was one called *Key Word in Context* (KWIC) that produced concordances from texts. I have, for many years, been

using a similar program written by William Ringle for analyzing Maya texts.

3. I was not the only beneficiary of Du Bois's concern for the academic welfare of Harvard graduate students during those years. Others are mentioned on pages 266–272 of Susan C. Seymour's recent biography, titled *Cora Du Bois: Anthropologist, Diplomat, Agent*, which was published by the University of Nebraska Press in 2015.

4. I rarely saw Cora Du Bois after that, but she must have thought about me from time to time, because at one of the annual meetings of the American Anthropological Association during the 1970s, she invited Harvey and me for a drink at our hotel. At some point in our conversation with her, she mentioned that one of the young professional couples she knew had decided that whoever received the best job offer should take it, and the other would come along and look for some kind of employment in the same area. She asked us what we thought of that. I replied that we had decided on a different approach to the search for employment, namely, to look for the best "package deal," rather than for the most prestigious position for one of us. That is what we were able to negotiate at Tulane, and although each of us received nibbles from more prestigious institutions in later years, we did not pursue them because there would have been nothing for the other spouse. Whatever personal ambitions we might have had ranked well below the value that we placed on our marriage.

5. Mother remained in Pullman for thirteen years until her retirement in 1982 at the age of 65, after which she returned to Seattle. While there, she volunteered in the library of the University of Washington, cataloguing books written in Hebrew for the Acquisitions Department. She moved to a retirement home in Bucks County, Pennsylvania, in 1996 to be near Frank and his family. She took care of the library while she was there, ordering books for the residents and supervising the shelving of books. Six years later, she moved to another retirement home just outside Baltimore to be near Michaela and her family. There also she took care of the library and also edited

the newsletter for the home. She died in August 2013, two weeks
after her ninety-sixth birthday.

6. That book appeared in 1969 with the title, *Zinacantán: A Maya
   Community in the Highlands of Chiapas*.

7. We stayed with the Staib family in their traditional farmhouse on
   Marktstrasse for several days. By then, Herr Koch had left farming
   and was making a living in industry in Waiblingen, leaving Herr
   Staib as the only full-time farmer in the family. The Kochs had
   moved into a new house next door to the Romaerschs. However,
   all three families still worked in their vineyards in the evenings and
   on weekends.

8. My first visit took place in 1960 during the five weeks I spent in
   England after participating in the Stanford-in-Germany program.

6

CHIAPAS:
EXPLORING MAYA HUMOR

On June 12, 1963, having completed my first year of graduate school, I set out for Mexico to undertake my first summer of fieldwork among the Tzotzil-speaking Maya Indians of highland Chiapas. I flew from Boston to Mexico City, where I spent a week, then went overland to San Cristobal las Casas, the principal town in the region occupied by Indians with whom I hoped to carry out anthropological research.

Upon arriving at the airport in Mexico City, I went to collect my luggage, only to discover that my sleeping bag was not there. Although my knowledge of Spanish had become rusty after eight years without use, the words I needed to communicate my dismay popped into my head: *es falta mi bolsa de dormir* ("my sleeping bag is missing"). The baggage agent told me not to worry, but to leave my tourist card with him and to call him after I reached the hotel to let him know where I would be staying in the city. However, before I left the airport, he came running up to me with my sleeping bag. But I forgot to reclaim my tourist card and had to call from my hotel anyway. My tourist card was delivered to me there later that night.

The next morning, George Collier, one of Vogtie's students, came to my hotel with Chep Apas, a friend of his from Zinacantan. They were in Mexico City because George's wife, Jane, was in a hospital there, expecting the birth of their first child. After their child was born, George planned to drive in their van to San Cristobal to meet the undergraduate students he would be placing in the field that summer. He would return to Mexico City ten days later to bring Jane and the baby to San Cristobal.

George suggested that I accompany him and Chep on their drive to San Cristobal. I agreed and stayed on in Mexico City to do some sightseeing until the baby was born five days later. I went with George and Chep to visit Jane and the baby in the hospital. There I met Bob and Mimi Laughlin for the first time. Bob was also one of Vogtie's students, who, like George, was carrying out fieldwork in Zinacantan that summer.

We set out for San Cristobal the next afternoon. We were accompanied by Shelley Zimbalist, one of the students who would be spending the summer in Chiapas. We spent the first night in Puebla and the second in a hotel on Lake Catemaco in the state of Veracruz before arriving in San Cristobal on the third day.

I spent the first night in San Cristobal at Na Bolom, the home of the archaeologist Frans Blom and his wife, Trudi. I remember that Frans was very ill when I arrived. Passing his bedroom door that night, I saw him lying in bed, his long white beard stretched out on top of the covers.

Frans Blom died during that very night, on Sunday, June 23, 1963, the day before the fiesta of San Juan in Chamula. By then, the remaining undergraduate students had arrived by bus from Mexico City, and George took them and me to Chamula to see the fiesta. On the next day, George took me to the ceremonial center in Zinacantan to place me with a family with whom I would live while I was learning to speak their Tzotzil language.

Some months before, I had spotted a special issue of the *Journal of American Folklore* lying on the checkout counter in the library at the Peabody Museum. The whole issue was devoted to joking. The topic appealed to me, and I thought that humor might be a suitable focus for my dissertation. Vogtie liked the idea of my writing a dissertation on Zinacantec humor, a topic that had not been investigated previously. However, it would require a considerable mastery of the Tzotzil language, and the sooner I immersed myself in the language, the better. Therefore, my first summer in Zinacantan was best spent on total immersion in the life of a family that spoke only Tzotzil.[1]

As it happened, the matriarch of the first family I stayed with was the only woman in Zinacantan who was bilingual in Spanish and Tzotzil. The members of her household included her two grown daughters and a son-in-law. The daughters also spoke some Spanish. It was not an ideal living arrangement for learning to speak the Tzotzil language.

When Vogtie arrived in Chiapas some weeks later, he suggested that I move in with another family, where the wife was a monolingual speaker of Tzotzil. In that environment, my knowledge of Tzotzil increased rapidly, and at the end of the summer I was pleased with the progress I had made on that front.

The academic study of Tzotzil was still in its infancy at that time. There was no textbook, comprehensive grammar, or dictionary of the language then. The Colliers had some fluency in speaking the language, having already spent several field seasons in Chiapas. Bob Laughlin had recently completed his dissertation on the folklore of Zinacantan, which involved the transcription, translation, and analysis of numerous recorded texts. Therefore, he had the greatest expertise in the language. He was already thinking about compiling a comprehensive dictionary, but that work did not begin until after I returned to Harvard for my second year of courses in the fall. In the meantime, the best way to learn the language was by living with monolingual speakers of Tzotzil, as Bob himself had done at first.

This was my first experience learning an unwritten language entirely by ear, without the possibility of consulting a grammar or dictionary when in doubt. It required a new approach to learning a language that I had to develop over time, beginning in the summer of 1964.

During my second summer in Chiapas, I benefited from the presence of Duane Metzger, the Stanford professor who had facilitated my admission to the graduate program in anthropology at Harvard. Duane suggested that I use a set of interviewing procedures called *formal eliciting* to investigate the kinds of humor recognized in Zinacantan. The advantage of this method was that it required only a rudimentary knowledge of the language, namely, the ability to form simple questions, which would elicit grammatically simple answers. Therefore, it meant that an entire interview could be conducted in Tzotzil, without the use of a contact language (Spanish). It would permit me to increase my conversational skills at the same time as I was acquiring information for my project.

Duane recommended that I begin such interviews with a general question, using vocabulary I was already familiar with. I did not then know whether Tzotzil had a specific term for "humor," but I did know that the word *loʔil* referred to verbal behavior in general. My task was to find out how many kinds of loʔil there were and what each of them was called. Once I had the names of each kind of loʔil, I could investigate their subcategories. Eventually, if I was lucky, my questions might identify one or more kinds of loʔil that would elicit laughter from speakers of Tzotzil.

This method proved to be very productive for my research. The Zinacantecs I interviewed mentioned a number of subcategories of loʔil, including one, *loko loʔil* "crazy talk," that looked promising, and offered to produce textual examples of each one. Once they realized that I was most interested in ones that provoked laughter, they took pleasure in writing descriptions of humorous incidents. I encouraged them to consult with each other as they were writing and to share their results. They worked in the same room at the Harvard Ranch, and their peals of laughter made it clear that I was getting good data.

It then became necessary for me to translate their texts into English so that I would understand what they were laughing about. I asked the writers who were bilingual in Spanish and Tzotzil to help me with this task. Their Spanish translations served as "ponies" from which I was eventually able to produce an English translation of the Tzotzil text.

The texts I collected that summer indicated that Zinacantecs had a robust sense of humor with interesting possibilities for my dissertation. It supplemented what I had been able to observe as humorous in Zinacantec households during the previous summer. From the texts I learned what Zinacantecs themselves thought about humor. From then on, I was no longer limited to speculating about what aspect of an incident might have provoked the laughter I heard as a participant-observer.

The texts had another more significant influence on the ethnologist I eventually became. They showed me for the first time how valuable an adjunct to language learning the translation of texts could be. Through them, I built up a passive vocabulary in Tzotzil and internalized the grammatical structure of the language, which improved my ability to engage in conversations and, eventually, to write letters in Tzotzil to friends in Zinacantan.

The Colliers' friend, Chep, had an important religious position that year as the junior Mayordomo Rey ("king's steward") on the first level of the cargo system. He and his senior counterpart served in the small chapel of Esquipulas next to the church of San Lorenzo, the patron saint of Zinacantan. Each Mayordomo Rey served for one month at a time, freeing the one who was not on duty to take care of his crops. At the end of the month, the one on duty was replaced by the other Mayordomo Rey in a ceremony during which the ritual objects in his care were inspected and then passed on to his replacement to be used in ceremonies during the next month.

Such a transfer ceremony happened to coincide with the fiesta of San Lorenzo in 1964. Chep invited me to spend the four days of the fiesta (August 7–11) in his house in Zinacantan Center and to tape-record the music that would accompany the transfer ritual on the night of August 8. This was a marvelous opportunity for me to observe an important ritual and, I hoped, to obtain additional experience in speaking Tzotzil. I did not realize until some months later that the tape itself contained not only music, but also evidence of a kind of humor that would become the focus of my subsequent research.

During the spring semester of 1965, Chep spent six weeks in Cambridge, assisting me with the teaching of Tzotzil to Harvard students who would be carrying out fieldwork in Chiapas that summer. Chep lived with the Colliers during the first two weeks, with Harvey and me during the second two weeks, and with the Vogts during the last weeks of his stay. Harvey and I had a tiny apartment on the third floor of an apartment building on Concord Avenue, and Chep was not very comfortable in our quarters. He was also homesick by then. At some point during the weeks he stayed with us, I brought out the tape I had made at his house the previous August and played it for him. He was thrilled with this reminder of home, and played it again and again during the rest of his stay with us.

One day Chep said to me: "You know that there is a lot of joking on this tape." All I could hear was the music and the fireworks going off from time to time outside, but he could understand the conversations in the background. I asked him whether he could transcribe all the words on the tape. He said that he could, and before he left Cambridge, he gave me a transcription and Spanish translation of everything on the tape, including the songs of the musicians.[2]

I arrived in Chiapas in the middle of August that year, after a delay of two months while taking lessons for a license that would permit me to drive a stick-shift vehicle. Such a license was necessary because I would be responsible for two Project vehicles, a relatively new Jeep and and an aged Land Rover, during the following months. This was my big year of fieldwork, when I would be on my own for eight or nine months collecting the most detailed information for my dissertation. I had a grant from the National Institute of Mental Health that would make it possible to pay a number of Zinacantecs to write texts on humor that would provide the principal data for my dissertation.

This experience would be different from those of the previous two summers, because after Vogtie and the students who had spent the summer in Chiapas returned to the States in the fall, I would be alone and responsible for the Harvard Ranch, as well as the two vehicles. I could have lived in the Vogts' house at the Ranch while they were away, but that did not seem to be a good idea for a woman alone. Instead, I decided to continue living at the Baños Mercedarios in the center of town, where I had rented rooms during the summers of 1963 and 1964, and use the Ranch as a place to work with consultants during the day.

It was also time for me to become acquainted with the local government of Zinacantan and request permission to carry out anthropological research within its borders. I appeared at the town hall one day and introduced myself to the Presidente Muncipal, José Sánchez, who served as the local magistrate, representing the lowest rung of the legal system in Mexico. With this matter in hand, I began contacting my Zinacantec friends from the previous year and inviting them to continue working with me.

By this time, I was well known in three hamlets of Zinacantan, and my use of the Harvard Jeep meant that transportation was not a problem for me. It was, in fact, an asset because it gave me the means to reciprocate the help offered by my Zinacantec friends.

For example, I received invitations to attend curing ceremonies in return for my willingness to transport curing parties from the hamlet to the sacred mountains and church in the township center. I regarded these invitations and the attendant obligations as opportunities to increase the scope of my knowledge of the culture and my circle of acquaintances. Although Zinacantan was in many respects a closed community and often hostile to outsiders, this system of mutual help mitigated whatever suspicions people might have had about my motives.

Nevertheless, as a woman alone, I had to consider carefully how to comport myself in a community where women were expected to keep a low profile. Like other members of the Harvard Chiapas Project, one of my first initiatives after arriving in San Cristobal in 1963 was to commission a weaver to make me a set of traditional women's garments: a navy blue tubular skirt, a red-and-white-striped cotton shawl, and two herringbone tweed woolen shawls to be worn under the cotton shawl when it was cold. The workmanship was superb, but the weaver misjudged my dimensions. The skirt was too short, and the shawls did not cover my elbows. I was not aware of these problems at first and did not realize that much of the laughter I heard concerned *me*, how ridiculous I looked in their clothes. Clearly my project would be a failure if much of their humor concerned me. Once I realized that my efforts to be less conspicuous by adopting their clothes were having the opposite effect, I went back to my own wardrobe and put away my Zinacantec skirt and shawls. No one commented on my appearance after that. And I discovered that when I did not dress like a Zinacantec woman, I was not expected to *behave* like one. This gave me greater freedom in my research, enabling me to observe the activities of men as well as those of women.

I also learned that, for me, the most important source of rapport in the community was my ability to speak Tzotzil. This was especially true of the women. The moment a woman realized that I could speak her language, she warmed up to me. Another thing that seemed to help was to pay lip service to their norms, even though I was not always able to follow them. This tactic developed gradually and partly by accident. In August, just before Vogtie left Chiapas, I talked with him about curing ceremonies—whether he thought I would have to agree to every request to drive a curing ceremony. He suggested at that time that I might make a point of only driving curing parties in which the patient was a woman. No one could object to this policy because it was perfectly understandable that I wouldn't want to be alone in the Jeep at night with a lot of men. So this was the policy I established, and it was well received.

Then the question arose as to whether I ought to give a ride to just any Zinacantec who came up and asked for one. I decided that, even though I was not afraid to carry a strange Zinacantec in the Jeep, it would probably make a good impression if I only carried people I knew or, if there were already friends of mine in the Jeep, people whom they knew. I had no hesitation about taking women. So, if a strange man walked up to me as I was getting ready to leave Zinacantan Center or one of the hamlets and asked me to give him a ride to San Cristobal, I would say, "No, because I don't know you," and he would walk away without being angry. But sometimes the man would reply, "Well, but my wife would be going along too. Would it then be all right?" and I would agree that it was, and he would put his wife in the front seat beside me and get in the back of the Jeep himself.

One day I overhead the wife of one of my friends talking with another old lady about me, saying words to the effect: Well, she's all right, even though she's a *gringa*. She doesn't deceive us. She will only drive curing parties in which the patient is a lady, and she won't take men she doesn't know in the Jeep. And the other old lady responded approvingly too. Clearly, it did not take long for gossip to make the rounds in Zinacantan.

However, not all such cultural differences could be reconciled so easily. In late September, I was invited by one of my consultants to attend a ceremony in his house in Zinacantan Center, during which he and his wife would be receiving gifts from the parents of their godchildren. The ceremonial visit would take place at night, and I arrived with my sleeping bag, prepared to stay there until the next morning.

When the visitors arrived, we all sat around the fire while my friends and the parents of their godchildren exchanged ritual greetings. As the evening progressed, I tried to participate in the exchanges, but I sensed that what I was saying was confusing my hosts and their guests and, in fact, was disrupting the flow of the exchanges. I then realized that I was behaving inappropriately, addressing people with terms of ritual kinship that only they could use. I decided that my only option was to retreat to my sleeping bag and to watch the rest of the ceremony from there as an observer, not a participant. As an outsider, I did not share kinship or ritual kinship ties with any of the participants and was therefore not qualified to participate in their ritual. It was a painful lesson about the limits of participant-observation as an anthropological technique.

The families I came to know best lived in Nabenchauc, the largest hamlet in Zinacantan. Most of it lies in a beautiful mountain valley, with a lake in the southwest corner that dries up during the dry season. The name *Nabenchauc* means "thunder lake" or "lightning lake." The hamlet had a chapel dedicated to the Virgin of Guadalupe, whose fiesta was celebrated on December 12. During that fiesta I had an experience that ultimately ensured my personal safety for the rest of the time I worked in Zinacantan.

While I was watching some clowns in the valley, someone in the crowd was busily pawing at me, while I kept digging my fingernails into his hand. After I finished watching the clowns, I slugged the Zinacantec who had been bothering me and ran off to look for someone I could sit with while watching the fiesta. As I was wandering around, one of my consultants came up to me and said that the Presidente would like to see me. I was surprised and told him that I had already talked with the Presidente and received his permission to photograph the clowns. But my friend said that I had better go to see him again, so I did. When I arrived, the Presidente asked me what happened, so I told him that I had decided not to take any pictures because the clowns wanted too much money. Then he asked me what else had happened, and then I noticed the Zinacantec who had bothered me standing there in the custody of two policemen, so I explained what he had done to me in terms that would be understood by a Zinacantec audience: "Oh, he tried to put his hand in my skirt!" This elicited great laughter from the crowd of onlookers. Whereupon the miscreant was thrown into the jail until the next morning, and the Presidente gave a speech about how such behavior must be punished and that I must be able to walk about Zinacantan without being molested. I never had any trouble from anyone in Zinacantan after that.

It seems that my friends had been unobtrusively "spotting" me as I moved about the valley. One of them must have seen me slug the miscreant and reported it to the Presidente, who sent the policemen to arrest him. I was totally unaware that this surveillance was going on, but appreciated it. I am sure that it continued whenever I went about in public at fiestas and on other occasions.

Most of my consultants were men or boys. It was fascinating to observe how they went about setting up opportunities for me when I was in the field, while at the same time behaving as though I didn't exist. My consultants would seldom greet me if I met them in Zinacantan Center. I discovered that the amount of recognition that a man could show me in public was a function of his relative age or status. An elderly man was not ashamed to speak to me. A Regidor or the Presidente would freely speak to me in public. But an unmarried man, a man who had never had a cargo, and sometimes a man with only a first-level cargo could not recognize me.

However, even though he ignored me in public, a man could work behind the scenes to make possible my participation in activities I needed to observe for my research. Before he left the house in the morning, one of my friends would instruct his mother, sister, or fiancée that someone ought to go with me to the churchyard at such and such a time so that I could see the bull-impersonators dance. Or, if I was watching some event going on and didn't seem to realize that the officials

were joking about it, he would surreptitiously poke me so that I would
turn on the tape recorder I was carrying hidden in a white cotton bag.
Sometimes when there was joking going on where I couldn't go, he
would come and get the tape recorder and carry it there himself and
turn it on. In this way I was able to accumulate data. I had to train
myself not to react negatively when friends ignored me—to realize that
in public contexts I would easily embarrass them.

I mention all this in part to emphasize that my fieldwork and the
data I collected were the product of a cooperative effort involving a
number of consultants and their kin. It happened that way because the
people I worked with found my research interesting and shared my
goals. They also enjoyed joking with me, as I increasingly became more
adept at participating in humorous conversations.[3] And there were
benefits for them as well, besides the small amounts I paid them for
recording, transcribing, and writing texts of their own. From the very
beginning, the Zinacantecs who worked for me saw the value of acquiring literacy in their language. This inspired some of them to go to
school, where they became literate in Spanish as well, skills that they
later used for serving their community in multiple ways.

My tape recorder broke down a few weeks after I arrived in Chiapas
and could not be repaired in San Cristobal. In late November, I went
to the annual meetings of the American Anthropological Association
in Denver, Colorado, on the way leaving the tape recorder at a repair
shop in Mexico City to be repaired while I was in the States at the
meetings.[4] Harvey met me in Denver, where we spent a few days together
before he returned to Harvard and I to Chiapas. I have two vivid
memories of those meetings. One of them was the elegant talk on
syntactic and semantic couplets in the *Popol Vuh* delivered by Munro
Edmonson, who became a close friend and colleague a few years later.
The other is of the earthquake we experienced in the bowels of the
hotel during the annual business meeting, when the pillars supporting
the upper floors seemed to move back and forth.

Harvey and I were reunited again in the middle of December 1965,
when he came to visit me for several weeks in Mexico. I drove the
Harvard Jeep to Merida to meet him, a two-and-a-half-day journey over

FIGURE 6.1. The Harvard Jeep returns from Merida over the Pichucalco road.
Photo by Harvey M. Bricker.

bad roads through some of the most beautiful landscape I have ever seen. My route took me over the Pichucalco road, which was under construction at the time and in some places almost impassible. I had to pick my way carefully around boulders and ford streams that first day (Figure 6.1).

As I rounded a bend on a mountain road later in the day, I found that the horn on the steering wheel did not toot, but did not realize what that meant. Then I came to a bridge that was only one-vehicle wide and had to stop because a truck was coming across it toward me. After the truck had passed, I found that I could not start the Jeep and realized that the battery was dead. As I sat there wondering what I should do next, several men jumped out of the bushes at the side of the road brandishing machetes. They offered to push the Jeep up the hill so that I could jump-start the motor as it rolled down. However, I did not know how to jump-start a vehicle using only the clutch. The men pushed me up the hill two or three times to no avail. Then another truck came across the bridge. The driver looked at me with great disgust, then told me to move over while he started the Jeep. He was barefoot and placed the big toe of his right foot on the brake and the rest of his foot on the gas pedal and started the Jeep after the other men had pushed it up the hill one more time. Then the truck driver told me not to stop for anything until I reached Villahermosa, where I could have the battery replaced. This was my first experience with the fabled helpfulness of the Mexican truck driver.

However, I was forced to stop in Pichucalco, when I found that I was going in the wrong direction around the main square. I leaned out the window of the Jeep and shouted to passersby that my battery was dead. About ten minutes later, a man showed up carrying a new battery. After he had installed it, I went with him to the automotive store nearby to pay for it. And then I was on my way again on the road to Villahermosa.

When I reached Villahermosa, I stopped at an intersection to ask directions of a policeman to one of the better hotels in the city. He took one look at my face and instead gave me directions to a less elegant hotel where I had stayed two summers before. After checking into the hotel and looking in a mirror, I understood why the policeman had not sent me to the better hotel. My face was almost black from the dust that had blown over the Jeep on the Pichucalco road!

On the second day of my journey, I drove from Villahermosa to Campeche on the coast road. In those days, there were no bridges to and from the barrier islands separating the Gulf from the Laguna de Términos, and I had to make four ferry crossings, one on a large raft, before reaching my destination.

I left Campeche early in the morning on the third day. The road wound over hills, and fog had collected in the dips in the road. Every time the Jeep entered a low area, the windshield steamed up, and it was impossible to see anything in the road ahead. I had to get out of the Jeep and try to clean the windshield. As time went on, the sun rose, burning off the fog in the low spots. Eventually I saw the pyramids of Uxmal ahead in the distance, a welcome sight because it meant that I would be in Merida before long. I stopped at the Hacienda Uxmal for a big breakfast in the dining room of the hotel. I reached Merida by noon and checked into a cheap hotel a few blocks from the main square, where I had stayed during a previous visit. I was told to take the Jeep to a nearby auto repair shop and arrange to park it there. Then I returned to the hotel and slept until the evening, when it was time to go to the airport to meet Harvey's plane.

After picking up Harvey at the airport and unloading his luggage at the hotel, I returned to the auto repair shop to park the Jeep. No parking spaces were available by then, but I was told to drive it onto the lift and leave it there.

The next morning, when we returned to pick up the Jeep, we discovered that it had a flat tire. The mechanic hoisted the Jeep on the lift and removed the damaged tire. He directed us to a tire shop several blocks away, to which we rolled the tire on the sidewalk. The condition of the tire was too bad to be repaired. We bought a new tire and rolled it back to the auto repair shop, where the mechanic placed it on the Jeep.

We had a wonderful time visiting the archaeological sites of Chichen Itza, Uxmal, and Kabah. In addition, because we had a Jeep, we were able to visit the sites of Labna, Sayil, and Xlapak that were only accessible to vehicles with four-wheel drive.

We celebrated our first wedding anniversary some days early in Alberto's Continental Restaurant in Merida, which had opened a few months before. Harvey's mother had sent along with him a chunk of our wedding cake that she had preserved in her freezer for one year and one of her famous shoo-fly pies. We ate the wedding cake while we were in Merida, but took the pie to San Cristobal to be consumed there.

Our return trip to Chiapas was uneventful. In the interim, the workmen had graded much of the road between Pichucalco and the entrance to the Pan American Highway. Nevertheless, I had to replace another shattered battery and worn-out tire on the Jeep shortly after arriving in San Cristobal.

Harvey and I spent Christmas Eve and Christmas Day in Zinacantan Center in the home where I had learned to speak Tzotzil during the summer of 1963. This was the first of the fiestas with ritual humor, in which stylized joking was an essential element of the performance of costumed actors. These actors, called *Grandfathers* and *Grandmothers*, pretended to ride stick horses and engaged in mock bullfights. I had brought my tape recorder along with me, but because the performances took place outdoors, the words of the actors were lost in the general hubbub of the crowd and were drowned out by the flute and drum music that characterized this fiesta.

It was not until later in the month that a solution was found for this problem. It turned out that such actors visited the homes of the religious cargoholders, where they put on their performances. In those cases, the tape-recording could take place indoors, where the walls of the house provided a better acoustical environment.

During the week between Christmas and New Year's, Harvey and I flew in a single-engine plane to visit the site of Palenque in the northernmost part of Chiapas, which, at that time, was not accessible by road. The views of the mountains from the plane were breathtaking on the way there. But clouds began to move in during the day, and the pilot tarried too long with his girlfriend in the town of Palenque, so that by the time we took off for our return flight to San Cristobal, the sky was socked in with clouds. San Cristobal lies at an altitude of 8,000 feet, and our small, unpressurized plane could not fly above 11,000 feet. It was impossible to see the San Cristobal airstrip from the air. But at the last minute, a hole developed in the clouds, revealing the airstrip directly below. The pilot brought the plane down through the hole and landed without incident. But it was a close call![5]

Harvey returned to Merida alone, first flying from Tuxtla Gutierrez, the capital of the state of Chiapas, to Villahermosa. From there he took a taxi to the train station in Teapa, where he boarded a train that brought him to Merida the next morning. I wrote out instructions in Spanish for him to show the taxi drivers in Villahermosa and Merida. He flew back to the States later that day, arriving in the Boston airport in a snowstorm, wearing a Panama hat and the thin cotton shirt called a *guayabera*.

On New Year's Day, the father-in-law of one of my consultants entered his cargo as Second Regidor. For this purpose, he had rented a house in Zinacantan Center, where he and his family would live throughout 1966. During fiestas, groups of costumed performers would visit his house, where they would sing and dance while musicians played traditional songs. The performers were expected to joke with each other, as well as with the musicians and members of the host's family, providing entertainment in honor of the fiesta.

Several consultants had written texts for me, in which they described some of the joking that takes place on such occasions, and I was anxious to witness it for myself. The incoming Second Regidor knew of my interest in this subject and offered to let me observe these rituals in his house if, in return, I would provide transportation for his elderly parents between their home in the hamlet and his house in Zinacantan Center (Figure 6.2). I was only too glad to oblige his family in this way, and he welcomed me as a guest in his house on those ritual occasions. He also gave me permission to tape-record the visits of costumed performers in his house.

I tape-recorded the visits of the Grandfather and Grandmother performers at his house on New Year's Day. A much more elaborate fiesta took place later that month in honor of San Sebastian. It included visits by two sets of performers called the *Senior Entertainers* and the *Junior Entertainers*. They were the men who had served as cargoholders during the previous year and had left office on December 31, 1965. They returned during the fiesta of San Sebastian to have a kind of "last hurrah," when they could impersonate animals such as jaguars, mythical figures such as feathered serpents and demons, and joke about their transformed roles. I recorded their visits as well.

I attended several other fiestas during the remaining months of my stay in Chiapas that year (1966), including Carnaval in February,

FIGURE 6.2.   A house in the hamlet of Nabenchauc like the one belonging to the parents of the Second Regidor.
Photo by Victoria R. Bricker.

which I expected to be as complex and rich in ritual humor as the ones in December and January. In fact, it was much less elaborate than the fiesta of San Sebastian, leaving me wondering whether the latter should be regarded as the Zinacantec counterpart of Carnaval in other highland Maya communities, where San Sebastian received less attention.

By the time I left Chiapas in the middle of April, the tapes of the recordings I had made in December and January had been transcribed, I had a sample of 300 humor texts in hand, and plenty of observed instances of humorous behavior for my dissertation. The tapes still had to be translated into English, as did many of the texts written by my consultants, but those tasks could be carried out elsewhere, thanks to Bob Laughlin's generous offer of a draft copy of his voluminous Tzotzil dictionary. I joined Harvey in Cambridge for a few days, where we attended the Vogts' spring party, and I had a chance to meet Munro Edmonson for the first time. He had been a visiting professor at Harvard that year. Vogtie urged me to get to know him (and him to meet me) because he had written his own dissertation on patterns of humor in a Spanish-American community in New Mexico some years before.[6]

I spent the next sixteen months in France with Harvey, while he collected data for his dissertation, and I did most of the writing of my own. Armed with Bob's Tzotzil dictionary, I translated many of my texts into English and then wrote chapters based on them. I sent copies of my typed transcriptions and translations to Nan Vogt, who was responsible for maintaining the Project archives. She read them and my field notes carefully and identified relevant passages in the field notes of other Project anthropologists, which she copied and sent to me. We had a lively correspondence that year that helped me feel connected to Chiapas in spite of my isolation in France.

As my dissertation took shape, I became more and more interested in ritual humor and the possible antecedents of the fiestas where it was performed. The use of small mirrors as adornments by the senior entertainers at the fiesta of San Sebastian reminded me of the mirrors on the masks of the men and boys in the traditional ceremonies in honor of Fasching before Lent that I had witnessed in Rottweil six years before. Were the performers, called *Blackmen* in the fiestas of San Sebastian and Carnaval, just impersonators of demons, or did they represent the Moors in what had once been a staged combat between Moors and Christians? And did the men costumed as feathered serpents have Precolumbian antecedents in Chiapas or the Valley of Mexico? These thoughts were flitting through my mind throughout the time I spent in France in 1966 and 1967, and I began to contemplate the possibility of pursuing some comparative fieldwork on ritual humor in other Maya communities after the completion of my dissertation.

That opportunity came during the year after I received my doctorate, when Harvey was invited to spend another twelve months in France during 1968 and 1969, helping his mentor, Hallam Movius, prepare a series of monographs on the Abri Pataud, the site where he had carried out his dissertation research. I decided to return to Chiapas during four months of that year in order to satisfy my curiosity about ritual humor in other Maya communities. A grant from the Harvard Graduate Society plus some funds from Vogtie's Harvard Chiapas Project made the additional fieldwork possible.

At the beginning of December, I traveled to Chiapas via Paris and Mexico City to begin the last phase of my research on ritual humor. I planned to stay in Chiapas for four months, from December 1, 1968, until March 31, 1969. My principal objective was to learn about the fiesta of Carnaval in Chamula. Time permitting, I also hoped to carry out a similar study of Carnaval in Chenalho, another Tzotzil-speaking town some distance north of Chamula. In theory, this would be possible because Chamula followed the Easter calendar in scheduling Carnaval, whereas the same fiesta was scheduled exactly four weeks after the fiesta of San Sebastian in Chenalho. Unfortunately, however, the two celebrations of Carnaval fell during the same week in February in 1969, which meant that I could only attend one of them. I chose the one in Chamula and relied on interviews with three inhabitants of Chenalho and photographs of the fiesta by Trudi Blom for data on ritual humor in the Carnaval in Chenalho.[7]

By scheduling the beginning of my field season well in advance of the fiesta of Carnaval in February, I was also able to return to Zinacantan in January for the performance of the Grandfathers and Grandmothers on Epiphany (January 6) and part of the fiesta of San Sebastian two weeks later. This enabled me to fill gaps in the data I had obtained for these celebrations in 1966.

In order to use my time most efficiently, I decided not to set up housekeeping at the Baños Mercedarios, as I had in previous years, but to live as a pensioner in Na Bolom, the home of Trudi Blom, where I would have well-balanced meals and access to her wonderful library. This was a fortunate decision, because my presence in Trudi's home meant that she was aware of my comings and goings. As I wrote in one of my letters to Harvey, on the day that she took a group of tourists staying at her house to Chenalho for the fiesta, "I jokingly remarked that maybe she should cover the fiesta there for me and take pictures for me. She took me seriously and apparently ran herself ragged trying to get pictures of all the costumed figures and their activities so that I wouldn't be disappointed."[8] Her photos served as stimuli for the interviews I carried out after the fiesta was over; my consultants from Chenalho identified the performers depicted in them and explained the relationship between the activities shown in the pictures and the fiesta as a whole.

It happened that Gary Gossen and his wife, Eleanor, were in residence at the Harvard Ranch that year, while Gary was carrying out his monumental study of the folklore of Chamula, the town whose fiesta of Carnaval I wanted to compare with the fiestas of San Sebastian and Carnaval in Zinacantan. Gary very kindly offered to help me with the logistics of getting started in Chamula. He went with me to Chamula Center to introduce me to the Presidente Municipal of that township, who agreed to my presence in Chamula for the purpose of studying its major fiesta, on condition that I took no photographs while I was there. He also assigned the town's scribe to serve as my bodyguard during fiestas.

Gary helped me in other ways as well. He arranged for me to attend a significant ritual in Chamula in January, and he introduced me to a number of literate Chamulans who could write texts on the fiesta of Carnaval to prepare me for what I would be witnessing in February, when the fiesta was scheduled to take place. The texts were written during December, giving me several months to become familiar with Chamula and to make arrangements to stay in the house of one of the cargoholders in Chamula Center during the fiesta. I learned that the festivities associated with Carnaval took place over a two-week period, beginning in the cargoholder's hamlet in a remote part of the township. When I arrived in the hamlet, I was instructed to park the Jeep in a small clearing in the woods at some distance from the cargoholder's home. Not long afterward, some boys let the air out of one of the tires of the Jeep, as well as the spare, which was mounted on the side of the vehicle, leaving me stranded many kilometers away from San Cristobal. This necessitated a forty-five minute hike over the mountains to Chamula Center in search of assistance. The cargoholder's daughter-in-law, who was a tiny woman and the mother of infant twins, agreed to accompany me on this mission as my guide and protector. She handed one of the twins to her mother-in-law to care for and tied the other twin on her back. Although she only came up to my waist, she was an excellent guide and companion. We chatted in Tzotzil as we walked over the mountains into town, where I encountered the scribe who had been assigned to me as a bodyguard. He took me to the Chamulan owner of a brand-new truck, who had an attachment for removing a spark plug and pumping air into tires powered by the motor. The scribe asked him whether he would do me the favor of going with me and my companion to inflate the tires on my Jeep, for a price of course. He agreed to do so, and we returned to the cargoholder's hamlet in his truck, where he reinflated the two flat tires on the Jeep.

After that, the cargoholder insisted that the Jeep be parked beside his house, both in the hamlet and later in Chamula Center itself for the principal days of the fiesta. He was counting on the use of the Jeep and me as chauffeur to run errands to San Cristobal on his behalf.

The Carnaval in Chamula Center was spectacular and far more elaborate than the fiestas of San Sebastian and Carnaval in Zinacantan. The entire town served as the stage for the celebration, which went on day and night. There was plenty of ritual humor in the houses of the cargoholders, as well as outdoors. The fiesta culminated in a mock battle that pitted two groups of men costumed as French grenadiers against each other. One group stood on the hillside and the other in the valley containing a sacred spring, flinging lumps of horse dung at each other. This was followed by all the performers running over burning thatch to purge themselves of the excesses of the Carnival season in preparation for Ash Wednesday the next day.

There were massive crowds in Chamula during the last five days of Carnaval, providing the perfect conditions for an epidemic. I and many Chamulans came down with various strains of typhoid and paratyphoid. I recovered in Trudi's house, where I was treated by a San Cristobal doctor. One of my Zinacantec friends was convinced that I was suffering from evil eye, which he blamed on my having gone to

Chamula for Carnaval, where people stared at me because they did not know me. He pointed out that, if I had gone to Zinacantan where I was well known, people would not have stared at me and, in so doing, given me the evil eye. He was undoubtedly right that I would have been better off in Zinacantan, where the sanitation conditions were better. He said that I needed to be treated by his wife's grandfather, who was a famous curer. I replied that I was too sick to go and see him, and he was too old to come and see me. My friend must have discussed my health with the Chamulan gardener at the Harvard Ranch, who was also a curer, for, as I described in a letter to Harvey, the gardener came to see me the next morning, "and before I knew what he was about, he was pulsing my wrists. Then he prescribed a mash of leaves and salt to be rubbed on my wrists and forehead."[9] I said that I did not know how to find such leaves. He replied that they would soon arrive. An hour or so later, I heard a thump outside my door. When I investigated it, I discovered that someone had dropped a small bunch of leaves in front of the door. I decided to follow the Chamulan curer's instructions, because they did not involve ingesting the leaves.

My fever broke that night. The San Cristobal doctor believed that he had cured me, but so also did the Chamulan gardener-curer at the Harvard Ranch!

Some weeks later, the Chamulan curer appeared outside my door complaining of being ill and asking me to take him to a doctor. By then, I was well enough to drive, and I took him to the clinic for Indians, but no one was willing to see him. I then took him to a pharmacy, where I described his symptoms to a pharmacist. The medicine he gave the curer was effective.

It was during this period that Harvey received an offer of a one-year visiting position in the Department of Anthropology at Tulane. This came about through a set of fortuitous circumstances. First of all, our friends George and Jane Collier were living in New Orleans at that time, where Jane was an anthropology graduate student at Tulane, and George had a two-year postdoctoral fellowship. Second, Harvey's close friend and archaeological colleague Berle Clay had a teaching position in the same department. And third, the anthropological linguist in the department, Marshall Durbin, had suddenly resigned in order to take up a position at Washington University in St. Louis. The Tulane department wanted to find a quick replacement for Durbin so that his position would not be lost.

George was not available for the position because he had just accepted a tenure-track position at Stanford. He and Berle persuaded the department to offer the position to Harvey. The offer included a vague promise to work out something for me after we got to New Orleans.

Harvey and I needed to confer about this offer, but with him in a hamlet in southwestern France and me in a small town in southeastern Mexico, this was not an easy matter in those days. There was a telephone in the home of the French family on whose farm we lived, and I had access to the telephone at Na Bolom. The call would have to be made through the undersea Atlantic cable. Harvey's first attempt to call me failed. The second, via Madrid, succeeded. We agreed that it was a tempting offer, and Harvey decided to accept the appointment, if the offer could be revised to include something specific for me. Tulane came back with the offer of a full-time visiting position for Harvey and a half-time visiting position for me. My position included the obligation to teach a beginning course in Spoken Yucatecan Maya. Evidently someone at Tulane—probably Munro Edmonson—thought that my experience teaching Tzotzil at Harvard qualified me to teach another Mayan language, of which I had no prior knowledge at all! (Equally incongruous was the decision to replace a linguist with a Palaeolithic archaeologist!) But the department promised to provide me with an assistant who was a native speaker of Yucatecan Maya, and I decided that the challenge was too good to pass up! So we accepted the offers.

Throughout our negotiation process, Trudi was enthusiastic about the possibility of Harvey and me becoming faculty at Tulane. Her husband, Frans Blom, had been the Director of the Middle American

Research Institute at Tulane before moving permanently to San Cristobal. She was delighted that we would be teaching at a place that was well known for Mesoamerican studies.

During my convalescence from the disease I had contracted in Chamula, I took advantage of Trudi's fine library to catch up on some recent publications in my field. Among the books I discovered in her library and read that month was Nelson Reed's history of the Caste War of Yucatan.[10] That book served as the inspiration for the project that would follow the completion of my study of ritual humor in highland Chiapas a few years later.

NOTES

1. I had already received some instruction in Tzotzil during the spring of 1963 from Lore Colby, whose linguistics dissertation was concerned with Tzotzil grammar. The following spring, training in Tzotzil was offered by Francesca Cancian, who had just completed her PhD in sociology. She emphasized the use of the language in conversation, an approach that I found helpful in establishing rapport in Zinacantan.

2. A digital copy of this tape is archived on the website of the Archive of the Indigenous Languages of Latin America (www.ailla.utexas.org), as is a transcription and English translation of it. The original tape is archived in the Library of the American Philosophical Society.

3. During my last field season in Chiapas, a two-week period in the summer of 1972 to finish collecting data for my book on *The Indian Christ, the Indian King: The Historical Substrate of Maya Myth and Ritual* (see Chapter 7), I visited the family in Nabenchauc that had been most helpful to me in my quest for data on Zinacantec humor. The visit went well, but as we were talking, I sensed that the people sitting there were waiting for something. Then I remembered, and I made a humorous remark. My friends collapsed with laughter, saying: "She hasn't forgotten!"

4. I picked up my tape recorder in Mexico City on my way back from Denver. The repair job was competent, and the tape recorder functioned without incident during the rest of my stay in Chiapas.

5. Our pilot died in a plane crash a few months later.

6. Munro S. Edmonson, "Los Manitos: Patterns of Humor in Relation to Cultural Values." PhD diss., Harvard University, 1952.

7. Although I could not be present in Chenalho during the fiesta of Carnaval itself, I was able to visit the town about three weeks before it began. I was accompanied on this trip by my good friends Marcey Jacobsen and Janet Marren and by my closest friend in Zinacantan. Our plan was to look for a cargoholder in whose home I could stay during Carnaval, but in the course of our search we learned that the fiesta was scheduled for the same days as Carnaval in Chamula, which meant that I had to abandon that plan. Nevertheless, our visit was fruitful in one respect, because it gave me an opportunity to meet friends of Marcey and Janet and Gary Gossen, who were willing to come to San Cristobal after the fiesta was over to be interviewed by me on what had transpired during Carnaval.

8. Letter of February 19, 1969, to Harvey M. Bricker.

9. Letter of March 19, 1969, to Harvey M. Bricker.

10. Nelson A. Reed, *The Caste War of Yucatán* (Stanford, CA: Stanford University Press, 1964).

7

TULANE:
SEEKING THE ANTECEDENTS
OF MAYA MYTH AND RITUAL

Harvey and I landed in New Orleans during the second half of September in 1969. As we emerged from the airport, we were engulfed by a wave of hot, steamy, flower-scented night air. Our friends Berle and Brenda Clay met our flight and took us to their home in the Uptown section of the city. We stayed with them for several days until we could retrieve from storage the furniture lent to us by a faculty member on leave and then moved into the house on the 900 block of Cherokee Street passed on to us by the Colliers, who had lived there for the previous two years.

We felt at home in New Orleans almost immediately. We liked the semitropical climate and the smell of Confederate jasmine, cashmere bouquet, and other flowers that perfumed the air. The house bequeathed to us by the Colliers was more spacious than anywhere we had lived since we were married. And we immediately made friends with Munro Edmonson (whom we knew as Ed) and his wife, Barbara, who lived only two doors away on the same block.

Ed took us under his wing and introduced us to campus life. He was active in university politics and brought us up to speed in that arena almost immediately. It was a heady experience for the novices that we were at that time.

Ed offered to let me teach his course on Middle American Indians during the first semester, which I gratefully accepted. The topic was one in which I had the most training and was relatively easy for me to prepare. Nevertheless, I found it challenging to provide enough content for each lecture to fill a 50-minute period, probably because I covered it too quickly in class. My students were sympathetic with my performance as a new teacher, and I found the entire course an exhilarating experience.

I taught only one course that semester because of the half-time status of my teaching position. I spent the rest of my time completing my book, titled *Ritual Humor in Highland Chiapas*, which I submitted to several university presses during the following semester. It was published in 1973 by the University of Texas Press.

During the second semester, Harvey taught only one course so that he would have time to work on his dissertation, and I taught two courses: Introduction to Cultural Anthropology and Spoken Yucatecan Maya. The latter was sponsored by the Center for Latin American Studies, which provided the funds to bring a native speaker of the language up from the town of Hocaba in the state of Yucatan in Mexico to help me with the instruction. His name was Ermilo Marín Mendoza. Fortunately, there was a textbook for this course, which gave me basic material, in addition to what I learned from my assistant. It was a struggle to keep one lesson ahead of the class, but the experience gave me a foundation to build on.

A number of the words in Yucatecan Maya have cognates in Tzotzil, but the grammatical structures in which they are embedded are so different that it is difficult to recognize the cognates in context. I realized that I was dealing with a totally unfamiliar language and tried to learn it as rapidly as possible.

The emphasis on conversation in our textbook was good for the students, but not for me, because in order to teach the language effectively, I needed to have a sense of the language as a whole. For this, I turned to Ermilo, from whom I elicited the paradigms that enabled me to place the material in the textbook in a more comprehensive grammatical context.

Because our teaching appointments were only for nine months, Harvey and I were also looking for jobs that year. Fortunately, Tulane wanted to keep us on in the same positions for another year. We said that we would stay if our appointments could be expanded to two full-time positions for two years. The department and the dean agreed to this upgrading of our appointments. Before the end of that two-year period, our positions were converted into tenure-track appointments. In due course, we received tenure and remained at Tulane for the rest of our teaching careers.

Tulane's Department of Anthropology was well known for its strength in Mesoamerican studies, which was enhanced by the Middle American Research Institute (MARI) and the manuscripts in the Special Collections of the Latin American Library. MARI dates back to 1924, when it was known as the Department of Middle American Research.

William Gates was its first director. He was followed by Frans Blom, in whose home in San Cristobal I had lived for four months in 1968 and 1969. Frans was succeeded after World War II by Robert Wauchope, an eminent archaeologist who became our friend at Tulane.

The Department of Anthropology was established much later than MARI, first as the Department of Sociology and Anthropology by 1947; it became an independent department only two years before our arrival in 1969. Ed Edmonson chaired the department during our first three years at Tulane.

It was during our second semester at Tulane that we first became aware of the central role that Mardi Gras plays in the social life of New Orleans. Ed Edmonson was an expert on this festival, having published a fascinating article on this subject in the *Caribbean Quarterly* some years before,[1] and he wanted to be the one to introduce it to Harvey and me on Mardi Gras Day (literally, "Fat Tuesday"). I was excited about the opportunity to participate in this event because it was the New Orleans counterpart of Fasching in Rottweil and Carnaval in highland Chiapas. I was curious to see how it compared with those variants of this festival with which I was already familiar.

Ed insisted that we had to mask for this occasion. I wore my Zinacantec woman's costume, and Harvey wore a Mexican charro outfit borrowed from Ed. Ed and Barbara were dressed in the traditional costumes worn in two different Maya communities of highland Guatemala, and their three daughters had put together disguises of their own. I remember that their eldest daughter, Evelyn, went as the Madwoman of Chaillot, wearing an enormous straw hat loaded with artificial fruit. Decked out in this fashion, we set out for the French Quarter, where Barbara had friends who had agreed to let us use their home as a base for viewing the festival.

The principal attraction in the French Quarter was the "He-Sheba Contest," during which gay transvestites competed for prizes for the most elaborate and outlandish costumes. Both before and after the contest, the contestants wandered through the streets of the French Quarter, showing off the costumes that they had spent the previous year designing and assembling. The Quarter was packed with people in other kinds of costumes as well, and we were glad that we were also in disguise. The spirit of abandonment that pervaded the crowd reminded me of what I had experienced on similar occasions in Germany and Mexico in earlier years.

In subsequent years, Harvey and I participated in Mardi Gras in other parts of town, both on Mardi Gras Day itself and during the weeks leading up to it. The entire city served as a stage for neighborhood parades that increased in number as the big day approached. In this respect, Mardi Gras reminded me of Carnaval in Chamula, where multiple events took place simultaneously in different parts of town.

I took advantage of Ermilo's presence in New Orleans during the Mardi Gras season to question him about how Carnaval was celebrated in his hometown. He responded by writing a detailed description of that fiesta in Maya. I was happy to see that, as in highland Chiapas, the fiesta in Hocaba had humorous elements, even though the principal themes were different. It seemed worth making an effort to see it in the future.

The spring of 1970 was also the semester when the students at Kent State University demonstrated against the Cambodian Campaign, and some of them were shot by the Ohio National Guard. There was similar unrest among the students at Tulane, in the course of which they occupied the University Center and poured glue in the locks on the building. It was interesting to see how Colonel Robert Scruton, the head of Security, handled the situation, compared to what I had seen after the occupation of the administrative building at Harvard the year before. He did not call in the New Orleans police, but let the students stay in the building, and when the students wanted to lower the flag in front of another building in mourning of the students who had died at Kent State, he did not interfere. As a result, the students showed their respect for him by renaming the auditorium in the University Center after him.

Ultimately, the university's administration decided to end the semester before the exam period. Grades were assigned based on exams taken and work already completed. As a beginning instructor, I found this way of ending the semester demoralizing, because the courses were not completed thematically or pedagogically. I was apprehensive about the possibility of the same thing happening in future years, but that did not come to pass during the remaining thirty-five years I taught at Tulane.[2]

Early in 1971, I received a letter from Ermilo, in which he invited Harvey and me to attend the Carnaval that would take place during the third week of February in Hocaba. He told me that he had made arrangements for us to stay in the home of his aunt and uncle during our visit. Harvey and I decided to accept his invitation, even though it would mean missing Mardi Gras in New Orleans. We flew to Merida and went from there in a cooperative taxi to Hocaba, a town of about five thousand inhabitants fifty kilometers southeast of Merida. Our presence in Hocaba aroused great interest. As honored guests, Harvey was asked to crown the Queen of Carnaval and I the Princess.

The themes of this Carnaval were different from the ones that characterized those in highland Chiapas. They touched on some painful events in the Colonial history of the Yucatan peninsula: (1) the Inquisition carried out by Bishop Diego de Landa during the 1560s and (2) the mistreatment of the Indians by the clergy during the nineteenth century. But the lighthearted and sometimes obscene joking that accompanied these more serious themes imposed a veneer of modernity on a turbulent past.

With this fiesta, I began to turn my attention away from my commitment to fieldwork in Chiapas toward a new interest in the language and culture of Yucatan. Tulane had close ties with scholars in Yucatan, and my responsibility for teaching Spoken Yucatecan Maya gradually pulled me away from my efforts to improve my knowledge of Tzotzil to mastering the native language of Yucatan. I had completed my book on ritual humor in highland Chiapas and was ready to undertake something new.

I had a much more ambitious project in mind for my next book, a comparison of Indian rebellions throughout the Maya area and their impact on myth and ritual. I already knew something about this subject for highland Chiapas,[3] but little or nothing about it for other parts of the Maya area, such as the Yucatan peninsula and highland Guatemala. The fact that I had already invested time in learning Yucatecan Maya made Yucatan the obvious place to begin my new project, as did the recent publication of Nelson Reed's history of the Caste War of Yucatan that I had read during my last month of fieldwork in Chiapas.

With a summer grant from the Wenner–Gren Foundation for Anthropological Research, I arrived in Merida in the middle of June with the intention of recording oral traditions about the Caste War of Yucatan in several Maya communities. Shortly after arriving in Merida, I went to pay my respects to the leading scholar of the region, Don Alfredo Barrera Vásquez, the director of the Instituto Yucateco de Antropología e Historia in the Palacio Cantón on the Paseo de Montejo. After I had described the research that I was hoping to carry out that summer, he told me that the Biblioteca Crescencio Carrillo y Ancona, which at that time was housed in the Palacio Cantón, had about 200 letters from the Caste War, many of them written in Maya, and he asked me whether I would like to include them in my study. Of course, I said yes, but that opportunity meant a significant change in the focus of my research for the summer and enlarged the scope of my project as a whole.

It had not occurred to me that some of the Indians were literate in their language during the nineteenth century. The existence of their letters meant that I would not have to depend entirely on oral traditions for a sense of how the Indians themselves felt about their domination by the descendants of the Spaniards. The letters could be compared with the official histories written by the other side. Perhaps in this way I could determine what the relationship was between myth and history.

But there was a practical problem in my working with those letters. I had only a very limited knowledge of modern Yucatecan Maya. I knew nothing about the nineteenth-century form of the language, nor whether I would be able to read or understand it.

It was then that an employee of the Palacio Cantón came to my rescue. It was Eleuterio Po'ot Yah, a member of the custodial staff, who had served as Marshall Durbin's assistant in teaching Spoken Yucatecan Maya at Tulane and later at Washington University in St. Louis. I had met him briefly during a layover in New Orleans on his way to St. Louis the previous year and again in Hocaba in February.

Elut (as he was known in Maya circles) was interested in learning about the Caste War of Yucatan and offered to help me translate the letters into Spanish in the late afternoon, when the Palacio Cantón was closed. I spent the mornings during the week transcribing the letters at the Palacio and the afternoons and some evenings going over my transcriptions with him and getting his advice on how to translate them. He also helped me find people known for their storytelling abilities who were willing to share their knowledge about the Caste War of Yucatan with me and have them recorded on tape. One of the raconteurs was a friend of his in Hocaba. For others, we made a special trip to Sotuta, where we recorded the accounts of several people we met there.

Harvey joined me in Merida at the end of the summer, and Elut went with us by bus to Carrillo Puerto in what was then the Federal Territory of Quintana Roo. This town had been the capital of the region controlled by the rebel Maya during the second half of the nineteenth century, when it was known as *Chan Santa Cruz* ("Little Holy Cross"). It was named after a cross that miraculously appeared in 1850, carved in the trunk of a mahogany tree near a sinkhole that became the headquarters of the rebel movement (Figure 7.1). I wanted to see the sinkhole on the outskirts of the town where the cross had first appeared and a small chapel had been built in its honor (Figure 7.2), as well as the large church built a few years later by the rebel Maya in the center of town (Figure 7.3). We stayed at a small hotel on one side of the square, next door to the church.[4]

After visiting the shrine on the edge of town, we returned to the square. From there, we began walking around town, looking for people who might be willing to tell us stories about the Caste War of Yucatan. We were unsuccessful at first, but eventually we reached a neighborhood that Elut thought might be promising. He walked ahead of us, looking in doorways. He poked his head in one doorway that led into a Maya

FIGURE 7.1. The sinkhole outside Carrillo Puerto where the Talking Cross first appeared.
Photo by Harvey M. Bricker.

barbershop, where a group of men had gathered in order to chat. He signaled that we should stop, because he had found the ideal context for carrying out our mission.

Harvey and I entered the barbershop and sat quietly in back. After some small talk about the price of beer in Carrillo Puerto, Elut got down to business and explained our mission. The names of several old men were proposed as informants. Then the man who was in the barber's chair, a rickety framework of unpainted wooden planks, announced that his father-in-law was General Francisco May, the Indian leader who had died in 1969. He suggested that we go and speak to his widow and son.

General May's widow received us graciously and began to show us various memorabilia: a photo of her husband when he was decorated

FIGURE 7.2.   The open chapel near the sinkhole outside Carrillo Puerto.
Photo by Harvey M. Bricker.

by President Cárdenas, a photo of him with an American consul, and so forth. We asked her whether she would be willing to tell us about her husband's life. She refused but suggested that we ask her son, who, she assured us, knew more about his father's exploits than she did. The son showed up a few minutes later. He was a young man in his twenties. He agreed to be interviewed. He gave us some excellent data about the Caste War.

After returning to Carrillo Puerto, we recorded a long interview with a descendant of Crescencio Po'ot, who had been the head of the rebel Maya in 1884. We sat outside next to the highway, with the traffic whizzing by, the sound of busses drowning out some of the words of the raconteur.

That evening, Elut went out alone with the son of General May, who made arrangements for a truck to take us the next morning to the

FIGURE 7.3.   The church in Carrillo Puerto built for the Talking Cross in 1858.
Photo by Harvey M. Bricker.

shrine village of Chancah. We set off the next morning for Chancah
by truck over an apparently seldom-used road. The men had to get
down several times to remove trees that had fallen across the roadway.
The entrance to Chancah was marked by a guardhouse, but there was
no one in it. I found the town of Chancah fascinating because it was
arranged like a Classic Maya ceremonial site. Each major structure sat
on a rather high platform mound. Other guardhouses were situated on
nearby mounds. The Patron's house sat on a mound directly across
from the church. The Patron was away working in his cornfield, so we
went off to look for other informants. We interviewed the man who
was the Patron of the Cross in 1959, when Nelson Reed visited the
town, and another old man.

All the interviews that Elut and I conducted in Carrillo Puerto and
Chancah were recorded on tape and were later transcribed and translated
into Spanish by him and subsequently translated into English by me.[5]

I had originally regarded the theoretical focus of my project as one of exploring the relationship between myth and history by comparing the oral traditions of the Maya with the written histories of the Spanish-speaking ethnic group. But my historical research in Yucatan during the summer of 1971 revealed that this approach was overly simplistic, because the nineteenth-century Maya were literate, and people of Spanish descent had their own oral traditions about the Caste War. It was therefore necessary for me to broaden the scope of my investigation to include the oral and written accounts of both ethnic groups.

I returned to the region in the summer of 1972 with the help of a summer grant from the Social Science Research Council, beginning with three weeks in the National Archives in Belize, which had a large collection of correspondence between the authorities in the British colony and the rebel Maya, who were encroaching on the northern border of British Honduras during the second half of the nineteenth century. I took advantage of my presence in Belize to tape-record accounts of the Caste War in the Yucatecan Maya town of Patchakan outside Corozal near the border with Mexico. From there, I crossed the Rio Hondo into Mexico and went by bus to Merida, where I completed the transcription and translation of the Maya letters in the Palacio Cantón.

Before returning to New Orleans, I made a short visit to highland Chiapas in order to record some oral traditions on an Indian rebellion involving Chamula and Chenalho between 1867 and 1870. This was my last field trip to Chiapas, where I collected data that could be compared with data from the new research I had undertaken in Yucatan and tied up some loose ends from my previous research.

But I was not finished with Chiapas! Later the same year, I received a letter from Edward E. Calnek, who had written a dissertation on the ethnohistory of highland Chiapas in 1964.[6] He had learned of my interest in Colonial Indian rebellions and offered to lend me, for an unlimited period of time, ten rolls of microfilm containing 6,000 pages of documents from the Archivo General de Indias in Seville (Spain) that were concerned with the Tzeltal rebellion of 1712. The uprising began in the town of Cancuc and subsequently spread to other towns in the

Tzeltal-speaking region, including Chenalho. For two years, I spent two afternoons a week, sitting in front of a microfilm reader in the library, indexing the documents and transcribing the ones that were relevant for my project. From them I determined that many elements in the fiesta of Carnaval in Chenalho could be traced to the rebellion that originated in Cancuc in 1712.[7]

Subsequently, Ed Edmonson pointed out to me that my coverage of Indian rebellions in the Maya area would not be complete unless I included Guatemala, especially the Totonicapan revolt of 1820, in my study. A brief trip to Guatemala in August 1974 to evaluate the summer program in Antigua sponsored by Tulane's Center for Latin American Studies provided me with the opportunity to visit the Archivo Nacional de Centroamérica in Guatemala City, where I ordered copies of the documents concerning the rebellion to be sent to me at Tulane. They arrived in good time and proved to be an excellent source of information on a rebellion with thematic ties to a Yucatecan uprising that had taken place some sixty years earlier.[8]

All this documentary research strongly influenced the courses I developed during the early 1970s. Ed Edmonson had generously let me teach his course on Middle American Indians during my first semester at Tulane, but this could not become a permanent arrangement. Instead, I decided to offer a course on Ethnic Relations in Middle America, which would consider some of the issues at the core of my ethnohistorical research. I also introduced a graduate seminar in Conquest and Colonialism, in which the students and I focused on a different topic each time it was taught. The course was populated by graduate students in anthropology, Latin American studies, business, and public health. The geographical scope of the course was not limited to Latin America, but often included Africa, North America, and Southeast Asia as well. The emphasis was on how the native peoples of these regions responded to colonial rule.[9]

Philip Thompson was one of the graduate students who became interested in this approach and adopted it for his dissertation. He initiated the archival research for his documentary ethnography of the

eighteenth-century town of Tekanto in 1974 and completed his dissertation on this topic in 1978, publishing a greatly expanded version of it
in 1999.[10] He was my first student, and both his dissertation and the
book based on it are highly regarded in the field of Latin American
ethnohistory.

In the meantime, Harvey had completed his work on the Abri
Pataud and was ready to begin a new set of excavations at the site of
Les Tambourets south of Toulouse in the foothills of the Pyrénées. In
December 1972, after we had turned in our fall semester grades, we
went to France so that Harvey could meet the landowner and the
director of the archaeological region in which the site lay and discuss
with them his plans for excavating the site during the summer of 1973.
We spent a few days with the Edmonsons in Paris, where Ed was serving
as the director of Tulane's Junior Year Abroad program that year. The
first night we were there we were so absorbed in catching up on news
about Tulane and the Edmonsons' experiences in Paris that we were
surprised by the first rays of the sun coming up outside the window
of their apartment. After a breakfast of onion soup, we retired to catch
up on the sleep we had lost staying up all night talking.

We took the train to Toulouse, where we rented a car and drove
to the hamlet of Couladére, where the owner of the land occupied by
the site of Les Tambourets resided. He and his wife welcomed us and
expressed their willingness for Harvey to begin his excavations in June.
We then drove to Foix to meet Jean Clottes, the director of the Circum-
scription of Midi-Pyrénées. He was equally supportive of Harvey's plans
to excavate Les Tambourets.

I accompanied Harvey to France during the summer of 1973 and
helped him with the initial survey of the field in which the site was
located to determine the best place to make an exploratory excavation.
A student from Newcomb College at Tulane joined him after that, and
I went off to England for three weeks, where I looked for additional
documents in the Public Record Office in London concerning the
involvement of the rebel Maya in the northern part of what was then
British Honduras. Although some of these documents were duplicates

of ones I had found in the National Archives of Belize the previous summer, there were many others that I did not find in Belize. The combination of documents from both archives gave me a more complete picture of how the presence of Chan Santa Cruz in southern Quintana Roo had affected the security of the northern boundary of the British colony.

The major excavation of Les Tambourets took place two years later during the summer of 1975. With the help of a grant from the National Science Foundation, Harvey was able to enlist the assistance of seven students from New Orleans and three from the University of Sheffield in England. I helped with the excavations in the mornings and supervised the lab in the afternoons.

I did not excavate during Harvey's last field season at Les Tambourets in the summer of 1980. There were only two student assistants that year, and I thought that their time was better spent in excavation, so I spent my time at the site entirely in the lab.

I greatly enjoyed our last two summers in southern France. The Pyrénées were usually visible in the distance, and the site itself was interesting. It covered an enormous area, much of which was under cultivation in soybeans in 1975. The excavations yielded many stone tools that had been manufactured by the last of the Neanderthals. The town of Cazéres where we stayed was picturesque, as were other towns in the region. From there it was less than a day's drive into northern Spain through the small principality of Andorra, where the Catalan language seemed to be a hybrid of French and Spanish. I found the differences between this region of the Pyrenean foothills and the Dordogne, where Harvey and I had lived for several years during the 1960s, interesting, especially the ways in which the pronunciation of French words was similar to what I knew from Spanish.

One other set of experiences during the first decade of our affiliation with Tulane had a significant impact on the rest of my professional life. When Harvey and I joined the Anthropology Department in 1969, there was already another husband-and-wife team on the faculty, Ann and Jack Fischer. During that year, they had agreed to become co-editors of book reviews for the *American Anthropologist*, the flagship journal of our national organization, the American Anthropological Association. However, Ann died during our second year at Tulane, and Jack did not want to continue with book reviews without her. Having only recently shipped all the books for review to Tulane, the Association was reluctant to pay for another expensive move of that office. For some reason, Jack (and perhaps one or two other senior members of the department) suggested me as a replacement for the Fischers, and the Association agreed. Six issues of the journal were published each year. Traditionally, each issue contained both articles and book reviews, but when Ann and Jack became book-review editors, the Association decided to separate articles from book reviews, with three issues devoted entirely to articles and the other three to book reviews.

I served as book-review editor for the *American Anthropologist* for two years. At the end of that time, the Association decided to return to the original format of the journal, with articles and book reviews in each issue, under a single editor. I assumed that my editorial career with the Association was over.

However, for some reason that to this day I do not understand, the Association asked me to assume the editorship of a new journal, called the *American Ethnologist*. I much preferred this assignment to the previous one, because I had a greater interest in articles than in book reviews, and under my editorship, only articles were published in the new journal.[11]

The number of publication deadlines I had to meet each year increased from three to four. In order to have the summers free for fieldwork (in Mexico, Belize, England, or France), I had to work on two issues of the journal at once during the spring semester. As time went on, my responsibilities within the department and the rest of the university were increasing. Eventually, my workload became too heavy and I gave up the editorship of the *American Ethnologist* after four years.

My experience as the editor of a journal was invaluable. From it, I learned how to communicate with the wider profession, and the task of copy-editing the manuscripts for the journal improved my own writing substantially. It was a wonderful opportunity for someone at the beginning of her career, as I was, and I am very glad that it came my way then.

As is often the case, one thing led to another. Bob Wauchope, the director of the Middle American Research Institute, had been serving as the General Editor of the *Handbook of Middle American Indians* for the University of Texas Press when I arrived at Tulane. After that series had been completed, he recommended me for the General Editor of what became the *Supplement to the Handbook of Middle American Indians*. Although this offer came only one year after I had relinquished my previous editorial position, it appealed to me because it was more closely related to my research interests, and, best of all, there would be no publication deadlines, and I could work at my own pace.

Thus, only a few years into my teaching career at Tulane, I was caught up in editorial opportunities that brought me into our national professional organization[12] and subsequently into contact with researchers in a variety of fields in my geographical area of research. I continued as General Editor of the *Supplement* series until a few years after my retirement from teaching at Tulane.

NOTES

1. Munro S. Edmonson, "Carnival in New Orleans," *Caribbean Quarterly* 4 (1956): 233–45.
2. However, my last semester of teaching ended in much the same way, because it happened to coincide with Hurricane Katrina, when Tulane had to close down for an entire semester (see Chapter 13).
3. During the two years that the Colliers lived in New Orleans, George had combed the Latin American Library for publications and manuscripts on Chiapas. He discovered that the Paniagua Collection in the library contained numerous pamphlets and articles on the history of the region around San Cristobal. He told me about them and gave me copies of many of them. In this way, he made me

aware of the possibilities for carrying out historical research on the antecedents of the rituals I had observed in fiestas in Zinacantan, Chamula, and Chenalho.

4. Elut had insisted that we buy hammocks for the trip because this hotel did not have beds. However, upon arriving at the hotel, we discovered that our room *did* have a double bed that occupied most of the space. Harvey dismantled the bed and placed the mattresses against two of the walls. We hung our hammocks and slept in them at night. The next morning we discovered that Elut had not used his hammock, but had slept on the bed in his room during the night!

5. The texts from the interviews with the descendant of Crescencio Po'ot and the former Patron of the Cross can be found in Appendix B of Victoria R. Bricker, *The Indian Christ, the Indian King: The Historical Substrate of Maya Myth and Ritual* (Austin: University of Texas Press, 1981).

6. The published version of Calnek's dissertation appeared in 1988 as *Highland Chiapas Before the Spanish Conquest*. Papers of the New World Archaeological Foundation, no. 55 (Provo, UT: New World Archaeological Foundation).

7. Digital copies of my transcriptions of these documents may be accessed at http://www.famsi.org.

8. Digital copies of my transcriptions of these documents may be accessed at http://www.famsi.org.

9. Unbeknownst to me, similar developments were taking place in the History Department of UCLA in California at that time, under the direction of James Lockhart. He became aware of my interest in this field only after the publication of my second book, *The Indian Christ, the Indian King: The Historical Substrate of Maya Myth and Ritual*, in 1981, when he was a member of the committee of the Conference on Latin American History that selected it for the Howard Francis Cline Memorial Prize in 1983. I met him subsequently during a visit he made to Tulane in 1987, when Richard Greenleaf, the director of the Center for Latin American Studies, arranged for Jim and me to have lunch together. It was only then

that I learned of our common interest in using sources written in indigenous languages for understanding the impact of the Spanish conquest and colonialism on Mexican Indian communities (the Nahuas of the Central Highlands in his case and the Maya of Yucatan in mine). He invited me to join his "school," but because I was deeply involved in unrelated projects in linguistics and epigraphy at that time, I declined.

10. Philip C. Thompson, *Tekanto, a Maya Town in Colonial Yucatán* (New Orleans, LA: Tulane University Middle American Research Institute Publication 67, 1999).

11. Book reviews were later added to the *American Ethnologist.*

12. I also served as a member of the Executive Board of the American Anthropological Association for three years between 1980 and 1983, where I participated in the publications committee.

8

ELUT:
TEACHING AND PRESERVING
THE MAYA LANGUAGE

My first encounter with Eleuterio Po'ot Yah, whom I came to know as "Elut," occurred on a blustery afternoon in February 1970, when he passed through New Orleans on his way to St. Louis, Missouri, to assist Marshall Durbin in a course he was offering on Yucatecan Maya at Washington University. Ed Edmonson went out to the airport to assist Elut in clearing Immigration and Customs, if necessary. Because Elut had a long layover in New Orleans, Ed brought him back to his house for a few hours and invited me to come over to meet this Maya Indian, who was originally from Hocaba, Yucatan, and a friend of Ermilo, who was helping me teach Spoken Yucatecan Maya at Tulane that semester. As I left our house to go over to the Edmonsons' house, a small whirlwind came down our street, snatching the screen door out of my hand. I hurried over to the Edmonsons' house on the corner to escape the wind and rain.

For me, this was not just an opportunity to become acquainted with the man who had assisted with the Spoken Yucatecan Maya course from its inception at Tulane in 1967. I had some questions about a verbal suffix that seemed to have the same function in Yucatecan Maya as in Tzotzil, and I wanted to see whether I could elicit some examples of its use in his language. It was clear that he was interested in what I had to say and corroborated my hypothesis. This was the beginning of a collaborative learning experience and friendship that was to last for thirty-six years.

The next time I taught the Spoken Yucatecan Maya course was in 1972. I worked out an arrangement with Marshall Durbin so that Elut would spend two months in New Orleans and two months in St. Louis, assisting with the teaching of the same course in the two universities. This cooperative arrangement between Tulane and Washington University continued for a number of years, until Marshall found a colleague in the Spanish Department at his university who was a native speaker of a different dialect of Yucatecan Maya to collaborate with. After that, Elut would come to Tulane for three months in even-numbered years until health problems made such travel unwise. He then trained a replacement so that the course could continue to be taught at Tulane, as it still is today.

Elut spent the first two decades of his life in Hocaba, where he was born on April 18, 1937, as the fourth of nine children of Pastor Po'ot Chi and Adalberta Yah Baas. The family was poor and illiterate. As soon as he was old enough, Elut began working on one of the henequen plantations near the town. He spoke only Maya during those years. But when he was drafted into military service at the age of nineteen, he was told that he had to learn to read and write Spanish and subsequently enrolled in an evening course in literacy offered by the city of Merida.

At the age of twenty-two, Elut moved with his wife and two children to Merida in search of better employment. He worked as a gardener and then as a stone mason's helper during his early years in Merida. Eventually, he obtained a position as a custodian in the Palacio Cantón.

The literacy training Elut received during his military service opened his eyes to the value of education, and after moving to Merida, he completed his formal education through the fourth grade in night school. He was an avid reader of the several daily newspapers published in Merida and was always au courant with current events in Mexico and the rest of the world. Later, his work at Tulane inspired him to purchase and read linguistics books available in Spanish translation during the rest of his life.

Elut's teaching and research activities relating to the Maya language of Yucatan began in 1967, when Marshall Durbin, my predecessor in the Department of Anthropology at Tulane, decided to undertake some research on that language. He contacted Professor Alfredo Barrera Vásquez in the Palacio Cantón and asked him to recommend a native speaker of the Maya language to come to New Orleans and work with him. In his request, Marshall stipulated that this person should have two Maya surnames, which he thought would ensure that the Maya language had been spoken in the home. Barrera Vásquez knew only one speaker of Maya who could do the job and also had two Maya surnames, namely, Elut, whose surnames were Po'ot Yah.

Elut's work with Marshall at Tulane took place during the two years when the Colliers were living in New Orleans. When George realized that Marshall was working on a dictionary of the Hocaba dialect of Maya with Elut, he offered his computer skills to the project, pointing out that because most of the roots in the language had a consonant–vowel–consonant structure (as in *sak* "white," s-a-k), the mainframe computer at Tulane could generate all possible combinations of such roots based on the twenty consonants and five vowels in the language, which could be used for eliciting entries for the dictionary. Marshall liked the idea, and George wrote the program that generated a list of all possible roots composed of such concatenations of consonants and vowels.

Elut was impressed with that list and wanted to have a copy of it. But Marshall was afraid that it might fall into the hands of a rival scholar in Merida and was reluctant to give it to Elut. Ever resourceful, after returning to Merida, Elut decided to imitate what the computer had done and generate his own list of roots, which he later typed up and had bound so that he could use it for his own research.

On the other hand, Marshall believed that linguists had an obligation to share their knowledge with consultants, that the relationship between the researcher and the person who spoke the language should be reciprocal and mutually beneficial. It was clear to me that Marshall had instilled in Elut an interest in the grammatical structure of his language and had given him some of the linguistic tools to analyze it. This made a deep impression on me, and I decided to follow Marshall's lead in this respect.

During the first years of my association with Elut, I did not share his interest in Maya grammar, beyond what I needed to know in order to co-teach our course. I was preoccupied with the research for my book on Maya rebellions and did not have the time to undertake such linguistic research.

It was very difficult for Elut to move back and forth between his low-ranking job as a custodian of a museum in Merida and his much higher position as an instructional assistant in anthropology at Tulane. In Merida, he was at the beck and call of higher ranking employees of the museum, whereas at Tulane, he commanded the respect of a teacher when he drilled students on the material covered in class. In addition, the evenings and weekends were especially difficult for him in New Orleans, so far from his family and friends in Merida. In order to occupy his time when he was not working with me or the students in our class, he pursued research projects of his own. During one semester, he wrote proverbs in Maya; during another, poems in his language; and during still another, songs.[1] It happened that one of the students in the class had a good voice and played the guitar well. I suggested to her that, for her class project, she learn the songs that Elut had written and perform them for the class, which then joined her in singing them.

As time went on, and my facility with conversational Maya improved, I became interested in the structure and function of verbs in the language. In order to explore this topic in depth, I needed to assemble a large corpus of verbs. I suggested to Elut that he come over to our house on Sunday afternoons to help me with this project (Figure 8.1). He was delighted with this proposition, not only because it would give him something interesting to think about, but also because it was something to look forward to on the weekends. He would arrive at 1:00 in the afternoon. We would work until it was time for me to prepare supper. We would work for a while after the meal, and then Harvey or I would drive him home to his apartment. In this way, I gradually came to share Elut's enthusiasm for the grammatical structure of his language. And once we began to collaborate on this project, he no longer wrote proverbs, poems, or songs.

What Elut really wanted us to collaborate on was a dictionary of his language like the one that Marshall Durbin had begun in 1967 but never finished. At the time, I was primarily interested in verbs and how they were conjugated. I suggested that we begin with a trilingual dictionary of verbs in Maya, Spanish, and English. We initiated this project during the summer of 1979, when I was living in Merida for a few months. We went through his self-generated list of all possible Maya roots in search of those that had verbal functions; there were 350 of them in all. The dictionary was authored by him, and I wrote the grammatical introduction, which was translated into Spanish by James

FIGURE 8.1.   Elut walking down Freret Street near Tulane in New Orleans.

Ward, a member of the staff of the Center for Latin American Studies at the time. The Center published the dictionary in 1981.[2] We used it as a supplementary textbook in our course for many years.

As Elut's knowledge of the grammatical structure of Maya increased, so also did recognition of his pedagogical talents in Merida. His first teaching position there—beginning in 1978 and continuing until 1983—was at the Seminario Conciliar de San Ildefonso next to the cathedral, where Maya has been taught for centuries as part of the training of priests for work in Maya-speaking villages and towns. He then taught for one semester in the Escuela de Enfermería—the School of Nursing—of the Hospital O'Horan in Merida, where he prepared future nurses for communicating with patients who spoke only Maya. He also taught Maya for a time in an evening class for adults sponsored by the State Library of Yucatan.

With the verb dictionary completed and published, we considered what we should do next. There was no point in moving on with separate fascicles on nouns, adjectives, et cetera. So I finally acceded to Elut's wishes and agreed to collaborate with him on a comprehensive dictionary of the Hocaba dialect of Yucatecan Maya. That work took place on Sunday afternoons in my home during the semesters when Elut was in residence at Tulane and in my hotel or at the headquarters of the Secretaría de Educación of the State of Yucatan whenever I was in Merida. By then, Elut had been transferred from his position as a custodian in the Palacio Cantón to a new position at the Secretaría, where he served as the watchman for the building all night and all day on weekends. He made arrangements for us to work in the conference room in that building, even when there were meetings of other employees there, as was sometimes the case on Saturdays. On such occasions, we were told to go ahead and use the conference room for our work, and the employee meetings took place elsewhere in the building. The Secretaría was within walking distance of Elut's home in the Barrio of San Sebastián. We would work there all day. His wife, Ofelia Dzul de Po'ot, would bring us lunch and join us in the meal, thereby reciprocating the dinners I had made on Sunday evenings in New Orleans.

By then, we had a personal computer at home, and Harvey had learned how to write programs in the Basic and Pascal languages. He generated for us a new list of all possible consonant–vowel–consonant roots in Maya, arranged in a format that was more convenient for our needs. This time, Elut received a copy of the list to take with him to use in Merida if he wished.

Ofelia accompanied Elut to New Orleans for the first time at the beginning of the spring semester in 1982, and she participated in our research on Sunday afternoons in my home. It soon became apparent that there was one domain of vocabulary that we could not handle alone, namely, the botanical names that are a necessary part of any dictionary. When asked for a gloss of a plant name, Elut or Ofelia would usually reply: *un tipo de planta* "a type of plant." I explained my dilemma to Arthur Welden, one of the botanists in the Biology Department, who was auditing our Maya course. He told me that he knew of someone who could help us. That person was Anne Bradburn, the associate curator of the Tulane Herbarium, across from whom I sat at a Center for Latin American Studies luncheon explaining my problem, to which she replied, "I can help you with that."

And help us she did! She accompanied me to Hocaba in August 1985 and spent a week showing Elut and me how to collect and preserve plant specimens and instructing us on the kind of information that should be recorded in field notebooks. We were assisted in this endeavor by Elut's wife, Ofelia, who had already worked with us on the dictionary in 1982 and who proved to have an expert's knowledge of native plants.

For six weeks, Ofelia accompanied Elut and me on almost daily trips by bus from Merida to Hocaba on plant-collecting expeditions (Figure 8.2). On the way to Hocaba, Ofelia would gaze out of the window of the bus in order to see which plants were in fruit or flower that day. Upon reaching Hocaba, we would stroll slowly through the streets of the town, while Ofelia looked over the low walls on both sides of the street into the gardens for plants that we had not already collected. When she saw a promising plant, she would call out to the owner of the house and ask whether we could have a look around her

FIGURE 8.2.   Elut and Ofelia collecting plants on the outskirts of Hocaba.
Photo by Anne Bradburn.

garden. We were always welcomed into the gardens and allowed to
take specimens of the plants that interested us.

Each specimen was placed inside a folded sheet of newspaper and
then in a field press, while I recorded its Maya name, possible uses,

and an identifying number in the notebook. The same number was written on the newspaper enclosing the plant. In this way, I became acquainted with different parts of the town, including one that seemed to be particularly hospitable for several kinds of cacti, which seemed to grow nowhere else. The train tracks at one end of town provided the only habitat for a bottle-gourd vine.

I remember one steamy morning, when Elut's father led us through some woods and into a cultivated field, where we collected specimens of such food plants as maize, beans, and squash. We also collected specimens of the weeds that grew near the stone walls on both sides of the unpaved streets. We collected everything that had a Maya name, whether it was considered a weed or not.

After returning to my hotel in Merida in the afternoon, I would take a nap. Then I would spend the evening preparing the specimens for the trip back to New Orleans. Because I had had surgery earlier that summer, I could not employ the usual method of drying them using a heavy press. Instead, Anne showed me another way of preserving the specimens by placing them in their folded newspapers in large plastic bags, pouring alcohol in them, and then sealing the bags with plastic tape so that the alcohol would not evaporate. After many bags of specimens came back to New Orleans with me, Anne spent days drying them in the Tulane Herbarium and supervising the work-study students who mounted them on archival sheets of paper and affixed the labels she had prepared with the information recorded in my notebooks. Duplicates of each mounted specimen were sent to the herbariums at the University of Yucatan in Merida and the New York Botanical Garden.[3]

I bought newspapers and alcohol almost every day during the six weeks that I spent in Yucatan that summer and fall. I read many newspapers before using them for the plants, and in that way became acquainted with the social and political life of the city. The price of alcohol went up by a few *centavos* each day, giving me a sense of the rampant inflation that Mexicans were coping with that year.

That experience made a great impression on me in several ways. It introduced me to aspects of Maya culture of which I had no prior knowledge. Plants have considerable significance in the lives of the rural Maya of Yucatan, and those six weeks of exploring the flora of Hocaba added another dimension to my understanding of their culture. I had never had the slightest interest in plants before, but after that experience, I cannot pass an overgrown bank of seemingly undifferentiated vegetation without noticing that it contains a variety of plants. And from then on, Harvey and I have made a point of visiting botanical gardens in whatever city we happened to visit in our travels.

Harvey and I attended an international conference on archaeoastronomy with the Edmonsons in Merida in January the next year (1986). This gave me an opportunity to collect specimens (with the help of Elut and Ofelia) of several kinds of native plums that were in flower at that time of year. Harvey and Barbara Edmonson joined us on this botanical field trip to Hocaba to see what was involved.

Ofelia accompanied Elut to New Orleans for the second time at the end of January the same year. I took them to the herbarium to see what had happened to the plants we had collected months before, and Anne showed them the mounted specimens with their labels. It turned out that Ofelia could recognize and identify dried, as well as fresh, specimens of plants. She spent a number of hours that semester assigning Maya names to specimens in other herbarium collections from Yucatan (Figure 8.3).

In June of the same year, Anne and I spent a week in Hocaba collecting plants that had not been in fruit or flower during previous field trips.

We completed our collection of plants one year later, in June 1987 (Figure 8.4). Ofelia decided to go out to Hocaba on the day before our last day of fieldwork in order to cook a large batch of *papadzules* at the house of Elut's sister, Alicia, for our lunch the next day and to distribute to the townspeople from whom we had obtained plants during the previous two years. *Papadzules* are a kind of soft taco made of maize tortillas filled with chopped hard-boiled eggs drenched in the ground seeds of round squash. They are delicious and a culturally appropriate expression of appreciation to the people who had helped us with our botanical research.

FIGURE 8.3. A botanical specimen identified by Ofelia and classified by Anne Bradburn.

FIGURE 8.4. Elut and Ofelia conversing with a shopkeeper in Hocaba.
Photo by Anne Bradburn.

Ofelia died of a heart attack in 1989. Despite his loss, Elut and I continued our work on the dictionary, checking the entries, adding example sentences where appropriate, and refining the translations and grammatical classification of the entries. He was the one who spent many weeks proofreading all the Maya words in the dictionary, while I was writing the grammatical sketch that placed the entries in context. Anne Bradburn contributed an alphabetical list of all the plants mentioned in the entries, arranged in alphabetical order by scientific names, followed by their Maya names.

From time to time, as he was working his way through the dictionary, Elut would draw my attention to interesting grammatical or semantic patterns. For example, on one Sunday afternoon, as we were working together, he suddenly realized that the five basic color terms (for black, green, red, white, and yellow) could serve as the base for evocative compounds that referred to texture, translucence, brilliance, and other striking qualities of objects. In order to show me what he had in mind, he suggested that we go into the garden behind our house, where he pointed out that Maya had a compound expression for describing the spiny fruit of the false canna that could be translated as *prickly green*. Then he described as "tender black" the newly sprouted, but dark leaves on a bush. He resumed this conversation a day or so later on an errand downtown, commenting from the back seat of the car that the windows of one office building were a "translucent green," that those on another building were a "translucent black," and that the paint on the car in front of us was a "shiny black." All the examples he mentioned had the same grammatical structure:

yáʔaš-p'oš-éʔen "prickly green"

yáʔaš-pik'-éʔen "translucent green"

ʔéek'-ʔol-éʔen "tender black"

ʔéek'-pik'-éʔen "translucent black"

ʔéek'-ȼan-éʔen "shiny black"

Each one begins with a color term (for either green or black) and ends with the same suffix (-éʔen).[4] It turned out that this kind of construction occurs in other Mayan languages as well, but Elut was the first person who recognized it in Yucatecan Maya.[5]

Because the Maya language of Yucatan was Elut's mother tongue, he had an intuitive knowledge of the language. Nevertheless, it was occasionally possible to point out a semantic or structural characteristic of his language that had escaped his notice. This was true of the class of intransitive verbs known as *positionals*. He was fascinated when I showed him that they could be distinguished from other intransitive verbs in terms of both formal and semantic criteria. Not only did they co-occur with a unique set of suffixes, but they also referred to physical states or positions, such as standing, sitting, kneeling, hanging, lying down, leaning, bending, and bowing that human beings, animals, and inanimate objects can assume. This was a revelation for him, and from then on, he quickly identified such verbs wherever they occurred in the dictionary.

Elut used a practical alphabet for writing Maya words that was adapted to a standard keyboard, whereas I preferred to use the International Phonetic Alphabet (IPA) that is widely recognized by linguists, for which I had special keys on my typewriter. I asked him how he felt about using IPA symbols for spelling Maya words in our dictionary. Without hesitating, he replied that his job was to provide the content of the dictionary and that the orthography and grammatical classifications were up to me. He wanted the dictionary to be useful to the greatest number of linguists, and he expected me to do whatever was necessary to achieve that goal. And that is why we used IPA in our dictionary, rather than one of the practical alphabets preferred by other experts on Mayan languages.

Our dictionary was published by the University of Utah Press in 1998, sixteen years after we decided to undertake the project.[6] Knowing that Harvey and I were on sabbatical leave during the spring semester of 1999 and would be vacationing in Yucatan with Anne Bradburn and her husband, Donald, in late January of that year, Elut invited me to

FIGURE 8.5.   At the recognition ceremony for the Maya dictionary in January 1999. *Left to right*: Alba Isela Aguilar de Marrufo, Elut, Victoria, Valerio Canché Yah. Photo by Harvey M. Bricker.

participate in a ceremony of recognition of the dictionary sponsored by Professor Alba Isela Aguilar de Marrufo, the Director of the State Library of Yucatan, where he had previously offered evening classes in Maya. The recognition ceremony took place in the evening on January 29. Elut and I sat at a table in front of a large room, flanked by the Director and Valerio Canché Yah, the man who would present our book to the audience (Figure 8.5). It began with a moment of silence in honor of Ofelia and was followed by introductory remarks made by the director and the presentation of the dictionary itself. There were also speeches by local scholars of the Maya language. A nice reception followed the ceremony, where we mingled with people in the audience, some of whom I had known for many years.

One day, in the second half of May 1999, I received a telephone call from the head of the Department of Tourism in the Municipal Government (Ayuntamiento Municipal) of Merida, María Teresa Gamboa Góngora, informing me that her city was interested in establishing a sister-city relationship with New Orleans. To that end, Merida would be sending a delegation of people representing various agencies and businesses involved in tourism to New Orleans in connection with the celebration of Mexican Independence Day on September 16. She told me that her office would like to include Elut in that delegation, if, in return, Tulane would be willing to offer him an award in a ceremony on campus in recognition of his many years of service to the university. I was stunned by this request, but said that I would have to talk to someone at Tulane to see whether that would be possible. I also pointed out that Elut had heart trouble, and I did not know whether he would be well enough to make the trip. She replied that the City of Merida would assume responsibility for any health problems he might have during the visit and that he would be provided with a companion, who would share a room with him at the hotel. I said that I would see what I could do at Tulane to facilitate this plan.

I spoke to Tom Reese, the Director of the Center for Latin American Studies at Tulane, and asked him whether the Center would like to sponsor such an award for Elut. He expressed an interest in doing this, and for the next four months, I served as the intermediary between María Teresa Gamboa and the staff of the Center in arranging Tulane's contribution to this event, which was substantial.

The delegation included not only representatives of the tourism industry in Merida, but also members of the Ballet Folclórico, who performed on campus on September 16. Tom Reese had a wonderful idea for scheduling their performance. He wanted them to perform at noon in the pocket park adjacent to the University Center, reasoning that students, faculty, and staff coming to the Center for lunch would hear the music, wonder what was going on, and watch the performance for a little while before entering the building in search of something to eat. And that is exactly what happened. The weather was beautiful that day, and a large crowd gathered to enjoy the performance of the traditional dances of Yucatan.

The award ceremony was convened later that afternoon by Tom Reese. I introduced the speakers, who included Will Andrews and Judie

Maxwell from the Anthropology Department, who talked about Maya archaeology and Maya language modernization in Guatemala, respectively. Then Elut expressed his appreciation to Tulane for everything the university had done for him since 1967, delivering his remarks in both Maya and Spanish, with me translating his words into English.

At the last minute, the mayor of Merida had decided to come to New Orleans to present the certificate of recognition that Tulane had been asked to offer to Elut. The text of the certificate read as follows:

Tulane University

City of New Orleans

Consulado General de México

Ayuntamiento de Mérida

join together to honor and to convey their deep appreciation to

Don Eleuterio Po'ot Yah

for 35 years of devotion to the preservation of the

Maya language of Yucatan

on this the 16th day of September of 1999

When he presented the award to Elut, the mayor of Merida, Xavier Abreu Sierra, asked: "Why am I at Tulane offering a recognition to someone who spends all his time in Merida?" And he replied to his own question, saying, "It is due to the interest that this university has in Maya culture."

The last speaker on the program was Miguel Angel May May, a well-known Maya writer and poet, who was Elut's companion during their visit to New Orleans. He spoke on the traditional dances of Yucatan in Spanish, and I summarized his remarks in English as he went along.

In the audience were many people who had come to know Elut over the years, including current and former students and members of the faculty from several departments. All in all, it was a fitting tribute to someone who had served Tulane well.[7]

During the early years of our association, Elut was impressed with the enthusiasm of Tulane students for learning the Maya language, contrasting their interest with the apparent indifference of his own people for preserving their language, and he commented on the irony of his having to travel to a foreign land to realize the value of his own language. By the time he died from a heart attack on April 2, 2007, sixteen days before his seventieth birthday, he had done much to preserve his language (Figure 8.6). It was at the Academia Municipal de la Lengua Maya Itzamná, sponsored by the Ayuntamiento de Mérida—the city government of Merida—that he realized his mission in life and the culmination of his career. Beginning in 1978, the Department of Education of the Ayuntamiento has sponsored courses in Maya language and culture for the benefit of the residents of the city; Elut was one of the founding instructors of that program. The courses were advertised in local newspapers, and a variety of people enrolled in them, including local teachers, tourists, students, and other visitors from the United States and Europe, and residents of Merida, whose first language was Maya. It was the third category of students—the native speakers of Maya—who captured his attention, for he saw in them a vehicle for preserving his language for future generations. They attended his courses because they wanted to become literate in Maya, which they spoke but could not read or write. Some of these students showed special aptitude for learning the linguistic structure of Maya, and he trained them to carry on his work in the future. His was truly a life well lived!

MERIDA
AYUNTAMIENTO 2004-2007

Ayuntamiento de Mérida
Dirección de Desarrollo Social

se une a la pena que embarga a las
familias Poot Yah y Poot Cob por el
fallecimiento, acaecido el día 2 en esta
ciudad, del señor

Eleuterio Poot Yah

quien fuera por 19 años instructor de la
Academia de Lengua Maya Itzamná.

Descanse en paz.

Mérida, Yuc., 6 de abril de 2007.

FIGURE 8.6.   Elut's obituary in a Merida newspaper.

NOTES

1. His proverbs were eventually published in Merida as *K'axt'aano'ob: Palabras enlazadas*. Collección Capital Americana de la Cultura 5 (Capital Americana de la Cultura, 2000).

2. Eleuterio Po'ot Yah, *Yucatec Maya Verbs (Hocaba Dialect)* by Latin American Studies Curriculum Aids (New Orleans, LA: Center for Latin American Studies, Tulane University, 1981).

3. My collections were deposited in the Tulane University Herbarium as Bricker 123 (NO), which are now housed in the Shirley C. Tucker Herbarium (LSU) at Louisiana State University.

4. ʔ is a glottal stop, "a sound produced by first bringing the vocal cords together and then releasing them so that there is a sudden escape of air" (John Lyons, *Introduction to Theoretical Linguistics* [Cambridge, UK: Cambridge University Press, 1968], 115).

5. For more examples of this process, see Victoria R. Bricker, "Color and Texture in the Maya Language of Yucatan," *Anthropological Linguistics* 41, no. 3(1999): 283–307.

6. Victoria R. Bricker, Eleuterio Po'ot Yah, and Ofelia Dzul de Po'ot, *A Dictionary of the Maya Language, As Spoken in Hocabá, Yucatán* with a Botanical Index by Anne S. Bradburn (Salt Lake City: University of Utah Press, 1998).

7. The celebratory dinner in honor of Mexican independence from Spain took place in the InterContinental Hotel downtown the next day (September 17). The dinner was hosted by the Consul General of Mexico, Alejandro de la Canal Knapp. As a result of a miscommunication among Mexican officials, the entertainment featured two groups of traditional dancers. One was the Ballet Folclórico of Yucatan, which was already present in New Orleans for the activities of the preceding day. The other was a group of dancers from Michoacan that had been brought to New Orleans for this celebratory dinner. Both groups put on wonderful performances of traditional dances from their regions. The Yucatecan dancers were familiar to me, but the "Dance of the Old Men" by the Michoacan dancers, was

spectacular and unforgettable. The impersonators of old men were bent over their canes, and, with longing eyes, hobbled after a young woman who danced just out of their reach to haunting music. I had known about this dance for many years because of the Old Men's resemblance to the Grandfather impersonators I had seen in Zinacantan decades earlier, but I had never had the opportunity to watch it before. It was a treat to witness such a fine performance of the dance in my hometown.

9

YUCATAN:
RELATING THE MAYA PRESENT
TO ITS PAST

When Don Alfredo Barrera Vásquez mentioned the collection of Caste War letters written in Maya in the Palacio Cantón to me in June 1971, he planted the seeds for a research program that would occupy me for several decades after I had finished my comparative study of uprisings in the Maya area. As I worked with those letters, extracting from them insights on why and how the Maya had initiated the Caste War of Yucatan and succeeded in maintaining their independence in the eastern part of the peninsula during the second half of the nineteenth century, I gradually realized their potential for understanding the grammar of Modern Yucatec, the language I had been hired to teach at Tulane. Subsequently, I discovered that Tulane's Latin American Library had original documents in that language from earlier centuries, including one written in 1569 and a late sixteenth-century copy of the earliest known Maya document in the Latin alphabet, the so-called *Crónica de Mani*, bearing a date of 1557. Because such documents usually mentioned the year, month, and day of their writing and the name of the town in which they were produced, they were suitable for exploring both the geographic distribution of dialects and the evolution of the language through time.

After a few years of teaching spoken Yucatecan Maya, I realized that, in order to speak it fluently, I would have to spend some time living in a Yucatecan village where Maya was the first and dominant language of most of its inhabitants. Anticipating that at some time in the future, I would want to explore the relationship between Colonial and Modern Yucatec, I chose for both purposes the small town of Ebtun, located about four kilometers west of Valladolid in the middle of the peninsula. Not only were the majority of Ebtun's three hundred inhabitants monolingual speakers of Yucatecan Maya, but the town's archive had once contained a large corpus of 125 Maya documents, known as the *Titles of Ebtun*, representing the years 1600 to 1833. The documents in this collection were published in 1939 by Ralph Roys, and, although the original documents had disappeared after Roys transcribed and translated them, a facsimile copy of the entire collection still existed in the Tozzer Library at Harvard.

The first opportunity to realize my goal of becoming fluent in Yucatecan Maya came during the spring semester of 1979, when I took my first sabbatical. I had told Elut about my plan to live in Ebtun during much of that semester. I must have explained to him that Hocaba had too many Spanish-speaking inhabitants to qualify for that purpose, and its town archive no longer had any Colonial documents, nor was I aware of their survival anywhere else.

Elut was proud of his knowledge of Yucatecan Maya and, before 1979, was not willing to recognize other dialects of the language as equally legitimate. As he explained to me later, he was concerned that when I encountered the use of other kinds of words and phrases in Ebtun, I would think that he had lied to me about the language. In order to maintain his credibility as a teacher of his language, he decided to visit Ebtun several weeks before my scheduled arrival in Yucatan in January. While there, he met the *comisario* of the town and informed him of my impending arrival. He also made a list of all the phonological and lexical differences between the two dialects that he observed to share with me when I arrived in Merida, so that I would not be taken by surprise when I heard them for the first time in Ebtun. From then on, he was more willing to recognize that not all departures from the Hocaba dialect were erroneous.

I flew down to Merida from New Orleans on January 7th. Also on the plane was a contingent of botanists from Tulane's Biology Department, including Anne Bradburn, who, a few years later, would collaborate with Elut and me on the Hocaba dictionary (as explained in Chapter 8).

After I had been in Merida for a few days, Elut accompanied me to look for a place to live in Ebtun. We took a bus to Valladolid and, from there, a taxi as far as the entrance to Ebtun. We walked slowly away from the highway on the road leading into town. We had gone only a few steps when an elderly woman stepped out of her house and said: "You know, my husband died three years ago!" Elut stopped short and engaged her in conversation. She invited us into her house, and we sat down, I in a hammock and the others on stools. In a very short time Elut had arranged for me to stay with her.

We returned to Merida, where I remained for a few more days before moving out to Ebtun. During that period, I met the cultural anthropologist Mary Elmendorf, who was carrying out research on family planning in Chan Kom near Chichen Itza. On one of my remaining days in Merida, she took Elut and me to Chan Kom, where she introduced me to the midwife and other friends of hers. She pointed out the house that belonged to the Mexican anthropologist Alfonso Villa Rojas that she used as an office while she was working in Chan Kom, and she invited me to return for a longer visit and spend the night there.[1]

From Chan Kom, Elut and I took a bus to Ebtun to confirm my move-in date. The trip took two hours instead of the thirty minutes we expected because of the many stops along side roads on both sides of the highway.

The name of the woman in whose home I lived for three and one-half months was Doña Francisca Cohuo Po'ot. She was a midwife, who occupied the lowest rung in the medical hierarchy in the state of Yucatan. She had received some training at the hospital in Valladolid and was permitted to sell a few medicines in her home. I could not have found a better person with whom to live. Because of her medical training, the level of hygiene in her home and the garden behind it was significantly higher than in other households in the town; as a result, I was in good health throughout the time I lived with her.

Another benefit of living in Doña Francisca's home was that it was located on the street leading from the highway into the center of town. People often stopped by to visit her on their way to the highway to catch a bus to Valladolid or on their way home. This gave me many opportunities to participate in conversations or simply to listen to the other people in the house talking. My fluency in the language increased rapidly in that environment.

Although I had come to Ebtun in order to improve my ability to speak Yucatecan Maya, people assumed from the outset that I was an expert in their language. Their positive appraisal of my knowledge of Maya was based on my familiarity with earlier forms of the language, not on how well I spoke their dialect. Because of the large number of

Spanish loans in Modern Yucatec, those who speak it regard it as "mixed," in contrast to the earlier forms of the language, which they assume was "pure" or "real." People would ask me to say something in "real Maya," implying that I knew the language better than they did.

The contrast with my experience with Tzotzil in the 1960s could not have been starker. In Zinacantan, people took it for granted that I would want to learn to speak their language, which they regarded as superior to mine, whereas in Ebtun, people regarded me as a linguistic resource, who could teach them something about the language of their ancestors. In Zinacantan, the "real" language was what they were speaking in the 1960s, whereas in Ebtun, the "real" language was what their ancestors had spoken.

My second goal in choosing Ebtun as the place for my sabbatical was to ascertain whether the people living there in 1979 were descendants of the people who wrote the documents in the *Titles of Ebtun*, for only in that way would it make sense for me to treat the dialect of Yucatecan Maya I was learning in Ebtun as directly related to the one recorded in the documents. The simplest way to tackle that task was to compare the surnames of the people living in Ebtun in 1979 with the ones mentioned in the *Titles of Ebtun*. Thanks to the location of Doña Francisca's house being so close to the highway, I was able to begin collecting such information almost immediately from the people who visited her.

However, I needed to have a more systematic method of collecting such information that would result in a complete inventory of surnames for the town. This entailed finding out who lived in each house on each street, in the course of which I discovered that much of the town was overgrown, suggesting that it must have once had a larger population. Some of the streets in the overgrown parts of town were still bordered by remnants of stone walls that must have originally been part of a grid.

This discovery forced me to take the historical context of Ebtun into account. The town has an enormous church that was completed in 1590 to accommodate a much larger population than the one living there in 1979 (Figure 9.1). During the Colonial period, people from

FIGURE 9.1.   The church in Ebtun.
Photo by Harvey M. Bricker.

the surrounding region had been forcibly settled there in a program called *congregación* to facilitate their conversion to Catholicism. There may have been as many as one thousand people living in Ebtun at one time, many of them occupying houses along the streets that were now overgrown.

It seems that even after people in the surrounding countryside were moved to Ebtun, they were able to retain ownership of their land, which extended west almost as far as the site of Chichen Itza forty kilometers away and up to thirteen kilometers north and south of the present highway. Many of the documents in the *Titles of Ebtun* are concerned with litigation to prevent the town of Yaxcaba near Chichen Itza from usurping these ancestral lands.

The population of Ebtun was much larger during the Colonial period than it is today. This larger population continued into the first two decades of the twentieth century. Only after the Mexican Revolution

of 1910–1917 was debt peonage abolished, freeing the Maya of Ebtun
and other towns in the region around Valladolid to live wherever they
pleased. Many people left Ebtun to live on their ancestral lands in the
west or, more recently, to find employment in cities like Cancun (see
the text that follows).

It did not take me long to realize that some of the residents of
Ebtun traveled long distances to the west to cultivate their fields. Their
preferred means of transportation was the Chan Kom bus, which made
daily runs between Chan Kom, about forty kilometers away, and Valladolid, with frequent stops en route. I was surprised that people expected
me to take the same bus on my occasional trips to Valladolid, even
though there were other buses and trucks that offered the same service
at the same price. I wondered what was special about that bus.

Eventually I realized that many of the people who lived in Chan
Kom had originally come from Ebtun. The appeal of that bus was the
likelihood that some of the passengers on it were relatives, with whom
they could converse on the way to Valladolid.

In this context, I was reminded of the trip that I had made to Chan
Kom with Mary Elmendorf and Elut a few days before I moved into
Doña Francisca's house and the circuitous route the Chan Kom bus
had taken between Chan Kom and Ebtun, traversing narrow roads
north and south of the highway to pick up or drop off people in small
villages along the way. Clearly, it was servicing the little communities
that had sprung up after people were liberated from debt bondage and
allowed to return to their ancestral lands. The trip from Chichen Itza
to Ebtun by car or bus normally takes half an hour, but the same trip
in the Chan Kom bus took two hours because of the detours north and
south of the highway, subtly demarcating the original holdings of the
people who had been congregated in Ebtun. Thus, the Colonial province
still has an economic, if not a political, reality and the Chan Kom bus
symbolizes that.

I saw Mary Elmendorf again after I had settled in Ebtun. She had
previously invited me to return to Chan Kom and spend the night in
Villa Rojas's house, and she reiterated this invitation when she realized

that Doña Francisca was a midwife. Having become aware of the genea-logical ties between the people of Ebtun and those in Chan Kom, I was interested in making such a return visit and recording the speech of some of the people there. Accordingly, I returned to Chan Kom during the first week of February, accompanied by Doña Francisca, who wanted to visit some of her relatives there.

At first, the people in Chan Kom did not take me seriously and insisted on speaking to me in Spanish, instead of Maya. But as the day wore on, their attitude gradually changed, and they began responding in Maya. The younger brother of the Presidente Municipal let me record his conversation with Doña Francisca, his wife, and me. Late in the day, we were able to get an audience with the Presidente Municipal himself, who agreed to tell me the history of Chan Kom and have it recorded. I turned on my tape recorder, and with the clearest pronuncia-tion of Maya I have ever heard, he told me the story of Chan Kom. I could understand virtually every word he said! When he finished, I played the whole text back for him to hear. The recording was as clear as a bell. I was able to transcribe it myself.

That was only the beginning. In exchange for the favor he had done me, he engaged me in conversation for the next two hours, entirely in Maya. Even when he said something I didn't understand, he did not switch to Spanish, but either repeated it or reworded it. It was just wonderful for me to have this opportunity to speak Maya at length on subjects such as the mass suicide at Jonestown in Guyana, the Pope's visit to Mexico, the several wives of Idi Amin in Uganda, and the likelihood of a third world war. It was an amazing experience, well worth the day-long wait.

Chan Kom was not the only Maya town in the region I visited with Doña Francisca in 1979. Her activities as a midwife and local health promoter were not limited to Ebtun. She provided the same services to some women in the nearby town of Dzitnup, two kilometers away, and occasionally in Cuncunul. Early in my stay in Ebtun, I accompanied her and her nurse supervisor to Dzitnup. We walked there from Ebtun along the dirt road that linked Ebtun with Dzitnup in the

east and Cuncunul and Kaua in the west. This had served as the main
street of Ebtun before the highway was built. It also leads to the town's
cemetery in the west.

The road departs from Ebtun to Dzitnup at the eastern edge of
town, where there are two altars composed of irregular slabs of stone
piled on top of each other, each surmounted by two wooden crosses
(e.g., Figure 9.2). I noticed that there were heaps of small stones in
front of the crosses on the top slab of stone. Doña Francisca told me
that people pick up three small stones (sometimes nine small stones)
and put them in front of the crosses on the way out of town so that
their legs will not become tired, and we followed suit.

During my first visit to Dzitnup, in a room adjacent to the sacristy
of the church, I witnessed a dance rehearsal that I immediately recognized as a variant of the medieval Christian play known as the *Sacrifice
of Isaac*. There was an "orchestra" consisting of two instruments: a
horizontal or slit drum and a harmonica. Two of the three dancers wore
old wooden masks and the third a mask of black leather. One of the
wooden masks was worn by "Isaac" and the other by someone called
"Señor." The leather mask represented the Devil. The men were preparing to perform their dance in Merida. I later learned that their performance had taken place in the library downtown where Elut worked
and that from them he had learned of my visit to Dzitnup.

When I arrived in Ebtun on January 18th, Doña Francisca's cousin
was skeptical of my ability to endure the much lower standard of living
than the one she assumed I was accustomed to and predicted that I
would give up and leave after one or two weeks. In order to convince
them of my staying power, I decided to remain in Ebtun without going
to Merida until a few days before Carnaval, five weeks hence, when
Harvey was scheduled to arrive in Merida to visit me. And stay I did,
with only short trips into Valladolid to retrieve letters from the post
office and indulge myself in a second breakfast of eggs and sausage. My
only overnight stay elsewhere was in Chan Kom with Doña Francisca.

Doña Francisca and her cousin must have been keeping track of
the days as the weeks passed, because on February 16th, exactly thirty-

FIGURE 9.2. Entrance crosses on the outskirts of Ebtun.
Photo by Victoria R. Bricker.

one days after I had arrived in Ebtun, on their own initiative, they took me on a tour of the town, moving systematically from street to street and visiting the people in each house along the way. As we moved from house to house, I recorded the names of the adults who lived in them. In that way, I was able to compile a list of the surnames of all the people living in Ebtun that I would later compare with the surnames mentioned in the *Titles of Ebtun*, a comparison that revealed an eighty-five percent overlap in surnames, implying a historical continuity between the two populations that justified my treatment of the modern dialect of Ebtun as directly related to the one documented in the *Titles*.[2]

After returning to the house, I immediately began drafting a map of the places we had visited that afternoon. I had barely started, when Doña Francisca looked over my shoulder at what I was doing and said casually, "Oh, you're making a map! I have a map of Ebtun that Lourdes [the nurse] made." She went over to her side of the house and pulled out a map drawn in pencil on graph paper plus the beginning of one drawn by her grandson to a larger scale on heavy white paper. She left the map with me while she went off to give someone an injection. Of course, I began tracing it immediately and had finished my copy by the time she returned.

In trying to relate the nurse's sketch map to the actual layout of streets in Ebtun, I discovered two misconceptions that distorted her map. The first was her placement of the highway in the very center of her map, showing it as bisecting the town, when, in fact, it cut diagonally across the grid of streets.[3] The second was her labeling of the short, paved road that led from the highway to the town hall as *calle principal* "main street." It was not then, and never had been, the main street of the town. In order to account for the other streets in the town, she had to draw irregular blocks instead of the rectangles that were formed by the streets in the grid.

Notably absent in her map was an intersection that was referred to as *cinco calles* "five streets," where the old road to Dzitnup met two of the streets in the grid (what in the northeastern part of the United States is called a *turkey foot*). The distortions imposed by her focus on the paved roadways represented by the highway and her *calle principal* made it impossible to modify her sketch map, and it was necessary to start over by laying out the grid and placing the highway and the *calle principal* correctly with respect to it. The map went through multiple revisions, first by me and later by Harvey, who paced through the streets holding a compass and redrew the map after our friend and colleague Edward Kurjack, who was making an aerial reconnaissance of archaeological sites during the months I was living in Yucatan, photographed the town from the air and sent me the result (Figure 9.3).

I found the notion of "five streets" intriguing as a landmark for reckoning the location of the church, the town hall, the mill to which women brought their boiled maize kernels to be ground for making into tortillas, and the stores. This concept was apparently not limited to Ebtun, for I was told that Valladolid had its own "five streets" that served as a landmark in the cultural geography of the city, and on one of my trips into Valladolid, I saw that its characteristics were similar to those of the "five streets" in Ebtun.

After five weeks in Ebtun, it was time for me to go to Merida to meet Harvey, who would be visiting me for a week. Because of a police strike in New Orleans, Mardi Gras had been canceled that year, and Harvey arrived in time to spend Carnaval in Yucatan instead. Also joining us for that week were Ed and Barbara Edmonson. Ed came from New Orleans like Harvey, and Barbara had come down from San Luis Potosi in northeastern Mexico, where she was carrying out her dissertation research on the Huastec language of that region. They arrived in Merida when the city was in the midst of preparations for Carnaval. The morning after Harvey arrived, the four of us drove to Valladolid, where we had lunch at the Cenote Saci, an enormous sinkhole that had been a major source of water for the Precolumbian town called *Saci*. From there, we went to Ebtun to visit Doña Francisca, giving Harvey and the Edmonsons an opportunity to see where I had been living.

Then we walked to the plaza, where we saw the town hall and the enormous ceiba tree in front of the Colonial church. We walked around

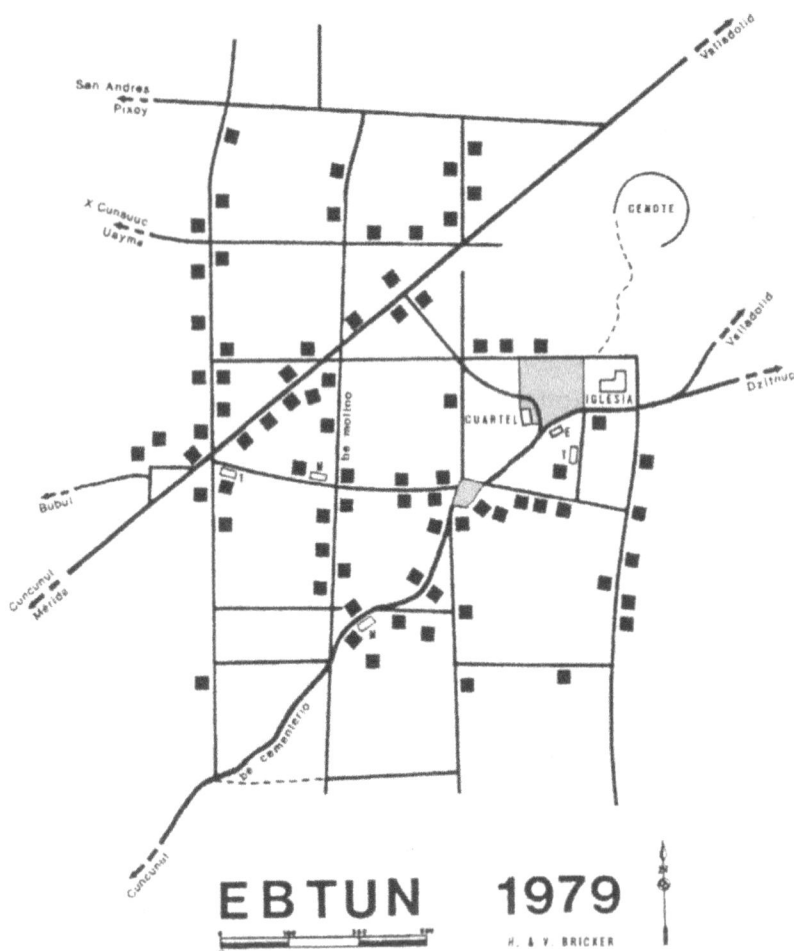

FIGURE 9.3.   A map of Ebtun.
Drawing by Harvey M. Bricker.

the north side of the church and followed the path into the dry sinkhole
with the natural staircase after which Ebtun is named.[4]

   We drove back to Merida after our visit with Doña Francisca in
time to get ready for a dinner party hosted by Joann Andrews, the stepmother of our Tulane friend and colleague Will Andrews. A delicious
roast armadillo in *achiote* sauce was the main course of the dinner.
Among the guests was the archaeologist Edward Kurjack, who gave us

advice about what we should do the next day. He recommended that we visit the site of Ake on our way to Izamal, our destination for lunch. Ake was well worth the visit. We climbed one pyramid, from which we saw several more and the plaza. I found the hacienda of Ake most interesting. The building that houses the machinery for rasping henequen looked like a Russian palace.

The roads we traveled on were rather narrow and went by field after field of henequen, the plant from which binder twine is produced. In this region, unlike the one around Hocaba, there was no sign of the decline of the henequen industry. We went through beautiful towns with large yards behind the houses full of fruit trees.

The famous convent in Izamal is built on top of a Precolumbian pyramid. It is a spectacular complex. The pyramid is so massive and has such a large top that the church has a huge plaza directly in front of it. From the top one can look down over the whole town, and we could also see another very large pyramid northwest of the town, which unfortunately we did not have time to visit. It would have provided a bird's eye view of the convent complex and the town. In the church in Izamal, we saw the original painting of Bishop Diego de Landa, the Franciscan priest who conducted the idolatry trials during the 1560s that I saw parodied in the Carnaval ritual in Hocaba in 1971.[5] There was also a painting of Bishop Crescencio Carrillo y Ancona, after whom the library in Merida where the Caste War letters are archived is named, and who seems to have been a native of Izamal.

From Izamal, we took the northern road back to Merida, passing through Motul, where we were caught in Carnaval traffic, which delayed us, as did Carnaval activity in Merida. We pulled up in front of our hotel at exactly 5:30, the time we had arranged to meet Elut, and he was there waiting for us to accompany him to his home for dinner.

In the car, Harvey gave Elut the electronic calculator he had brought along as a gift. Elut was very pleased, and as soon as he had served his guests with beers and *refrescos*, asked for an explanation of how to use it. Ed and Harvey showed him the basic operations. Then Elut set up a problem as he normally calculates it: How to determine how much the client and the agent get with a 25/75 split. He worked the problem as follows:

A   Total sum
B   Half of total sum
C   Half of B (agent's share)
D   Sum of B and C (client's share)
E   Sum of C and D = A (original sum)

Harvey worked the problem on the calculator and showed him how quickly he could calculate the split. Elut understood immediately and called to his wife: "Ofelia, this is going to save you a lot of time!" I assumed that she was less adept at mental arithmetic than Elut, and thus was likely to be the real beneficiary of the gift.

Their living room was as neat as a pin, with a fresh tablecloth and flowers on the table and a complete setting of silverware at each place. The dinner consisted of *relleno negro* served in a new way. Ofelia brought out a huge tray of parts from two chickens that had been boiled in the burnt chile sauce, surrounded by the stuffed eggs that are called *b'üut'*. In addition, each person received a cup of the burnt chile broth to be sipped separately. The chicken was served on plates and eaten with tortillas. The chile sauce was thinner than usual and was made from chicken broth.

I asked Ofelia how she made the stuffed eggs, and it turned out to be the reverse of the way we make them in the United States. First of all, the chicken is boiled in water until it is barely tender. Then the burnt chile mixture is stirred into the broth.[6] Whole tomatoes are allowed to cook in the broth and are taken out later and discarded so that there won't be seeds in the bottom. Then the chile mixture that has sunk to the bottom is scraped up and mixed with the ground meat (pork) and chopped boiled egg whites. Then this mixture is formed around whole boiled egg yolks into a ball, which is then sliced. Thus the whites end up on the outside as part of the stuffing, whereas the yolks remain whole on the inside. The slices go back into the broth to cook for a while.

A masked krewe marched past the house while we were eating, and we rushed outside to watch. After dinner, Elut disappeared for a moment and returned with a handful of Mardi Gras beads, which he threw to each of us. So we had our Mardi Gras after all. It is ironic that the one year all four of us decided not to spend Mardi Gras in New Orleans, it was canceled there.

The next morning, we headed back to Valladolid with a stop in Chan Kom. It was raining when we arrived in Chan Kom. A cold front was going through. We pulled up in front of the two-story house on the plaza that belonged to the Presidente Municipal. At that point, his younger brother, with whom I had conversed during my last visit to Chan Kom, walked by, looked into the car with a startled expression, recognized me, and then beckoned us to back up in front of his house. He then urged us to enter his house.

Although I expected him to be friendly, I was quite unprepared for the urgency with which he ushered us into his house. After we had all been seated, I found out why. His wife began to talk about an insect with silken wings like an airplane called a *tulix*. For a moment, I thought that a glider had landed in Chan Kom the day before. Barbara finally realized that she was talking about a dragonfly (*libélula* in Spanish). It turned out that a dragonfly had flown into the house the day before and circled several times before leaving. This sometimes happens before a rain, such as we had experienced. Dragonflies announce the impending arrival of visitors, which they had interpreted as *American* visitors. So we were the fulfillment of a kind of prophecy, and it was important to them that we actually set foot in the house!

After chatting with them in Maya for fifteen minutes or so, we took our leave and went to explore the enormous sinkhole that takes up the center of the town. It had recently been landscaped and presented a spectacular view. The rain had stopped in the meantime, and the sun had come out again, so we were able to take pictures. The church was open, so we went inside. Some men were dipping candles beside the side door. Then we continued on our journey.

We spent the rest of that day and most of the next in Valladolid. I had become familiar with the town during my weekly visits to the post office and to one of the restaurants on the plaza for a second breakfast, where I had often had long conversations with the owner's wife. The town was comparable in size and function to San Cristobal las Casas in highland Chiapas, but it differed markedly in one respect: Everyone who lived there spoke Maya, even people of Spanish descent. This meant that I could (and did) speak Maya with everyone I met in Valladolid, including the employees of the post office, the owners of the hotels and gift shops, and the staff at the hospital to whom I had been introduced by Doña Francisca.

Yucatecan Maya is a tonal language, in which the vowels in some words are long and have high or rising tone and are long with low or falling tone in other words. The words with long vowels and high tone resemble the "drawl" in the southern dialect of English. The presence of both kinds of tone in Yucatecan Maya gives the spoken language a musical quality, which was evident in the speech of members of both ethnic groups. Words containing these two kinds of vowels have different meanings, as do words with short vowels, which do not have tone.

One day, the bilingual wife of the owner of the restaurant I frequented in Valladolid began reading to me from her copy of a monolingual Maya dictionary with extensive glosses in Maya.[7] The dictionary employed the traditional alphabet, which did not distinguish between long and short vowels or high and low tones. As she read, I realized that she was lengthening the vowels and producing the appropriate tones without textual cues. From her, I learned an important lesson: Fluent speakers of a language who are literate do not need a writing system that marks vowel length and tone, because they automatically supply them when they read out loud. Only linguists and students learning Yucatecan Maya benefit from the use of accents and special marks for recording the distinctive features of a language. This was a humbling experience for me.

Over time, as my passive vocabulary increased, I found that I too was able to read texts without representation of long vowels and tone and pronounce the vowels in them correctly, in the same way that native speakers of English can read texts in English, where spelling often does not correspond to pronunciation. I realized then that the traditional alphabet for writing Yucatecan Maya was adequate for both monolingual and bilingual speakers of the language (if not for foreigners), and it was presumptuous of me to think that they would benefit from an alternative, more linguistically inspired alphabet.

This is a contentious matter in anthropology and linguistics. There are those who insist on what they call a "practical" alphabet that is different from the one introduced almost 500 years ago by Colonial authorities based on the Latin alphabet. I do not hold this view.

The next morning, we headed north to visit Ek Balam, a little-known site that had been previously inaccessible by road. It was a cool morning, the perfect weather for visiting an archaeological site. In Temozon, we inquired about the road to Ek Balam. The man, a Maya, told us that there would be a sign on the road, where we should turn off. What he didn't tell us was what was written on the sign. He probably couldn't read. Anyway, we turned east on the road marked "Hunuku." It was a narrow gravel road, but passable. When we reached Santa Rita, we asked for directions again and were directed to an even narrower road that consisted of two tire ruts. This was the new road to Ek Balam that had been completed the previous November. We followed it for what seemed like ages and finally arrived in the town of Ek Balam.

I left the car and asked someone about the ruins. I was directed to the *comisario*, who told us that we would need a guide. That was fine with me. In the end, we had three guides: the *comisario*, the former *comisario* (an elderly man), and the official guide, a young man who cleared a path for us with his machete. Ed commented that this was the first time in his life that anyone had cleared a trail for him. It reminded us of the travels in Yucatan of John Lloyd Stephens in the 1840s.

We hiked into the woods for a kilometer or so. We passed one mound with part of a stone wall still in place, then climbed a much higher mound to look over the site. From there we could see what had probably been the main plaza of the site. We also saw two pyramids far off to the southeast. We asked what they were, and our guides told us that they were the two pyramids of Coba. We could hardly believe it—Coba is about forty miles (or kilometers?) away.[8]

On our way into the site, our official guide suddenly leaped into the air and shouted "¡Víbora!" The old man took over the situation. He cut a branch off a tree and used it to club the snake to death, then flipped it into the bush some distance away. It was evidently poisonous, a fer-de-lance. After that I was rather careful where I stepped.

We expressed an interest in inscriptions, so we were led to five pieces of sculpture, first a figure of a bound captive, whose head, legs, and arms had been hacked off by looters, then four stelae, one of which had a date carved on one side.[9]

While Harvey was taking pictures of the stelae, the *comisario* asked me whether they were going to be shown on television. I learned then that the village was hopeful that it would get some of the tourist trade. The governor himself had participated in the inauguration ceremonies in November. The former *comisario* had petitioned for the road for many years. Now he was agitating to have the road extended into the site, and he thought that we might have recent information about that possibility. Of course, we didn't.

I had the same feeling that I had had in Chan Kom the day before, namely, that the people of Ek Balam had received an omen that we were coming and had certain expectations of us. Perhaps they had also been visited by a dragonfly. This impression was reinforced later, when we had finished touring the site and went to the store to buy some *refrescos*. The woman who served us also began the conversation as though she had expected us and asked me for information about where the road into the site would be built.

Our drive back to Valladolid was uneventful. We took it easy during the rest of the day. In the evening, I played my tape of the history of Chan Kom for Ed. He was impressed with the clarity of the tape, much of which he could understand, and howled with laughter when he heard the part about how progressive Chan Kom was.

The next morning, we returned to Merida via the northern route, stopping for lunch in Tizimin on the way. Near the plaza, we encountered Carnaval crowds in costume. We were all surprised at how large and modern Tizimin was, compared to Valladolid, and how few Maya were evident in their traditional clothes.

Harvey and Ed spent a full day in Merida before flying back to New Orleans on March 1st to continue with their courses at Tulane. Barbara remained in Merida for two more days in order to consult with me about her dissertation and then returned to the Huasteca to resume her fieldwork.

I did not return to Ebtun right away after they left. Elut and I worked for several days on what eventually became our verb dictionary, which was the precursor to our comprehensive dictionary of the Hocaba dialect of Yucatecan Maya (see Chapter 8).

After my arrival in Ebtun on March 7th, my life continued in much the same way as it had during the second half of February. Doña Francisca and I made several more visits to Dzitnup during March. At my request, Harvey had brought along a compass, with which I was able to verify the layout of the streets of the town. I decided that it was time for me to begin recording texts as a way of documenting the modern dialect of Ebtun. I began with Doña Francisca, from whom I obtained texts about her early life and her work as a midwife. Then I played the tape back so that she could help me with the transcription. From other people, I obtained texts on the history of the town and transcribed them with the assistance of Doña Francisca.

I enjoyed a visit from both Elut and Ofelia on March 24th. Ofelia came prepared to make lunch for all of us. She sailed into the house and then moved into the kitchen while Elut and I went off to buy *refrescos*. When we returned, Ofelia was making ham-and-cheese sandwiches. Doña Francisca looked like a cyclone had hit her, but she was gamely chatting away with Ofelia. I had never seen Ofelia with other Maya women before, and I was surprised at the way she took charge in an unfamiliar setting.

I also had not realized how much Ofelia knew about curing and ethnobotany. In our walk to the center of the town, she kept pointing out plants on the roadside and describing their medicinal properties to everyone she met.

I had invited my mother to visit me while I was living in Ebtun. She was scheduled to arrive at the end of March, and I left Ebtun two days earlier to make sure that we would have the hotel room in Merida that I had reserved.

After several days of sightseeing in Merida, we took a taxi to Chichen Itza, where we stayed at the Mayaland Hotel for one night. Our room was on the third floor of the main building at tree-top level, where we could see birds flitting through the branches. We visited the site early the next morning while it was still cool and then took a second-class bus to Valladolid, which served as an introduction to the rigors my mother would encounter later in the day. After checking into our hotel, we took a taxi to Ebtun. Doña Francisca was expecting us, and Mother had her first glimpse of what it was like to do fieldwork in a Maya village. On our walk along some of the streets of the town we were greeted by friends I had made during the months I had lived in Ebtun.

We returned to Valladolid on a second-class bus with standing-room only. Mother clung to me for dear life. Fortunately, it was only a short distance to Valladolid, and we arrived without incident.

The next morning we visited the market in Valladolid, where Mother had a wonderful time because it reminded her of some of her experiences in Shanghai. She mentioned it to the salesman at one of the stalls, who produced a coolie hat and a pair of cloth shoes that had been made in China! She wanted to take a hammock back to the States with her. There was a hammock salesman in the street outside the market, with whom I bargained in Maya. A crowd gathered around us, and she told me later that it reminded her of my father bargaining in Chinese in Shanghai.

We took a first-class bus back to Merida that afternoon. Elut was interested in meeting my mother, and we spent some time together in a cafe, where she talked about my father, his interest in Chinese, and his mother's complaint that he had learned a language that no one in his country spoke and that no one could understand. I heard Elut mutter, "So that's where she gets it!" a reference to my interest in Yucatecan Maya.

I returned to New Orleans with Mother, where she stayed for several days before flying back to Seattle. I remained with Harvey in New Orleans for the rest of the month of April.

On May 2nd, I flew to Merida and went on to Ebtun the next day, where I learned that Doña Francisca and I had been invited to attend a dance at the *cenote* in Dzitnup two days later. The *cenote* had been carefully developed for tourism. In addition to a *refresco* stand and attached palm shelter, there were bathrooms with running water piped in from the *cenote*. There were two major attractions at the site: a rock shelter that served as a stage for dances and the spectacular *cenote* itself. The *cenote* was quite large, and the surface of the water was far below the single restricted opening in the ceiling. It was well lighted to show off its stalagmites or stalactites. The water was a deep blue and a wonderful place for swimming. As a cave, it was better than anything I had seen in France or elsewhere in Mexico.

A team of movie photographers and interviewers was there to film the event. They used a small Uher tape recorder like mine to record the music.

The "dance" was a performance of *The Sacrifice of Isaac*, a rehearsal of which I had seen in the church of Dzitnup during my first week in Ebtun in January. The two masked performers (Isaac and Señor) danced inside a ring of men with wood and metal rattles. The Devil approached the group and tried to get inside the ring. He succeeded, but Isaac and Señor slipped out of it at the same moment. The men chased the Devil and pushed him to the ground. They carried him to a rock at the back of the shelter and mauled him. After a while he got up, and the routine was repeated. The dance-drama was accompanied by a slit drum, a harmonica, and a woman singing in Maya.

During February and March, Doña Francisca had received periodic visits from a male cousin who had once lived in Ebtun, but was then living in Cancun, where he supported himself by selling fruit and a sweet made from tamarind to school children during recess. The whole fruit and the tamarind sweet called *tamarindito* came from Ebtun. Doña Francisca would often serve as the intermediary in those fruit-buying expeditions, negotiating with people in Ebtun as the fruit on the trees in their gardens ripened and became available for sale. The cousin was in town on such a mission and had accompanied us to Dzitnup.

Cancun was founded in 1974, the same year that the former territory of Quintana Roo became a state. The city was a creation of the federal government, envisioned as a popular tourist destination on the Caribbean coast of Mexico that would rival Acapulco on the Pacific Coast. The task of creating a city from nothing was enormous. Constructing the necessary infrastructure created numerous employment opportunities for road builders, masons and their assistants, plasterers, and painters, and once completed, in service jobs. Men from all over the peninsula had flocked to Cancun to fill those positions, leaving their families behind in towns and villages like Ebtun, Dzitnup, and Chan Kom. One of Doña Francisca's grandsons sold ice cream from a bicycle-driven cart on the streets of Cancun, sending a portion of his earnings back to his parents in Ebtun from time to time. He had invited his fourteen-year-old sister and grandmother to visit him, and they wanted me to accompany them, but I regarded Cancun as a tourist trap and demurred at first.

However, Doña Francisca's cousin had a completely different perception of the place. He described Cancun in glowing terms, as if it were the Mecca of Yucatan. He marveled at the plate-glass windows on shops, the marking of prices directly on the merchandise, eliminating the need for haggling, and the *barrios* with people from all over the peninsula. I had already learned that all the workers from Chan Kom lived in one *barrio*, and it sounded like that might be true of other towns as well. As time went on, I began to realize how important Cancun was in the lives of many people in Ebtun, and I developed an interest in visiting Cancun, not as a tourist center, but as a place with a tremendous attraction for the Maya of the peninsula.

That opportunity came the week after I had returned to Ebtun in May. Doña Francisca, her granddaughter, and I went on the Chan Kom bus as far as Valladolid and on another bus from Valladolid to Cancun. Arriving at the bus station in Cancun, we took a taxi to the crossroads where we had arranged to meet her cousin. He was there selling plums, but because it was a holiday (Mother's Day), he had almost no business. He led us immediately to his house, about eight blocks away. He lived in a neighborhood of tiny houses constructed of poles and thick, water-proofed cardboard roofs and shared a small yard with about five other households. His house was too small for us to spend the night there.

After lunch, our host took us sightseeing with great pride. We took a bus downtown to a large department store and walked around from there. We did some window-shopping then visited the main plaza of the city. The church there was a real surprise, with a thatched roof, a bamboo ceiling beneath it, and instead of a crucifix over the altar, an open, cross-shaped window behind it. The sides of the church had walls of pierced cement that let the air through. It was a breathtakingly modern church, surprising for a Catholic church in Mexico, but appro-priate for a "Newtown" like Cancun.

Doña Francisca commented that there were very few images in the church. Her cousin replied that there weren't many believers in Cancun either. There was one image of the Virgin in front of the altar that seemed to receive special attention. Votive candles were burning before it, and it was covered with garlands of frangipani. Except for that, the church was like a chapel on a college campus—antiseptic and modern. Beside it was a large air-conditioned movie theater.

We had met Doña Francisca's grandson pedaling his bicycle-driven cart near the department store and had arranged to spend the night in the ice cream factory that served as his home and workplace when he was not cycling through the streets with his wares. The ice cream factory was about ten blocks from the cousin's home in a much better neighborhood not far from the water. The owner of the small ice cream factory was a Maya. The factory had two rooms of the same construction of poles and thick, waterproofed cardboard as the home of Doña Francis-ca's cousin, but the rooms were much larger and had cement instead of dirt floors. We were offered the room where the ice cream machinery was kept, which is where Doña Francisca's grandson slept. The floor was wet because ice was kept there, and the place was full of mosquitoes. The owner apologized for the mosquitoes. I said that I had brought some repellent. He also told us that there wasn't any water at that hour, so I pointed to my canteen. He told us that there was a bathroom, but it didn't have any light. Doña Francisca jumped in and said that I had brought my flashlight. "Ah, so then you've come well prepared!" And we all laughed.

We spent the early part of the evening in the movie theater next to the church we had visited during the afternoon. It was playing the movie *El Ministro y Yo* ("The Minister and I"), starring the popular Mexican comedian Cantínflas, and I enjoyed it thoroughly. This was the first time I had been to a movie in Mexico since I worked in Chiapas, and I was delighted to discover that I could follow the witty repartee without difficulty. Doña Francisca enjoyed the movie, too, although she couldn't have understood much of the dialogue. Her bilingual grandchildren did not have the same difficulty.

We returned to the ice cream factory about 10:00 p.m. I slathered myself with repellent with Doña Francisca's help and climbed into my hammock. I was not bothered by mosquitoes and slept very well.

I was awakened the next morning about 5:00 a.m., by the sound of Doña Francisca moving about. Twenty minutes later, four large blocks of ice were delivered, and I quickly got up and folded up my hammock. They were brought into our room and immediately began to melt. The floor, which had dried up during the night, was soon sopping wet again.

Our breakfast of scrambled eggs and sausage was prepared on a stove by Doña Francisca. I had to show her how to light the stove because she had never used a stove without a pilot light before.

Doña Francisca's grandson had been given the morning off from work to take us sightseeing. We walked all the way downtown, visiting some beautiful residential areas on the way. The whole city was full of beautiful avenues named after archaeological sites (Yaxchilan, Tulum, Bonampak, etc.) with ornamental bushes and flowers in the median strips. Even in the *colonia* where Doña Francisca's cousin and grandson lived, these avenues were only a few blocks away. It was possible for even the poorest and most humble people to take a vicarious interest in the city, for they were free to roam through all parts of it at will. They could spend all day enjoying the beauty of the streets as they went about their business, spending only the nights in their very modest abodes.

We returned to Ebtun in the afternoon, where we were met by Doña Francisca's *compadre* from Dzitnup, who invited us to attend his daughter's fifteenth-birthday party the next day. We said that we would come.

Her *compadre* (the godfather of one of her children) lived in a very large house on the edge of Dzitnup. The house had plastered walls and three or four doors and windows, suggesting that he was a man of means. His wife had given birth to seventeen children, of whom thirteen or fourteen had survived. They had many sons, some of whom cultivated their fields near Dzitnup and others worked in Cancun. The sons were well spaced in age, so that as soon as an older son married and had to support his own family, a younger son was ready to go to work in Cancun. In such an arrangement, nothing would be gained by limiting family size, and it was possible for the family to continue living on the land and prosper, as long as there was a steady stream of younger sons who could replace the ones who married. Because the families remained in the countryside, they did not complete the "demographic transition" to smaller families characteristic of families that migrated to the cities. Declining agricultural yields resulting from bad weather and population pressure on the land were counterbalanced by wage labor in Cancun. There was, therefore, no incentive to decrease family size and, in fact, large families with many sons were economically better off than small families or large families with many daughters. Thus, the migration to Cancun had the unanticipated effects of keeping people on the land and favoring high fertility rates in the rural hinterland.

While I was at the party, one of the sons of the family came up to me and asked whether I would be willing to have my picture taken with his family. I misunderstood at first and said that I hadn't brought my camera with me. No, they had their own camera. They wanted to take *my* picture. I was amused at having the tables turned on me and agreed to have my picture taken. I was photographed with the birthday girl and her sister and with the host and his wife, as well as with other members of the family.

That night we attended the first of a series of novenas in the church in Ebtun.[10] Doña Francisca had volunteered to provide new clothes for the Virgin, and she brought along with her several bunches of red and yellow frangipani, candles, and two buckets of rice cooked with milk and a dozen small gourds. When we arrived at the church, Doña Francisca ladled out the rice mixture into five or six gourds, which she placed on the main altar and in the two side chapels. The church filled up with men, women, and children, and the novena began. The ceremony was conducted by two men in the community called *maestro cantor* and *prioste*, who served as lay clergy.

After the ceremony was over, the rice gruel was served to the congregation. The novenas continued each night until the end of May, with a different woman responsible for the offerings each night.

The last novena was scheduled for May 30th. It was preceded by a mass at 6:00 p.m., and was conducted by a priest who arrived in a truck. His assistant played a portable organ and sang. For a moment, I thought that the priest was going to conduct the entire service in Maya, which would have been ironic in comparison with the novenas, which were conducted entirely in Spanish. But except for his opening remarks and the sermon, the service was conducted in Spanish.

It was a beautiful, carefully orchestrated service. The church had been cleaned up, an altar was set up, and all the lights functioned. The pews were filled. The moment the service ended, the organist closed up his organ, and he and the priest left the church by a side door. A few minutes later, I heard the truck drive off.

For the last novena, the Virgin of Guadalupe was lowered onto the platform and candlesticks placed before her image. Women went up and placed monetary offerings in a plate before her.

I could not help but contrast the polished and almost theatrical performance of the priest and his organist with the devout, off-key novenas I had attended on preceding nights. The mass was the most vibrant and warm mass I have ever attended. The use of the vernacular (Maya) for part of the service gave it a very human touch. If the town could have had such masses on a regular basis, the Church would have been a driving force here. But I was left with a feeling that I had seen something like a television performance, beautifully choreographed and executed, timed to the minute, then to vanish off screen, the props carried off in a sound truck. I was reminded of something that the most respected man in Ebtun had told me that afternoon about how, in some towns, tape recorders instead of *maestros cantores* provided the music for novenas.

All along, I had been working on my map in my free time. I had accompanied Doña Francisca on a visit to the part of town north of the highway, where she informed people of the forthcoming visit of a doctor to vaccinate children. I took advantage of the opportunity to extend my mapping to that part of town and expand my surname list. I had taken compass readings at each intersection north of the highway, so I knew that that part of the map was correct. The problem came in fitting it to the part of Ebtun that lay south of the highway. Doña Francisca suggested that I do the same thing for the southern part of town that I had done for the northern sector earlier that day: Walk over it with her, street by street, with a compass, clipboard, and pencil. That was the only way I could hope to get it right. And she assisted me with this task in subsequent days. However, no matter how hard I tried and how much help I received from Doña Francisca, I was unable to determine the correct configuration for the *cinco calles* on my map. That had to wait until later in the summer, when Harvey arrived and surveyed the area with a Brunton compass and pacing, and after we had received the aerial photograph from Ed Kurjack.

It was only near the end of my stay that I finally understood why the lands attributed to Ebtun in the *Titles* of the same name were so distant and dispersed. Apparently, the town itself had never owned the land in question. Instead, it had been familial land owned by lineages in small Precolumbian settlements some distance away, who had been forced to relocate to Ebtun by Spanish missionary priests to facilitate their conversion to Catholicism. It was they who retained title to the land during the Colonial period and afterward. Once liberated from debt peonage after the Mexican Revolution during the early decades of the twentieth century, the descendants of the original owners were free to move closer to their land, and it was then that they founded towns like Chan Kom and Xcalacoop near Chichen Itza.

Thus, Ebtun did not "lose" its lands after the Revolution. Its "title" to the lands was an artifact of Colonial policy, as was its heterogeneous population. It is in a sense misleading to call these documents *The Titles of Ebtun*. The lands belonged to people who happened to live in Ebtun. They now belong to people who have been allowed to return to them.

The fiesta in honor of San Antonio de Padua began on the evening of June 12th with a novena, followed by a procession from the church to the home of the couple sponsoring the celebration that year. An object called a *ramillete* was near the head of the procession. It was a large cylindrical object, about three or four feet high, consisting of a wooden frame covered with colored-paper streamers with doll-shaped cutouts that represented the saint's flowers (see cover image). We joined the procession and, as we left the church, the band fell in behind us playing. We moved up the road to the highway, then east down the highway, stopping traffic on the way. We entered the part of town north of the highway and went to the home of the fiesta's sponsors. The small images of San Antonio and San Bartolomé (the patron saint of Ebtun) were removed from the altar and used in the procession (the larger images of the saints remained behind on the altar). The images were taken into the house and placed on the family's altar. The *ramillete* was also brought inside and hung from some of the rafters.

A raised platform had been set up outside the house in a clearing, which served as a dance floor. A gasoline lantern borrowed from Doña Francisca provided the light. The young dancers were rather stilted. A boy would go up to a girl and offer her his hand. She would pretend not to notice him and wait a suitable interval before getting up, pretending reluctance, and going to the dance floor with him. The couple would dance without looking at each other. Often, before the dance ended, the girl would break away and leave the dance floor. Sometimes the boy went and got another partner. The dancing lasted until 3 a.m.

The next morning, shortly before 11:00, we heard music, and the band marched past our house. We followed the band to the house on the other side of the highway where we had been the night before.

When we arrived, a table was being set up for the Dance of the Pig's Head (see cover image). The head of a pig had been stripped of its meat. Only the snout still had skin on it. The skull was placed in a galvanized tub with some *relleno negro* sauce in the bottom of it. The snout pointed up and out of the tub. In its jaws was a large crescent of bread called a "half moon" (*media luna*). The tips of the crescent pointed up, too.

A bottle of rum, a stack of twenty-five tortillas wrapped in a cloth, several packs of cigarettes, and a candle were put on the table. One of the men picked up the wrapped stack of tortillas and danced in front of the man carrying the pig's head, pretending to offer them to spectators. Other men carried the rum, cigarettes, and candle. They danced around the table, pretending to offer things to the spectators.

I could not help comparing this performance of the Dance of the Pig's Head with the one I had first seen in Telchaquillo in November 1971.[11] They differed in several respects. First of all, in Telchaquillo, the flesh and skin were left on the pig; in Ebtun, they were not. Second, the cigarettes and ribbons were attached to the pig's head in Telchaquillo; in Ebtun, perhaps because of the *relleno negro* in the bottom of the tub, the pig's head was not adorned. In Telchaquillo, girls held on to the ends of the ribbons during the dance. Women did not take part in the dance in Ebtun, nor were ribbon streamers used. Instead, the *ramillete* of paper streamers was carried during the dance. And, of course, the performances were associated with different feast days: Concepción on November 12th in Telchaquillo and San Antonio on June 13th in Ebtun.

June was also the month when rainmaking ceremonies took place in Ebtun, but, unlike Hocaba, it was entirely a male affair, with men preparing all the food offerings for that occasion. I became aware of them only because the husband of one of the women whom I taught how to knit participated in such a ceremony and suggested that I be invited to partake of the leftover food that he brought home with him.

It was on that occasion that I saw the special tortillas called *naabal*, which were made of four large, thick tortillas pressed together, with a cross formed by ground pumpkin seeds on top. They had been wrapped in leaves and baked in a pit oven. I was also served a dish called *ya'ach*, consisting of broken up tortillas made of *atole* lees (similar to grits) and ground pumpkin seeds covered with the thick, dark-orange sauce called *kol*, and some pieces of chicken.[12]

My friend's husband and sons had already eaten in the field where the ceremony had been performed north of town. He was surprised to learn that I had not heard of such ceremonies being carried out in other parts of town. Of all the people I met in Ebtun that year, he had the most intuitive understanding of my interest in the customs of the town. He was the only person who invited me to attend a religious function. It was he who thought of showing me the *naabal* and explaining how they were made.[13]

He also told me that he would be attending the fiesta of San Juan in Cuncunul the following Saturday. He would be taking the image of San Bartolomé to Cuncunul to pay his respects to San Juan. He mentioned the towns involved in the saint exchange: Uayma (Santo Domingo), Cuncunul (San Juan Bautista), Tekom (San Pedro y Pablo), Dzitnup (San Andrés), Tixcacalcupul (Santiago), and Ebtun (San Bartolomé).

What I found interesting about the exchange of saints was that its roots must lie in the Colonial past, and the towns that exchange them were frequently mentioned in the *Titles of Ebtun*. They seemed to have formed a group in Colonial times.[14]

On June 23rd, Doña Francisca and I took the bus to Cuncunul to join the group that had escorted the smaller image of San Bartolomé to greet the image of San Juan Bautista in the church in the center of town. The delegations from the other towns had already arrived, and each delegation was being entertained in a different house in Cuncunul. We were served food and drink in the house assigned to the delegation from Ebtun. Then we repaired to the church for the mass. The image of San Juan was in the central niche over the altar. Below it, on a staircase-like platform, were arranged the five visiting images—from Ebtun, Dzitnup, Uayma, Tekom, and Tixcacalcupul.

The priest went to the door of the church and awaited the arrival of the *gremios* "sodalities," which were accompanied by a band. I counted three sets of banners and flags. One *gremio* was sponsored by the women of Cuncunul. Another was sponsored by the farmers (*agricultores*) of Cuncunul. The third was sponsored by the youth of the town. After the mass, the *gremios* led a procession that wound through the streets of the town.

I took advantage of my presence in Cuncunul that day to seek out a woman who had invited me to visit her there. I had met her in one of the overcrowded taxis that plied the highway to Valladolid one day. She was delighted that I had followed through on my promise to visit her sometime in Cuncunul. She invited Doña Francisca and me to have lunch with her, and we did. I was touched by her generosity.

I spent much of the next day with Doña Francisca at her daughter's house in Valladolid. The family was gathered there for the baptism of her daughter's youngest child. I arrived too late to attend the ceremony itself, but partook of the celebratory lunch with members of the family, neighbors, and friends.

That event coincided with the end of my stay in Ebtun. Elut and Ofelia arrived in a taxi the next morning (June 25th) to help me move my belongings to a hotel in Merida. From then on, I would visit Doña Francisca from time to time in Ebtun, but I would no longer be a member of her household. Doña Francisca had arranged to spend that night in Valladolid with her daughter to ease the transition to living alone again.

I spent the next five days in Merida, where Elut and I completed the elicitation for our verb dictionary. On June 30th, I moved out of the hotel and transferred most of my belongings to Elut's house, before taking the train to Palenque that evening for a week-long workshop in Mayan linguistics. The highlights of that workshop are mentioned in subsequent chapters.

At the end of that week, I returned to Merida by train with my friend and colleague Louanna Furbee. The train station in Palenque was crowded with people like us who did not have reserved seats. Louanna and I found a spot on the floor for our luggage and then sat on my suitcase (squashing it) until it was time to buy tickets. Maya Indians were sprawled out all around us on the floor.

A young Indian couple sat on a bench near us, and I decided to try to find out what language they spoke. They were Tzeltal speakers from Yajalon on their way to their *colonia* near their fields. I tried speaking Tzotzil with them, making the necessary shifts in pronunciation and grammar that I knew differentiated the two languages. Louanna chimed in in Tojolabal (the third Mayan language spoken in Chiapas). Amazingly enough, we were able to communicate quite well in the three languages, better than if we had used Spanish.

Elut met us in the train station in Merida. He told us that the long-distance bus drivers were on strike in the state of Yucatan, which explained why the train was so crowded. I was thankful that I had persisted with my original plan to take the train back to Merida instead of going by bus, which would have taken less time. Otherwise, we would have been stymied at the Campeche border with Yucatan.

We had to wait a long time for a taxi. Elut suggested that we take a horse and buggy to the hotel, which would have been a picturesque ending to a trip that began with a trilingual Maya conversation, but someone else got to it before we did. So Elut went off to get a taxi at the Mejorada plaza.

After resting briefly in our room at the hotel, Louanna and I went over to Elut's house. His son, Aguileo, was married that day. We were too late for the ceremony, but we arrived in time for lunch. It was the most relaxed celebration of any kind that I had ever attended in Yucatan. I knew most of Elut's family: his parents, nieces and nephews, sister, and brothers. Everyone talked to me in Maya. I also spent some time talking to the bride's mother, who was originally from Calkini in the state of Campeche, and to Elut's aunt, his mother's sister.

The next day, Louanna and I had lunch with Norman McQuown, the well-known linguist, who was on his way home from the Palenque meetings. We were joined by Don Alfredo Barrera Vásquez, who I arranged to visit the following day.

At Don Alfredo's house the next morning, I met his assistant, Domingo Dzul, who was transcribing a tape from Nunkini in Campeche. He was a Presbyterian minister from Becal, with two parishes in Merida. He recited some stories to me in Maya, most of which I understood.

Señor Dzul suggested that I might go along with him the next time he went on a tape-recording mission in Campeche. I was enthusiastic about the possibility, and we mentioned it to Don Alfredo, who endorsed it, but no definite plans were made that morning.

The next afternoon, I received a telephone call from Weldon Lamb, a graduate student at Tulane, saying that he had visited Don Alfredo in the morning and that Señor Dzul was planning to go to Ah Canul tomorrow for tape-recording, and would I like to go along? I was happy to accept the invitation.

Señor Dzul picked me up at my hotel early the next morning and Weldon and his mother after that. We stopped for about an hour in Becal to visit Señor Dzul's family. Becal is the center of the "Panama" hat-making industry. There was a large display of oversized hats made of plaster in the town square. Each family in Becal had its own cave in its back yard, where the members of the family make the hats. Hats had to be woven in caves where it was damp so that the palm was flexible. We visited one of the caves, a small man-made cavern cut into the limestone, in which it was impossible to stand upright.

From Becal, we went through Calkini on the way to Nunkini, a town of twelve hundred people. We pulled up at a house, and Señor Dzul engaged a middle-aged woman in conversation. We recorded some conversation with her and a text on the 1910 revolution. The conversation included some information on stars for Weldon, who was interested in astronomy.

From there, we went to the house of a woman who made reed mats. The reeds (*po'op*) from which she wove the mats grew in nearby swamps, called *peten*. She worked with both natural and dyed reeds and wove them into intricate geometric patterns. One of the designs was called armadillo (*uech*). It consisted of a group of three wavy lines, which I assumed resembled the plates on an armadillo. She was a lively woman, and I obtained an excellent tape of our conversation with her.

On July 15th, I returned to Ebtun for the first of several visits since I had moved to Merida. Doña Francisca was very happy to see me again, and we caught up on what had happened in our lives during the preceding weeks. She also cleared up a point of grammar in the Ebtun dialect that had puzzled me for some time.

During July, I spent much of my time in Merida transcribing the texts I had recorded in Chan Kom and Ebtun for Elut to check. For the most part, they were narrative, not conversational texts, and I wondered how narrative style compared with conversation. I mentioned this to Elut and asked him whether it would be possible to tape a natural conversation in Hocaba. He replied that his father had a friend who loved to talk and that his father, that friend, and two other old men would often get together and talk for hours. He offered to explore the possibility of my recording one of their get-togethers.

That recording session took place on July 19th in the house of Elut's sister in Hocaba. Two men were already there when we arrived, and the loquacious man joined them soon after. He did indeed love to talk and would have gone on all afternoon, if we had had sufficient time, tape, and battery. He was completely oblivious to the microphone. He told jokes, talked about curing, and gossiped with the other two men. It was an amazing performance. About a dozen women and children gathered in the doorways to listen. It was the first natural conversational situation I was able to record in Yucatan.

Those three old men loved to get together and converse. Elut told me that they sometimes talked until two o'clock in the morning. I couldn't have asked for a better sample of conversation. Elut's father came in eventually and joined in the conversation. When they stopped more than an hour and a half later, the house was full of people enjoying their repartee.

Those men were conversationalists, not storytellers. They were hesitant about telling stories and claimed that they did not know any. I was interested in the apparent dichotomy between people who were good storytellers and those who were known as avid conversationalists.

I received a visit from Doña Francisca two days later. She came with the granddaughter who had accompanied us to Cancun and with her daughter who lived and worked in Merida, whom I met for the first time. Doña Francisca wanted to inspect my living conditions and to see how I was getting along. I promised to return the visit one week later and did so.

Harvey joined me in Merida on July 30th, and we set out for a vacation on the East Coast, where we visited the archaeological sites of Chunyaxche, Coba, and Xcaret in Quintana Roo. On the way back to Merida, we visited the site of Kuluba north of Valladolid. We stopped in Ebtun for a few hours to see Doña Francisca. She accompanied us to *cinco calles*, where she watched in amazement as Harvey paced each street leading into the intersection in order to determine its correct location on my map of the town. And that is how my fieldwork in Ebtun that year came to an end.

NOTES

1. Alfonso Villa Rojas was the first ethnographer to carry out fieldwork in Chan Kom in 1930 and 1931. He co-authored *Chan Kom, a Maya Village* with Robert Redfield, which appeared as Publication 448 of the Carnegie Institution in 1934. He was a visiting professor during one of the years I was a student at Harvard, and I corresponded with him about my fieldwork while I was living in Ebtun.

2. Although Ebtun was apparently abandoned during the Caste War, a comparison of the surnames for Ebtun in the 1841 and 1883 censuses shows substantial continuity when the town was repopu-

lated after the Caste War (Rani Alexander, personal communication, February 18, 2008).

3. According to Doña Francisca, construction of the present highway between Valladolid and Merida that cuts Ebtun in two began in 1930 and was completed in 1935 (the same year that Roys visited Ebtun). Before 1930, there was no road between Ebtun and Merida; people took the train to Merida. The old road between Ebtun and Valladolid (with the branch that we followed during our walks to and from Dzitnup) was used primarily by horse-drawn carts. She thought that it ultimately led to Kaua.

4. *Ebebtun* means "stone staircase"in Maya.

5. Years later, we visited Cifuentes in Spain, the city of his birth, and the church in the walls of which his remains are interred. A copy of the same painting hangs in the church.

6. To do so at an earlier stage would mean that everything would sink to the bottom. The chiles are burnt outdoors on a large griddle over an open fire. Anyone standing downwind of the fire will be overcome by the corrosive smoke, as we discovered one night when attending a celebration in a Maya town. The carbonized chiles are then ground on a *metate* before being added to the broth.

7. Santiago Pacheco Cruz, *Hahil Tzolbichunil Tan Mayab o Verdadero Diccionario de la Lengua Maya* (Merida: Méjico, 1969).

8. We visited Ek Balam for the second time a few years later, when two of our former graduates students, William Ringle and George Bey, were excavating there.

9. This was Stela 1, later reassembled and re-erected by Mexican archaeologists working at the site. The date in the Maya calendar corresponds to January 20, AD 840 in our Gregorian calendar.

10. *Novena* refers to the recitation of a prayer on nine consecutive days or nights. However, in Ebtun, there were novenas on nineteen consecutive nights.

11. I saw the Dance of the Pig's Head in Telchaquillo as the guest of Joann Andrews who, upon learning of my interest in Maya fiestas during the summer of 1971, invited me to return in November for

that purpose. Telchaquillo lies south of Merida near the archaeological site of Mayapan.

12. I attended such a ceremony in Hocaba in July 1971. The dish called *x-ya'ach'* was prepared by the men. Women were not far away making tortillas, but they were not permitted to approach the altar. I was told that I could take photographs at a distance of ten meters from the altar, which gave me an excellent view of the ceremony.

13. I was not invited to the ceremony itself because women were regarded as polluters. This is why all the food had to be prepared by the men.

14. I witnessed the same kind of saint exchange during the fiesta of San Lorenzo, the patron saint of Zinacantan, in 1963.

10

COLONIAL DOCUMENTS: THE PAST SPEAKS IN MAYA

My interest in Colonial Maya documents came from their accessibility in the Latin American Library at Tulane. Having transcribed a large number of nineteenth-century documents concerning the Caste War of Yucatan in connection with my book on Maya rebellions, the logical next step for me in documentary research was to move gradually back in time, from the known to the unknown, until I reached the first document, written in 1557, which would give me an idea of what the language was like at that time.

This was not a path generally chosen by linguists. For example, Norman McQuown of the University of Chicago had produced a grammatical sketch of what he called "Classical Yucatec (Maya)" that was published in Volume 5 of the *Handbook of Middle American Indians* in 1967. That work was based on the voluminous late sixteenth-century dictionary known as the *Calepino de Motul*. And Ortwin Smailus at the University of Hamburg was working on a more comprehensive grammar based on the same source during the months leading up to the time I spent in Ebtun. He had sent me a copy of the preliminary version of his grammar, which I took with me to Ebtun; my notes and comments on that manuscript were recorded on many pages of my field notes as I was reading it.

The Latin American Library at Tulane had a facsimile copy of the *Calepino de Motul* and the edition of that manuscript published by Juan Martínez Hernández in 1929. In leafing through the latter, I noticed that many of the example sentences represented Maya translations of Biblical passages from the Old and New Testaments, a Spanish catechism, and Catholic prayers. I wondered about the authenticity of the Maya expressions recorded in that work. It seemed to me that documents written by native speakers of the Maya language were more likely to be authentic than a dictionary compiled by Spanish priests. That is why I have always preferred to use such documents as sources in my research on Colonial Yucatecan Maya.[1, 2]

It was Ortwin who pointed out in a letter to me dated June 6, 1979, that "colonial and modern Yucatec are, although historically related, in fact two different grammatical systems and one has to be very careful in taking proof from one system to the other." As I moved back in time from the nineteenth to earlier centuries, I soon learned how right he was and adapted my methods accordingly.

Elut had been very helpful to me in translating the Maya letters written during the Caste War of Yucatan, but when I began transcribing documents of the late eighteenth-century, I discovered that they contained grammatical structures that were no longer in use by the middle of the nineteenth century, when the Caste War began. For example, the late eighteenth-century documents still used two forms of the first-person plural possessive pronoun, one (spelled *c*) before nouns beginning with a glottal stop and the other (spelled *ca*) before nouns beginning with other consonants. The *ca* variant had dropped out of use by the 1840s, and the *c* variant appeared before nouns beginning with all consonants, as is also the case in Modern Yucatec, except for one holdover from the Colonial period, *ca yumil ti Dios*, that shows up in Maya translations of Catholic prayers.[3] *ca yumil ti Dios* meant "our Father who is God" in Colonial Yucatec, but Elut and other speakers of Modern Yucatec translated *ca yumil* into Spanish as *segundo padre* "*second* father" because *ca* only means "two" today. For this reason, I did not ask him to help me in translating Colonial documents.

The first Colonial Maya document I transcribed and translated came from the town of Chunhuhub in the southeastern part of the peninsula. It was part of a *visita*, a tour of inspection conducted at the end of a parish priest's term of office that took place in 1784. This document, as well as other documents in the dossier, catalogued the misdeeds of the priest while he was in office. A copy of the entire dossier (including pages from the *cofradia* book of the years in question) was lent to me by Philip Thompson, my first graduate student, who had discovered it in the cathedral archive in Merida while he was carrying out ethnohistorical research for his dissertation.

The Chunhuhub document contained some interesting grammatical constructions that I had shared with Ortwin before leaving New Orleans for Yucatan in January 1979. Ortwin was at the Mayan Linguistics Workshop at Palenque that I attended during the first week of July that year, and we had some useful conversations about Colonial Maya grammar there and two weeks later, when he came through Merida on his way back to Germany.

I transcribed two other, much longer late eighteenth-century manuscripts as part of another, unrelated project that is described in Chapter 11. I mention them here because of their use in concordances that provided me with an efficient method for analyzing large sets of Colonial Maya documents.

As I explain in the next chapter, by the 1980s, I had become interested in the possibility of documenting the grammatical structure of Maya hieroglyphic texts by comparing them with texts written in lowland languages like Colonial Yucatecan Maya. For this purpose, I needed to have some method of retrieving information on the prefixes and suffixes used in texts. Bill Ringle, a Tulane graduate student in archaeology who was also interested in hieroglyphic decipherment, offered to produce a concordance of the *Book of Chilam Balam of Tizimin* on Tulane's mainframe computer, if I would prepare a digital copy of the manuscript on my Apple II home computer. After transcribing and keyboarding the text on the computer and proofreading it against the facsimile of the Tizimin in the Latin American Library, I hyphenated the prefixes and suffixes in each word, so that they would be alphabetized separately in the concordance. This would allow me to assess the relative frequencies of alternative spellings of the pronouns in the text so that they could be compared with the frequencies of possible candidates for them in hieroglyphic texts. If the frequencies were roughly the same, then this would be an argument for assigning that function to those glyphs.

I turned next to the *Book of Chilam Balam of Chumayel*, for which there was a facsimile edition in the Latin American Library. The digital copy I produced of my transcription was also transformed into a concordance.[4] The *Books of Chilam Balam* were less useful for my linguistic research because they could not be provenienced very accurately in space and time. As pilot projects, the concordances based on them were valuable as examples of what might be done with the provenienced documents in the Latin American Library and other libraries and archives.

The first set of provenienced documents I tackled for this purpose were in the *Documentos de Tabi*, a five-volume collection of hacienda papers that Tulane had purchased in the 1920s and 1930s. Craig Hanson, an archaeology graduate student in the Department of Anthropology, made the initial transcription of each Maya document, and I followed by proofreading his digitized transcription against the original documents.

Then I tackled a much larger collection of about 550 Maya documents from the town of Tekanto that Philip Thompson had found and microfilmed in the notarial archive of the state of Yucatan in Merida. His dissertation and the book resulting from it were based on those documents. He lent me his microfilms to use in my linguistic research, and a local company made printouts of each page from them. It took me and a number of graduate student research assistants many years to transcribe, digitize, and proofread them all. In addition to the small stipend they received, I taught them paleography in return for their hard work.

From time to time, John Chuchiak, then a graduate student in Latin American history, has augmented my collection of provenienced documents with Colonial documents he found in the national archives in Mexico City and elsewhere, including some from Tahmek near Hocaba, as did colleagues like Bill Hanks, who sent me a facsimile copy of the famous Landa letter of 1567, and Mark Christensen, who gave me a digital copy of an eighteenth-century *cofradia* book from Hocaba itself. And during the summer of 2004, I spent two weeks in the Tozzer Library at Harvard, checking my digitized transcription of the Maya documents published in Roys's *Titles of Ebtun* against the facsimile copy archived there.

Bill Ringle made concordances of my entire collection of digitized and hyphenated documents from the Hacienda Tabi papers and the sixteenth- and seventeenth-century documents from Tekanto. As the memory on desktop computers increased, it became possible to make the concordances at home. Harvey and I purchased an IBM software package that allowed Bill to write a concordancing program tailored for a desktop computer that I was able to run myself, and I produced concordances for two of the Talking Cross documents from the Caste War of Yucatan, the documents and *cofradia* book from Chunhuhub, and a large number of documents from Tekanto from the second half of the eighteenth century. These concordances proved invaluable when the time came for me to write my historical grammar of Yucatecan Maya.

In the meantime, I had been invited to collaborate with a German colleague and friend, Helga-Maria "Pauline" Miram, on a translation of a third *Book of Chilam Balam*, the one attributed to Kaua, a town a few kilometers west of Ebtun. Pauline (the name I had known her by since the 1970s) wanted to prepare a critical edition of this Colonial manuscript and, knowing that I had been working with Colonial Yucatec, she asked me to help her with its translation into English. She and her husband, Wolfgang Miram, visited me in New Orleans during the fall semester of 1987, in the course of which she made the request.

It was a tempting offer because of the collateral material she had already gathered for interpreting the *Kaua*. In those days, the *Books of Chilam Balam* were regarded as reliable sources on Precolumbian Maya culture, uncontaminated by European accretions. Archaeologists relied on these manuscripts for insights in understanding the artifacts they unearthed during their excavations. Pauline had found European texts that were reproduced in Maya translation, in whole or in part, in the *Kaua* (and to a lesser extent in the *Books of Chilam Balam of Chumayel* and *Tizimin*) and planned to make the European antecedents of much of the *Kaua* the centerpiece of her critical edition of the manuscript. I was intrigued with this method of evaluating the relative inputs of the Maya and European cultures in these works.

However, I was already immersed in other research projects, such as the Hocaba dictionary, that were requiring much of my time, and I was reluctant to delay their completion by taking on a new project that would require my full attention at that time. Also, I knew that I would soon be entering a three-year term as chairman of the Anthropology Department that would also involve much of my time.

My solution to this dilemma was to apply for a research grant from the National Endowment for the Humanities that would include as one of its components support for a one-semester leave from teaching and administration, during which I would spend all my time on the *Kaua*. The grant was awarded for a three-year period, from July 1990 through June of 1993.

My leave was scheduled for the fall of 1990. Pauline joined me in New Orleans for the entire month of November so that we could go over her transcription of the *Kaua*, my draft translation of the first part of the manuscript, and discuss the kind of information we wanted to include in the footnotes.

After my leave ended, I continued working on the translation **part time** for the next eighteen months. Pauline commented on my translation and suggested revisions by fax and letters and contributed to the footnotes as I went along. We spent another five weeks together during the summer of 1992, this time in Wedel near Hamburg in northern Germany where she lived., That was when we wrote the first draft of the long introduction to the book that resulted from our collaborative effort.[5]

For the transcription, Pauline and I had worked from copies of photographs of the original manuscript of the *Kaua* taken by Teobert Maler sometime before 1887 and archived in the Ibero-Amerikanisches Institut Preussischer Kulturbesitz in Berlin. A few pages of the manuscript were missing from our copies of the photos, and we had difficulty reading some of the pages we did have. Our solution to these difficulties was to spend a few days at the Institut in Berlin, examining the problematic pages.

Harvey had planned to meet me in Hamburg at the end of my time in Wedel, after which we would fly to Prague and then go on to Brno in Moravia, where he wanted to visit the Palaeolithic site of Dolni Vestonice. Therefore, our trip to Berlin took place after our visit to Prague and Brno.[6] We flew from Prague to Berlin, landing at the old, by then seldom-used Tempelhof airport, where I and sixty-seven other Stanford-in-Germany students had arrived in Berlin thirty-two years earlier.

My return to Berlin took place only three years after the wall had come down, and it was fascinating to see the city again under those conditions. I felt like I had entered a time warp. The Kurfürstendamm, the main shopping street and showcase of Western opulence in West Berlin in 1960, had not changed a bit, but after more than thirty years, it looked quaint and antiquated, compared with its counterparts in other parts of Western Europe and the United States. We saw Russian soldiers walking around aimlessly with no place to go after the wall had come down and their own country had disintegrated. Russian uniforms and decorations were being sold in the area where the wall had been, particularly at the Brandenburg Gate.

In 1960, the part of East Berlin near Checkpoint Charlie where the wall was later erected had been covered with rubble from the Second World War that we had to pick our way through in order to reach the theater where we had seen *Swan Lake* performed. The rubble was removed after the wall went up, and drab high-rise apartment buildings were constructed very close to the wall.

Pauline and Wolfgang met us in Berlin after traveling by train from Hamburg. While Pauline and I worked with the Maler photos at the Institut, Harvey and Wolfgang took an extended walking tour of downtown Berlin. The copies of the Maler photos we saw at the Institut were much more legible than the ones that we had in our possession, and we were able to complete our transcription of the *Kaua* manuscript that day. We spent the rest of our time in Berlin revisiting parts of the city I had first seen in 1960, with side trips to Potsdam and the palace of Sans Souci.

As I worked on the documents for my Colonial database, I became more and more aware of how much variation there was in the spelling of the Maya and Spanish words they contained. The ones that did not conform to the canonical or standard spellings could have been considered errors, marking the scribes who produced them as incompletely literate, but I decided to preserve the original spelling as much as possible, hoping that they might reveal something interesting in the future. My decision was influenced by an experience I had had many years before, in the mid-1960s, when I was training native speakers of

Tzotzil in Zinacantan, Chiapas, to write texts in their language (see Chapter 6). For that purpose, I introduced them to a practical alphabet that members of the Harvard Chiapas Project had developed for writing Tzotzil. Most of the Zinacantecs who were learning to write Tzotzil understood immediately the need to use a consistent alphabet and system of word division for representing utterances in their language. However, a few did not understand the importance of spelling words consistently and continued spelling them in more than one way.

I soon realized that as long as the texts were intelligible to me, it did not matter how consistently the words in them were spelled. What I did not realize at the time, but benefited from later, was that some of the aberrant spellings represented the actual pronunciation of words in the language more faithfully than the spellings I preferred.

The value of treating alternative spellings as clues to pronunciation can be illustrated by comparing the conventional spelling of two words in English with their popular spelling:

Conventional	Popular
through	thru
though	tho'

The words *through* and *though* differ only in the presence or absence of the consonant *r*, but they have significantly different meanings, and the vowel cluster *ou* in them is pronounced differently, as *oo* in *through* and as *ō* in *though*. The popular spellings of these words, which show up in informal contexts, reflect the pronunciation of their vowels better than the conventional spellings and lack the consonants *gh* at the end of both words, which are never pronounced at all.[7]

Returning to the Colonial Maya texts of Yucatan that are the focus of this chapter, the Latin-based alphabet in which they were written did not have symbols for all the sounds of the language and therefore did not, and, in fact, could not represent the pronunciation of the language adequately. In their training, Maya scribes were introduced to canonical, or standard spelling of words, which many of them used, but other scribes, whose training may have been inadequate or incomplete, did not, a situation that paralleled my teaching of literacy in Tzotzil in Zinacantan. As time went on, I became fascinated with the possibility of learning how the words in Colonial Maya texts were actually pronounced by analyzing the variations in how they were spelled. In this way, I was able to prove, with the help of my linguist friend and colleague, Nike Orie, that Colonial Yucatec had *six*, not five vowels, even though the Colonial alphabet contained only the five vowel symbols of Spanish. The sixth vowel, called *schwa*, is the one represented by the *a* in *sofa* and *e* in *the* in English because English has no symbol for schwa. The same kind of variation, but between *a* and *i* served as the clue to the presence of schwa in Colonial Maya.[8] Other kinds of spelling variations revealed that hieroglyphic principles of writing continued for a while after the Spanish Conquest in alphabetic texts and the problems Colonial Maya scribes encountered in incorporating Spanish loans into their texts.[9] These discoveries encouraged me to move ahead with a historical grammar of Yucatecan Maya based on Colonial and nineteenth-century documents, the dictionary that Elut and I had produced for the Hocaba dialect of Modern Yucatec, and what I had learned about the Ebtun dialect during the months I spent in the town in 1979.

NOTES

1. My misgivings about the authenticity of entries in the *Calepino de Motul* were later corroborated by William Hanks, who demonstrated that the *Motul* and other Colonial Maya dictionaries contained a "reduced" form of the language that was used in the missionary effort. Nevertheless, I eventually realized that, flawed as it was, the *Calepino de Motul* was the most comprehensive source of lexical items in the language of the sixteenth century, and after I retired from teaching at Tulane, I spent four years becoming familiar with its contents by translating it into English and distributing each of

its example sentences under the appropriate lexical entries (see Chapter 15).

2. I had a different reason for questioning the validity of the grammars of Colonial Maya produced by the Franciscan missionaries. Their grammars, like those produced by priests in other parts of Latin America, were couched in terms of the categories of Latin grammar, and as such distorted the structure of the Maya language. In this, I was in agreement with both Bill Hanks and Ortwin Smailus, whose approaches to Maya grammar were similar to mine.

3. This was an excellent example of what Hanks calls *maya reducido* "reduced Maya" that has persisted into recent times. See William F. Hanks, *Converting Words: Maya in the Age of the Cross* (Berkeley: University of California Press, 2010).

4. Bill Ringle asked me to prepare two additional manuscripts for concordancing to aid his own epigraphic research: the "Crónica de Chac Xulub Chen" from the town now known as *Chicxulub* and the "Pax-bolon-Maldonado Papers" of Colonial Chontal.

5. Victoria R. Bricker and Helga-Maria Miram, *An Encounter of Two Worlds: The Book of Chilam Balam of Kaua*. Tulane University Middle American Research Institute, Publication 68 (New Orleans, LA: Tulane University, 2002).

6. We took a bus tour of Prague that included a visit to the Jewish Quarter, where one of my mother's ancestors had lived during the sixteenth century.

7. A more technical explanation of these examples appears on page 425 of Victoria R. Bricker, "Where There's a Will There's a Way: The Significance of Scribal Variation in Colonial Maya Testaments," *Ethnohistory* 62, no. 3 (2015): 421–44.

8. Victoria R. Bricker and Olanike O. Orie, "Schwa in the Modern Yucatecan Languages and Orthographic Evidence of its Presence in Colonial Yucatecan Maya, Colonial Chontal, and Precolumbian Maya Hieroglyphic Texts," *International Journal of American Linguistics* 80, no. 2 (2014):175–207.

9. Victoria R. Bricker, "The Use of Logosyllabic Principles of Writing in the Book of Chilam Balam of Chumayel," *International Journal of*

American Linguistics 51, no. 4 (1985): 351–53; Victoria R. Bricker, "Abbreviation Conventions in the Maya Inscriptions and the Books of Chilam Balam," *Anthropological Linguistics* 29, no. 4 (1987): 425–38; Victoria R. Bricker, "Where There's a Will There's a Way: The Significance of Scribal Variation in Colonial Maya Testaments," *Ethnohistory* 62, no. 3 (2015): 421–44.

11

MOVING BACK IN TIME: READING MAYA HIEROGLYPHS

My interests in ethnology and later, ethnohistory, have had two foci: (1) human behavior and (2) both oral and written texts in whichever Mayan language was relevant for my research at the time. At first, Tzotzil was the language in question because it was the principal vehicle for the humor of the Zinacantecs that served as the subject of my dissertation. However, my responsibility for teaching the Spoken Yucatecan Maya course at Tulane meant that I had to become conversant with the grammar of that language as well, and this need was encouraged by the opportunity to work with Elut, who had his own interest in revealing the grammatical intricacies of his language.

Harvey was more interested in the behavioral and ethnohistorical aspects of my research than in the purely linguistic approach I was moving into during the 1970s. He saw an opportunity for me to apply my knowledge of Yucatecan Maya grammar to the decipherment of Mayan hieroglyphs, an endeavor that was more in line with his archaeological interests. To that end, he began buying me books containing hieroglyphic texts, including Eric Thompson's commentary on the Dresden Codex,[1] Michael Coe's book on the Grolier Codex,[2] and the Yaxchilan fascicles of Ian Graham's *Corpus of Maya Hieroglyphic Inscriptions*,[3] never dreaming that one day he would embark on a study of the eclipse table in the Dresden Codex himself. These works joined several books on Maya hieroglyphs that I had inherited from my father, including Thompson's *Maya Hieroglyphic Writing: An Introduction*,[4] which he had collected for the purpose of applying his ideas about comparative semantics to the decipherment of Maya hieroglyphs when he retired, but he died before that was possible.[5]

I was reluctant to make a significant investment of time in the study of Maya hieroglyphs, fearing that it could become a bottomless pit from which I might never be able to extricate myself. I had another project that I was anxious to complete, namely, research for *The Indian Christ, the Indian King*, for which I was still collecting data.

In the meantime, however, others had begun to approach the decipherment of Maya hieroglyphs from a linguistic point of view. Floyd Lounsbury had made some significant breakthroughs in demonstrating the logosyllabic nature of the script, and John Justeson had confirmed it with his comparative analysis of the Maya script with other, previously deciphered writing systems. And Linda Schele was popularizing the study of Maya hieroglyphs with academicians and lay people.

The ultimate catalyst for me was not the growing popularity of the subject, nor Harvey's subtle efforts of persuasion, but rather what I perceived to be a misuse of dictionaries for highland Guatemalan Mayan languages, especially K'iche' and Kaqchikel, for deciphering a writing system that had been developed and used in the Maya lowlands. In the archaeology courses I took at Harvard, I had been trained to control space, time, and form in the analysis of artifacts. Therefore, decipherments based on highland Mayan dictionaries were unlikely to be correct unless the terms in question were shown to have cognates in lowland languages. I realized, however, that my methodological objections would not be taken seriously unless and until I had achieved some mastery of the writing system myself.

I was initially not sure whether I was capable of working with such a highly pictorial script. I had no talent for drawing and wondered whether I had much of a visual memory. I decided to test my capacity for undertaking such a task by spending one month during the summer of 1978 working full time on a research project based on Maya hieroglyphs. I would then set it aside and come back to it one year later to see whether I had remembered what I had learned during that month. In the meantime, I finished preparing the manuscript of *The Indian Christ, the Indian King* for submission to the University of Texas Press.

After the year had passed, I found, to my delight, that I did have a visual memory for hieroglyphic signs. I also learned that my inability to draw glyphs was not a serious handicap because of the availability of copy machines for reproducing the glyphs that interested me, which could then be cut out and arranged as I wished (Figure 11.1). My preferred approach to learning a new subject was to immerse myself in some research project, rather than to work through a textbook systematically. This was a technique that had served me well in learning Tzotzil in Chiapas and French in France, and I thought it might be

FIGURE 11.1. Arranging glyphs on an illustration.

effective for becoming acquainted with Maya hieroglyphs. There were no textbooks for learning Maya hieroglyphs at that time anyway, even if I had chosen that route. I selected the emblem glyphs in the inscriptions of Yaxchilan as a research topic and explored the question of whether they represented site names or lineage names. I cannot say that I solved that problem during the month I worked on the inscriptions of Yaxchilan—there were arguments in favor of both interpretations—but that was enough for me to become sufficiently familiar with the inscriptions of that site to recall what I had learned about them one year later.

With that test completed, I considered what I might be able to contribute to the decipherment of Maya hieroglyphs. I thought that a grammatical approach to the problem might be useful, especially if the Mayan languages that were selected were limited to those spoken in regions where hieroglyphic inscriptions have been found. At the Maya Linguistics Workshop I attended at Palenque during the first week of July in 1979, I heard a brilliant talk given by Barbara MacLeod, in which she showed that some hieroglyphic texts contained verbs that took the same positional suffixes as those that are characteristic of the Modern Cholan and Yucatecan languages. It seemed to me that the task of decipherment might be simplified if the glyphs in the writing system could be classified in terms of grammatical categories, because, as I stated at the beginning of my book *A Grammar of Mayan Hieroglyphs*, "a classification as transitive verb, intransitive verb, noun, adjective, or particle limits the number of possible meanings, and hence phonetic readings, appropriate to its form class."[6] This approach to decipherment proved to be fruitful and demonstrated that much could be learned about the morphology and syntax of the language(s) recorded by the hieroglyphs without appealing to the dictionaries and grammars of the highland Mayan languages. My research on this topic was supported by a grant from the John Simon Guggenheim Foundation that enabled me to work full time on this project during the summer and fall of 1982.

As I was collecting the data for my grammar of Maya hieroglyphs, I noticed some thematic parallels in the representation of New Year's ceremonies on Classic Maya monuments, in the Maya codices, in early Colonial sources on the Precolumbian religion of the Yucatecan Maya, and in Chamula, where I had conducted ethnographic fieldwork more than a decade earlier. I presented my findings at a conference in San Cristobal las Casas in Chiapas during the summer of 1981. In it, I had drawn attention to the way the performers in these different media sprinkled incense over a brazier, and I pointed out that some of them wore high-backed sandals, whereas others had bare feet.[7] The Mexican students in attendance put out a newsletter at the beginning of each day with a cartoon on the first page that ribbed one of the scholars who had spoken on the previous day. On the day after I gave my presentation, I was portrayed as "Big Foot" on the front page of the newsletter, with huge feet and pellets of what were probably intended to represent incense falling from my right hand (Figure 11.2)!

The focus of most scholars doing hieroglyphic research during the 1970s and 1980s was on what could be learned about dynastic history from texts carved on Classic period monuments. The meetings called *round tables* organized by Merle Greene Robertson at Palenque during the summer provided a forum for sharing the results of this research, as did the workshops organized by Linda Schele at the University of Texas in Austin during the academic year. I began attending the "round tables" in 1980, where I presented talks on my research on the grammar of Maya hieroglyphs and other topics.[8]

The screenfold books known as *codices* were not concerned with dynastic history and for that reason were rarely considered by other epigraphers during the 1980s and 1990s. Because I have always been more interested in the grammatical structure of hieroglyphic texts than in their content, I paid as much attention to the ones in the codices as to the ones on stone monuments that engaged the attention of other scholars. The codical field was wide open at a time when most epigraphers were preoccupied with monumental inscriptions, and I would be treading on few toes if I focused on the codices. Some of the students in my seminars joined me in this endeavor, and Tulane became known as a center of research on the Maya codices in the late 1980s and 1990s.

FIGURE 11.2.   "Bigfoot" cartoon.

My epigraphic research on the grammar of hieroglyphic texts
proved useful for understanding the calendrical structure and content
of the Maya codices. The well-known scholar J. Eric S. Thompson
favored a reading order for codical texts that was different from the
one on monumental texts. Using a method that I called *astronomical
syntax*, I proved that the reading order of codical texts was the same
as the basic reading order in monumental texts: date–verb–subject (*not
verb–subject–date*).[9] This discovery was based on research on astronomy

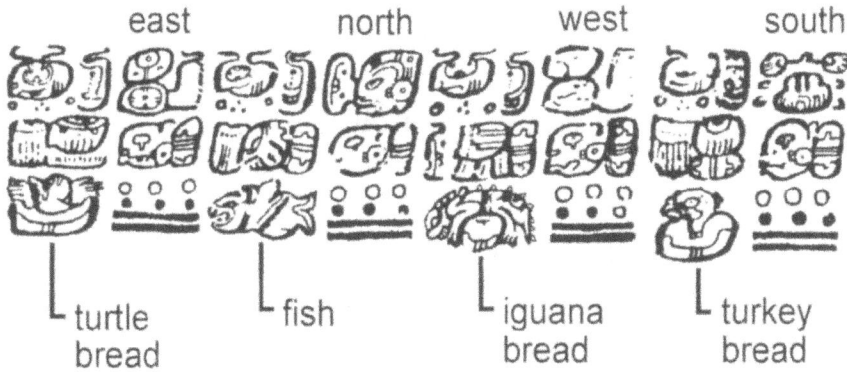

FIGURE 11.3. Offering glyphs in the rain-making almanac on pages 29b–30b of the Dresden Codex.

After the second edition of *Códices mayas*, by J. Antonio Villacorta C. and Carlos A. Villacorta, pages 68, 70. Guatemala, Tipografía Nacional. 1976.

in the Maya codices that Harvey and I were engaged in at the same time that made it possible to place such texts in historical time, where the astronomical glyphs mentioned in the texts corresponded to actual astronomical events when the basic reading order was invoked, but not with the reading order favored by Thompson.

Once the question of reading order had been settled (and accepted by most, if not all, epigraphers), I discovered that one of the almanacs in the Dresden Codex described the rainmaking ceremonies scheduled at 13-day intervals during the growing season at each of the four cardinal directions of a town (four sets of two bars and three dots in Figure 11.3). As it happened, I had witnessed such a rainmaking ceremony in Hocaba during the summer of 1971, which took place at the southern end of the town, and I had been told that such ceremonies were also performed at fortnightly intervals at the other three sides of the town. The offerings made during such ceremonies were mentioned in the Dresden almanac: turtle-bread in the east (the head and feet of a turtle emerging from the glyph for *tortilla* or *tamale*), a fish in the north, iguana-bread in the west (a glyph representing an iguana lying on the glyph for *tortilla* or *tamale*), and turkey-bread in the south (the head of a turkey rising out of the glyph for *tortilla* or *tamale*; see Figure 11.3). A similar offering was made during the rainmaking ceremony I saw in Hocaba, with chicken heads and feet substituting for the turkey head shown in the offering glyph in the codical almanac. The same kinds of offerings (including one for fish-bread) were mentioned in connection with other ceremonies in the Dresden Codex, plus a fifth offering of deer-bread (the head of a deer rising out of the glyph for *tortilla* or *tamale*). The names of these animals, spelled syllabically, replaced their images in a few contexts: *cay* "fish," *cutz* "turkey," *huh* "iguana."[10]

My experiences collecting plants and their names for the Hocaba dictionary were relevant for deciphering one of the almanacs in the Dresden Codex, which pictured the rain god sitting in six trees and on an agave plant. The Maya used the sap of four of the trees as vegetable dye and the juice of the agave is described as "divine juice" in the caption above the picture.

Topics like these were more relevant to my previous experiences as an ethnographer, ethnohistorian, and lexicographer than dynastic history, and for that reason I found them more challenging and interesting than events in the lives of the rulers of Classic-period sites. This was not by design, but was a result of the fact that I already had a foundation for recognizing them and understanding their significance whenever I encountered such themes in codical texts. My growing familiarity with the almanacs led me to explore other avenues of content, most notably astronomy, a special interest shared with Harvey.

NOTES

1. J. Eric S. Thompson, *A Commentary on the Dresden Codex, a Maya Hieroglyphic Book,* Memoir 93 (Philadelphia, PA: American Philosophical Society, 1972).

2. Michael D. Coe, *The Maya Scribe and His World* (New York: The Grolier Club, 1973).

3. Ian Graham and Eric von Euw, *Corpus of Maya Hieroglyphic Inscriptions. Volume 3, Part 1* (Yaxchilan) (Cambridge, MA: Peabody Museum, 1977); Ian Graham, *Corpus of Maya Hieroglyphic Inscriptions. Volume 3, Part 2* (Yaxchilan) (Cambridge, MA: Peabody Museum, 1979).

4. J. Eric S. Thompson, *Maya Hieroglyphic Writing: An Introduction* (Norman: University of Oklahoma Press, 1960).

5. With these and the more recently published books that Harvey gave me, I had almost everything I needed to undertake hieroglyphic research. When I finally succumbed to the temptation to undertake such research, I had to purchase only two additional books in order to get started: J. Eric S. Thompson, *A Catalog of Maya Hieroglyphs* (Norman: University of Oklahoma Press, 1962); and David H. Kelley, *Deciphering the Maya Script* (Austin: University of Texas Press, 1976).

6. Page 1 of Victoria R. Bricker, *A Grammar of Mayan Hieroglyphs*, Publication 56 (New Orleans, LA: Tulane University, Middle American Research Institute, 1986).

7. Victoria R. Bricker, "Las ceremonias de año nuevo en los monumentos clásicos mayas," in *Proceedings of the XVII Mesa Redonda of the Sociedad Mexicana de Antropología*, Volume 1 (Chiapas, Mexico: San Cristóbal Las Casas, 1984), 227–46.

8. I participated in them in 1983, 1986, 1989, and 1993 as well. I attended three of Linda's workshops in 1992, 1993, and 1997.

9. Victoria R. Bricker, "Astronomical Syntax in the Dresden Codex," *Journal of Mayan Linguistics* 6 (1988): 55–78.

10. Victoria R. Bricker, "Faunal Offerings in the Dresden Codex," in *Sixth Palenque Round Table*, Volume VIII, eds. Merle Greene Robertson and Virginia M. Fields (Norman: University of Oklahoma Press, 1986), 285–92.

12

HISTORICAL ASTRONOMY: MAYA RECORDS OF THE SKY

Neither Harvey nor I had any expectation of becoming involved in collaborative research when we decided to marry each other. My interest in Maya ethnology and his in Palaeolithic archaeology were too far apart to find common ground, and our field sites in different hemispheres—mine in the highlands of southeastern Mexico and his in southwestern France—meant that we lived apart for long periods of time.

However, these barriers to collaboration did not prevent us from helping each other in our diverse activities, as the need arose. I ran the lab for him during the summers of 1975 and 1980, when he was excavating with students at the site of Les Tambourets in the foothills of the Pyrénées, and he provided technical illustrations for my first book and computational assistance with other projects. We supported each other's research, but did not take an active role in its design or interpretation.

During the early days of my epigraphic research, I decided to ignore the calendrical and astronomical statements that usually introduced hieroglyphic texts, focusing instead on the narrative portion that followed, which I assumed was more likely to contain the grammatical elements that interested me. I mentioned this strategy to David Kelley after the first Palenque Round Table that I attended in June 1980, when we shared a cab to the airport in Villahermosa for our return flights home. Dave quickly disabused me of this notion, saying that phonetic signs and grammatical elements could appear anywhere in an inscription, and in order to understand the function of such elements, I would have to consider all parts of a hieroglyphic text. I realized that he was right and that I would have to take a more holistic approach in my research.

In order to incorporate the calendrical portion of hieroglyphic texts in my research, I needed to find some way of making the necessary transformations from one calendrical notational system to the other *accurately*. Calendrical statements usually consisted of an initial series date based on the Maya era of ca. 5,125 years and a calendar-round expression composed of a *tzolkin* date, representing a position in a 260-

day cycle, and a *haab* date, representing a position in a 365-day cycle, which, when permutated against each other, refers to a single day in a 52-year cycle. For example, the inscription on Stela M at Copan in Figure 12.1 represents the initial series date, 9.16.5.0.0, followed by the *tzolkin* date, 8 Ahau, and the *haab* date, 8 Zodz. I needed some method for moving easily from one cycle to the other, without introducing errors in computation.

My needs happened to coincide with the first availability of hand-held programmable electronic calculators. We were short of funds at that time, so Harvey decided to redeem some savings bonds that his family had purchased in his name during World War II and to use the proceeds to purchase a TI-58 programmable calculator. He went on to write TI-58 programs for converting one calendrical system to the other. With the accuracy provided by those programs, I felt comfortable about including the calendrical portion of hieroglyphic texts in my investigations.[1]

When our linguist colleague Thom Smith-Stark learned of the calendrical programs that Harvey had written for the calculator, he said that it would be much easier to use such programs on Tulane's DEC-2030 mainframe computer, and proceeded to produce a set of programs for that purpose. Inspired by Thom's programs, Harvey saw ways that they could be made more flexible and therefore more useful for my research if we had a personal computer. Accordingly, we purchased an Apple II+ computer, for which he wrote a completely new set of programs that incorporated elements that Thom's programs lacked (including routines for converting Maya dates to dates in the Gregorian calendar and vice versa). He dubbed this set of programs "Mayacal," and it became the mainstay of all further research that I and later he undertook in Maya calendrics and astronomy.[2]

These developments gradually transformed our relationship from one of helping each other with our respective activities to one of collaborative research on topics of mutual interest. In the course of writing programs for the TI-58 calculator, Harvey became very familiar with Maya calendrical cycles and, ultimately, with the glyphs that recorded them and their variants.

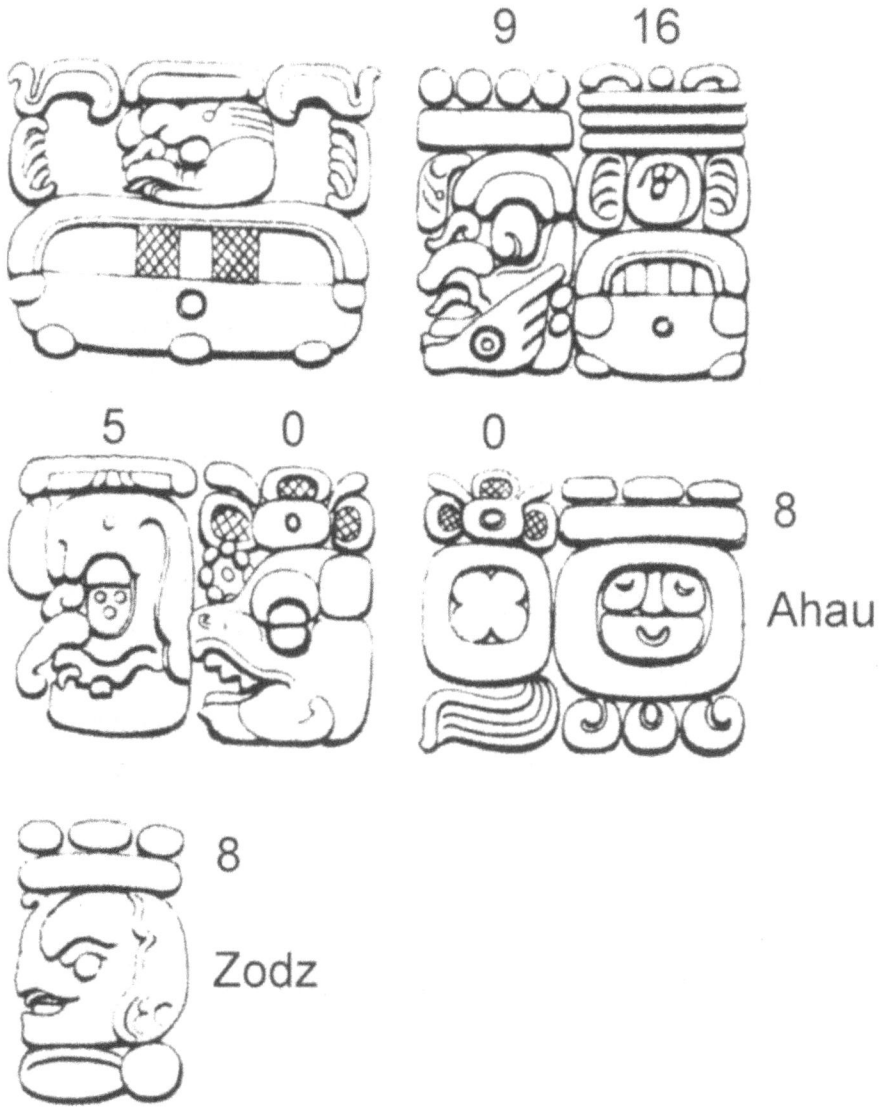

FIGURE 12.1.   The initial series and calendar round on Stela M at Copan, Honduras. After *Archaeology Biologia Centrali-Americana*, by A. P. Maudslay, Vol. 1, Plate 74. London. 1889–1902.

It was during the spring of 1981 that I first began offering a course with the title, "Introduction to Maya Hieroglyphs." I intended it to be a real introduction to this subject, beginning with the Maya number system and the different glyphs for recording them, followed by a unit on the different calendrical cycles and their notational systems. I illustrated this part of the course by pointing out the relevant glyphs on the plaster cast of the large tablet in the Temple of the Sun from Palenque, which was mounted at one end of the exhibition hall in the Middle American Research Institute. Only after the students had demonstrated their ability to perform the necessary calculations for moving from one system to another, first by hand and then using Thom's suite of computer programs, did we move on to dynastic history, using the inscriptions of Piedras Negras and Yaxchilan for this purpose. The last unit of the course was devoted to the history of phonetic decipherment and the grammatical structure of hieroglyphic texts. (I later added a few lectures on the relationship of the Maya script to other writing systems in Mesoamerica.)

Early one morning, about halfway through that semester, I came downstairs to breakfast holding some pages containing a facsimile copy of the eclipse table in the Dresden Codex, saying: "I wonder how this table *really* worked." Harvey looked up from his meal and snatched the pages out of my hand, muttering, "Here, let me have a look at that!" I heard nothing more about it from him for two months, when he presented me with a solution for the table that agreed with the calendrical information in the introduction to the table and predicted all the solar eclipses that had taken place in the world between AD 755 and 783, the beginning and ending dates of the table.

Harvey wrote up his findings in an article that he wanted to submit to *Current Anthropology*. He insisted that I be listed as a co-author because he was afraid that such an article written by a French Palaeolithic archaeologist would not be taken seriously unless it was co-authored by a Mesoamerican specialist. Although I had participated in the project by evaluating his analysis of the table and suggesting ways that his argument might be refined, I wrote only one paragraph in it, suggesting how the table might be recycled, based on information in its introduction.

"Our" article was published in *Current Anthropology* in February 1982. To it were appended several "CA comments" by reviewers, plus a response to them by us. Among the scholars who commented on our article were Floyd Lounsbury, whom I had met two years earlier at Palenque, and the astronomer Anthony Aveni, whom we met for the first time at the Palenque Round Table in June 1983. By then, Floyd had demonstrated how the information in the introduction to the Venus table in the Dresden Codex could be used for calculating the entry date for the table, a discovery of primary importance for understanding the function of other astronomical tables in that codex. Tony became our astronomical mentor and good friend, sending us copies of relevant publications in his field and guiding us in naked-eye astronomy.

Harvey's work on the eclipse table in the Dresden Codex served as the opening wedge and often the reference point for all our later discoveries in Maya astronomy. With it, I was able to work out the method that we call *cross-dating*,[3] whereby eclipse glyphs in almanacs containing only *tzolkin* dates could be cross-referenced with eclipse dates in the eclipse table or one of its multiples, which could be correlated with dates in the Gregorian calendar. This was the case with the zodiacal almanac in the Paris Codex, so-named because its middle and lower registers picture a series of animals biting solar eclipse glyphs, each of which represents one of the thirteen constellations of the Maya zodiac (Figure 12.2).[4] The almanac begins with the *tzolkin* date, 12 Lamat, which is the same *tzolkin* date found at the beginning of the eclipse table, and it introduces none of the several hundred other almanacs or tables in the Maya codices. The 12 Lamat *tzolkin* date in the eclipse table is accompanied by a long-count date that Harvey had demonstrated could be accepted in historical time as written. The same *tzolkin* date in the zodiacal almanac lacks such a long-count date and for that reason cannot be placed in historical time.

Or so it seemed at first. However, it occurred to me that because no other almanac in the Maya codices begins on 12 Lamat, it may have

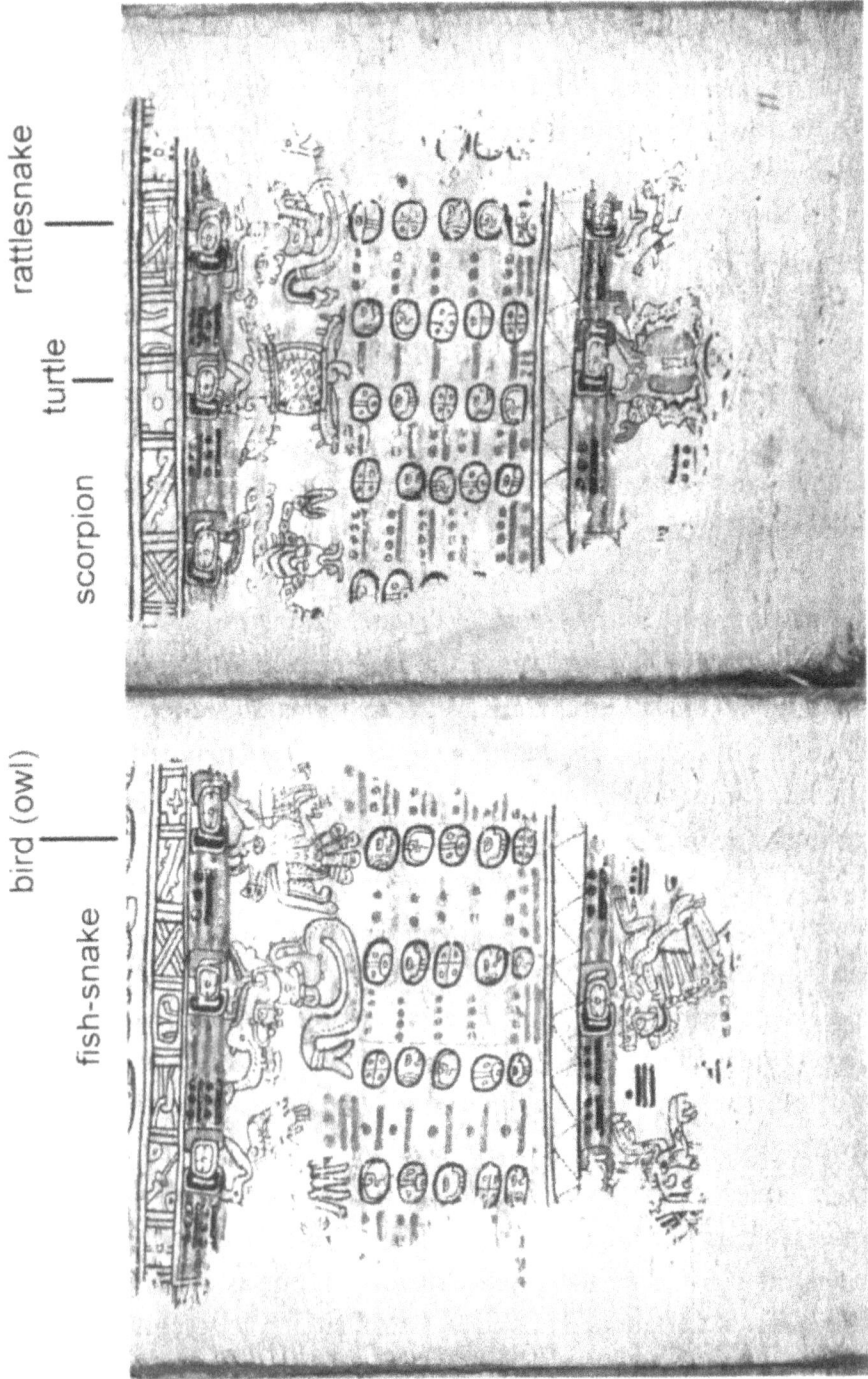

FIGURE 12.2.   Animals representing constellations in the zodiacal almanac on pages 23 and 24 of the Paris Codex.

been intended to represent the 12 Lamat date at the beginning of the eclipse table, and I decided to test the possibility that it began on the same day in the Gregorian calendar, in other words, cross-dating it with the eclipse table.

The sixteenth-century Maya dictionary known as the *Calepino de Motul* associates three of the animals in the zodiacal almanac with well-known Western constellations: the rattlesnake with the Pleiades in Taurus, the turtle with Orion,[5] and the scorpion with Scorpius (see Figure 12.2). The Pleiades and Orion are adjacent constellations, but Scorpius would have been at the opposite end of the ecliptic from Orion, leading Harvey to suggest that the animals in the zodiacal almanac represented *pairs* of constellations at opposite ends of the sky, a hypothesis that was later confirmed by a text on the façade of the Governor's Palace at Uxmal (see the text that follows). Cross-dating the zodiacal almanac in the Paris Codex with the eclipse table in the Dresden Codex correctly placed the Pleiades on the western end of the horizon at sunrise on November 10, AD 755, and Orion and Scorpius at opposite ends of the horizon—Orion in the west and Scorpius in the east—one month later on December 8 in the same year. (The animal to the right of the rattlesnake, much of which is no longer visible, would then have represented Libra, which appeared opposite the Pleiades on November 10, 755). These relationships result from cross-dating the zodiacal almanac with the eclipse table.[6]

The basis for cross-dating in the example just described was the use of the same *tzolkin* date—12 Lamat—for beginning the table and the almanac. However, sometimes an internal date associated with similar pictures can be used for cross-dating an almanac with a table. The two instruments in question are the Venus table in the Dresden Codex and an almanac in the same codex that is also concerned with the movements of Venus, but unlike the Venus table, does not have a long-count date that would permit it to be correlated directly with the Gregorian calendar, and their initial *tzolkin* dates are also different (*1* Ahau in the Venus table and *11* Ahau in the thematically related almanac). Although the dates have the same name (Ahau), their coefficients are different ("1" in the table and "11" in the almanac), and they are 140 days apart in the *tzolkin*. Clearly, they are not useful for cross-dating. The picture they share is one associated with the summer solstice, namely, the image of a deity seated on a skyband with a star or Venus glyph as one of its elements (Figure 12.3). The almanac contains nine pictures and 20 rows, with a column of 20 *tzolkin* dates associated with each picture.

The summer solstice is the theme of the sixth picture in the almanac (Figure 12.3b). The *tzolkin* date associated with that picture in the fourth row of the almanac is 11 Cib. So also is the date in the fifth row of the third column associated with the summer solstice picture on the first page of the Venus table (Figure 12.3a), a date corresponding to June 13, AD 968, in the Gregorian calendar. The summer solstice fell on June 21st that year and was followed two days later by a heliacal rise of Venus. Both events are accommodated by intervals associated with the 11 Cib date and the solstitial picture. The long-count position of the 11 Cib date in the Venus table can be used for determining the long-count position of the beginning of the almanac and placing it in historical time.

This example illustrates the principle of "triangulation" that under-lies the cross-dating method, namely, that three independent kinds of information are necessary for making such a connection, in this case: (1) a *tzolkin* date shared by the almanac and table (11 Cib), (2) a reference to a heavenly body (Venus), and (3) a reference to a station of the solar year (the summer solstice). The *tzolkin* date and one refer-ence to an astronomical event are both necessary for the triangulation. The third piece of information may also be astronomical, or it may refer to an event in another kind of cycle: a ritual associated with a day in the 365-day *haab* (e.g., New Year's Day), or an agricultural activity, such as planting, that is restricted to a season of the tropical year. Tables and almanacs contain cultural as well as astronomical information, always associated with *tzolkin* dates, which facilitate the task of cross-dating by means of triangulation.

The calculations involved in working with the multiple cycles of the Maya calendar require an understanding of modular arithmetic, a

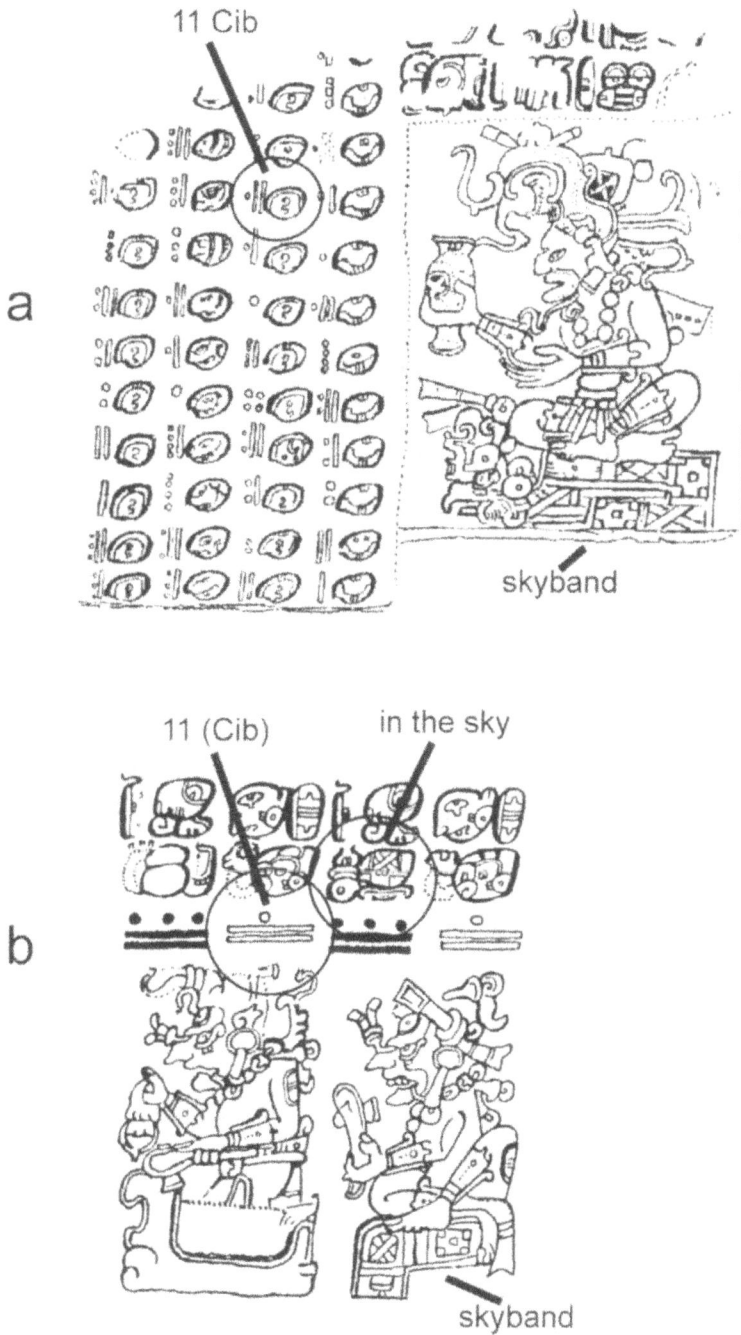

FIGURE 12.3. Summer solstice pictures in the Venus table and almanac in the Dresden Codex. a. D.46a. b. D.32c.

After the second edition of *Códices mayas*, by J. Antonio Villacorta C. and Carlos A. Villacorta, pages 76, 102. Guatemala, Tipografía Nacional. 1976.

subject I was first exposed to in seventh grade, where I was taught how to check multiplication by "casting out nines" Also necessary is an ability to work with multiple notations and to convert one notation to another. My somewhat delayed training in trigonometry was ideal for this purpose, because trigonometric functions like sine, cosine, and tangent are notations that can be transformed into each other.

During the period when Harvey and I were decoding the astronomical tables and almanacs in the Maya codices, I often found myself engaging in thought experiments, which, if they seemed promising, I would check with an electronic calculator. If those calculations held up, I would ask Harvey to modify one of his calendrical programs to fit the conditions I had in mind so that I could check them in historical time. This was the approach I used in the two sets of examples described previously, and it was one we both applied to other astronomical tables and almanacs in the Maya codices.

By 1987, I felt that our research on the Dresden Codex was far enough along that it was time to share it with some of the graduate students at Tulane. To this end, I decided to offer a graduate seminar on the Maya codices during the fall semester of that year. Ten students signed up for that course. My lectures and the course readings were based on the tables and almanacs in the Dresden Codex. The students were assigned chunks of the Madrid Codex to analyze. I saw this as a way to extend what Harvey and I had learned about the Dresden Codex to the analysis of thematically related sections of the Madrid Codex. Harvey and Mary Elizabeth Smith, our colleague in the Art Department, also attended the class meetings. Harvey decided to undertake his own research project for the class, selecting a pair of almanacs in the first part of the Madrid Codex that seemed to have affinities with the seasonal tables in the Dresden Codex. By the end of the semester, he was able to show that they represented the counterpart in the Madrid Codex of those tables in the Dresden Codex, suggesting that it might be possible to relate other parts of the Madrid Codex to tables or almanacs in the Dresden Codex.

I offered the Codex seminar again two years later, in which seven students enrolled. Merideth Paxton, who was a visiting professor in the Art Department while Betsy Smith was on leave, participated in the 1989 seminar as well.

At that time, the Madrid Codex was relatively unknown territory. Several of the student papers from the two seminars had interesting insights. One of the more enterprising students in the first seminar suggested that I should prepare an edited volume containing the most interesting papers. That seemed like a good idea to me, because it would give the authors of the chosen papers experience in preparing an article for publication and responding to reviewers' comments.

One student, Gabrielle Vail, who participated in both seminars, had developed a keen interest in the Maya codices, which became the focus of her dissertation and later career. When she also expressed an interest in becoming an editor, I suggested that she join me as a co-editor of the collection of student papers, which eventually bore the title, *Papers on the Madrid Codex*. It contained chapters by Cassandra Bill, Donald Graff, Christopher von Nagy, and Gaby based on their seminar papers. I wrote the introductory and concluding chapters.[7]

As I explained in my introduction to the volume, the papers broke new ground "by relating the calendrical structure of almanacs to their pictures and captions."[8] When the almanacs in a section had a common theme, it was sometimes possible to show that they referred to events taking place at the same time in different years (Vail). In another section, the partial overlap in pictures and their associated dates in multiple almanacs suggested a sequential relationship within a single year (Bill). And it was possible to provide both absolute and relative dates for the almanacs in still another section (Graff). A section with unusually long texts inspired a glyph block-by-glyph block transcription and translation and a comparison of their content with related ethnohistorical and ethnographic accounts (von Nagy).

Harvey's and my interest in astronomy was not limited to the Maya codices. In our work with the zodiacal almanac in the Paris Codex, we had become familiar with the signs for the constellations, which were also represented in murals and on the façades of buildings at Classic-period archaeological sites, such as Bonampak and Chichen Itza.

In January 1993, while we were on vacation with Anne and Donald Bradburn in Yucatan, I announced that I would like to spend a day working with Elut on our dictionary of the Hocaba dialect of Yucatecan Maya (see Chapter 8). When Harvey asked me what he and the Bradburns could do that day, I suggested that they visit the site of Uxmal, which they did.

After they returned from Uxmal at the end of the day, Harvey exclaimed: "Why didn't you tell me about the hieroglyphic text on the façade of the Governor's Palace?" I replied that there wasn't one! He said, "Wait until my slides come back!" And sure enough, there were several rows of hieroglyphic signs on that façade, some of which were recognizably astronomical—Sun, Moon, and Venus.

The presence of the glyph for Venus in the second row of the text on the façade of the Governor's Palace was not surprising, because Tony Aveni had demonstrated that the building is aligned to an extreme position of Venus on the horizon.[9] What caught Harvey's eye was that some of the glyphs in that text were thematically similar to some of the animals in the zodiacal almanac in the Paris Codex: a scorpion, two snakes, a frog, two birds, a human skeletal head, and a bat or peccary. Four of the animals appear in the top row of the Uxmal inscription: one of the snakes, the scorpion, the frog, and one of the birds (Figure 12.4).

One of the snakes in the zodiacal almanac in the Paris Codex is depicted with rattles and has been identified with the Pleiades, as discussed previously. The other snake has a forked tail and is commonly called "fish-snake"; we have identified it with Sagittarius in that almanac (see Figure 12.2). Sagittarius and Scorpius are adjacent constellations in the sky, and the fish-snake glyph shares the left side of the first row in the façade text on the Governor's Palace with the glyph for Scorpius occupying the position at the left end of the row (Figure 12.4).

In our research on the Paris zodiacal almanac, we had postulated that the bird (an owl) to the right of the fish-snake referred to Gemini.

FIGURE 12.4. The hieroglyphic text on the façade of the Governor's Palace at Uxmal, Yucatan, Mexico. Drawing by Harvey M. Bricker.

The glyph on the right end of the first row of the Uxmal façade text resembled the head of a bird. If it referred to Gemini, it meant that it was paired with Sagittarius at the other end of the row. We were able to show that these constellations appeared at opposite ends of the horizon at sunrise on the day when Venus could be seen reaching its maximum northerly extreme, thereby confirming Harvey's interpretation of the layout of the zodiacal almanac in the Paris Codex. Thus, this particular configuration of constellations was what was actually visible in the sky at Uxmal at the several times when this Venus extreme took place during the period when the Palace was occupied. Ultimately, this discovery led to a joint publication relating this inscription to the architecture of the building and a Venus alignment.[10]

Harvey and I returned to Uxmal one year later so that he could check the accuracy of his drawing by examining the inscription through binoculars. His mother, who was on vacation with us in Yucatan at that time, accompanied us to the site. The steps leading up to the platform on which the Governor's Palace was built were steep and had no railing. His mother went up the steps on her hands and knees. Once there, she sat on a large rock in the shade while we were at work. After we finished, she approached the steps gingerly and hesitated. Two young men, seeing her plight, lifted her by her elbows and trotted her down the stairs. This was but one of the memorable experiences she had traveling with us in Yucatan.[11]

Some years later, Harvey spotted a photograph of a carved stone bench with glyphs for the Sun, Moon, and Venus in an exhibition catalog. The bench was originally located along the back wall of a vaulted stone structure in a residential complex at Copan in Honduras. With the help of David Webster, the project director, who provided us with information on the orientation of the building in which the bench had been found, we were able to determine that it was oriented to the horizon position of sunset of solar zenith passage and that the references to the Moon and Venus were consistent with a visible lunar eclipse and the first and last visibility of Venus as the morning star that took place during solar zenith passages in the late eighth century AD. Our first opportunity to see the bench itself came in 2001, two years after we published our report on its astronomical significance,[12] when we were invited to participate in a conference at Copan.

Our most recent detour away from Maya codices into monumental texts came in 2012, when an article appeared in the journal *Science* announcing the discovery of murals containing astronomical records on the walls of a small building at the site of Xultun in Guatemala.[13] My contribution to the analysis of these records was the decipherment of a hieroglyphic text containing glyphs for a lunar eclipse and the constellation Orion, which were accompanied by dates in the 260-day cycle known as the *tzolkin*. We were able to show that one of those *tzolkin* dates referred to a total lunar eclipse that would have been visible at Xultun on 7 December AD 792, a date consistent with other information on the possible age of the building. For the publication, we teamed up with Tony Aveni, who had been a co-author of the *Science* article.[14]

These forays into the astronomy of stone monuments led to the replacement of the Maya Codices seminar I taught in the late 1980s with one I co-taught with Harvey covering astronomical topics appropriate for both Maya archaeology and codices. We offered the seminar called "Maya Archaeoastronomy" three times before we retired, in 1996, 2001, and 2003, to both undergraduate and graduate students.

The well-known art historian Elizabeth Boone replaced Mary Elizabeth Smith when she retired from Tulane in the mid-1990s. At Elizabeth's suggestion, we co-taught a seminar on Mesoamerican divinatory codices during the fall of 1998, in which twenty-two students enrolled. I, of course, emphasized the astronomical texts in the Maya codices, and Elizabeth covered the divinatory almanacs in the Central Mexican codices. It was from her that I first learned about the Venus almanacs in Codex Borgia, to which I applied the same method of analysis that had proved useful in studying Maya codices. It was as much a learning experience for me as for the students.

At a reception during a professional meeting near the end of the 1990s, our friend and colleague John Justeson came up to me and said that he thought that it was time for Harvey and me to collect into a single volume the articles on Maya astronomy we had written over the years. In discussing this suggestion with Harvey later, we agreed that we did not want to assemble already published articles together in a collected work. Instead, we decided that it would make more sense to go back to our original work, update it as necessary, add new information that we had discovered in the meantime, and work it together into an integrated volume to be called *Astronomy in the Maya Codices*. That proved to be a very ambitious undertaking that we completed five years after we retired from Tulane, more than a decade after we began the project (see Chapter 14).

In our analysis of the astronomical texts and pictures in the codices, we emphasized three general themes. First, we placed our current knowledge about the tables and almanacs in its developmental context, tracing the history of European and American research on those instruments from the mid-nineteenth to the early twenty-first century. Second, we attempted—usually successfully—to place the astronomical, meteorological, and other phenomena actually mentioned in the codices in historical time, most often in the seventh through the sixteen centuries AD. This was possible because, although in the codices these phenomena are dated in terms of Maya calendrical cycles, it has been possible since the mid-twentieth century to correlate the Maya calendar with the Western—Julian and Gregorian—calendar. And third, we emphasized the theme of the "commensuration" of multiple astronomical cycles in a single text, which often proved useful for placing them in historical time. Thus, the text in the synodic Mars table in the Dresden Codex mentions an eclipse season coinciding with a retrograde period of Mars. Similarly, the seasonal table in the same Codex aligns eclipse seasons with solstices and equinoxes in the tropical year.

Our work with Maya astronomy reconnected me with the natural sciences, especially physics, whose problem-solving methods I had enjoyed learning about in high school and my first year of college, before shifting my attention to the humanities, especially philosophy, and later, in graduate school, to the social sciences, specifically anthropology. Because, for the Maya, naked-eye astronomy served as a tool for astrology, the texts in their astronomical tables and almanacs were also concerned with other matters that were central to their lives, namely, agriculture, meteorology, procreation, and several kinds of recurrent rituals. The task of decoding those texts benefitted from the multiple kinds of research I had engaged in earlier: epigraphy, to be sure, but also ethnography, folklore, linguistics, ethnohistory, and ethnobotany, enabling me to integrate what I had learned before in addressing a new set of problems. In this sense, our work with what has to be called *cultural astronomy* represents the culmination of my intellectual journey, one to which I have devoted more than 30 years of my career.

Recognition of the value of my scholarship came suddenly and from an unexpected quarter. One day in late April 1991, I received a telephone call from Vogtie with the most amazing news that I had just been elected to the National Academy of Sciences. It came as a "bolt from the blue," for I had no idea that I was being considered for this honor. Other members of the Anthropology section of the Academy came on the line to congratulate me as well, and in the days that followed, I received congratulatory letters from additional members and other colleagues who learned about my election to this national organization.[15]

The National Academy of Sciences was established in 1863 by an Act of Congress at the instigation of Abraham Lincoln. It has the mission of providing scientific advice to the U.S. government.

My induction took place one year later in Washington, DC. Three members of my family (Anne, Frank, and my mother) and three members of Harvey's family (his mother; sister Helen; and her daughter, Elizabeth) joined us on that occasion. Harvey and I hosted a dinner on one of the evenings we were in Washington that included, in addition to the members of our families, Vogtie and Nan and Frank's friends Andy Vogt (no relation to Vogtie) and his wife, Barbara, in whose home in Washington my relatives were staying. Because the Reiflers (my family) who attended had been "China hands," we chose a Chinese restaurant for this occasion, at which we had a delicious meal because Anne gave our orders in Chinese.

In 2002, I was informed that I had been elected to the American Philosophical Society in Philadelphia, the oldest scholarly society in the United States. The American Philosophical Society was founded by Benjamin Franklin in 1743 for the purpose of "promoting useful knowledge." It does so today with lectures in all fields of knowledge at semi-annual meetings in April and November, in publications, in a research library of manuscripts and other collections internationally recognized for their enduring historical value, [16] and in several grants and fellowship programs.

I was inducted during the April meeting in 2003. Harvey accompanied me, and both of us enjoyed the program of lectures and the collegial atmosphere so much that we regularly attend the meetings at least once a year. After we retired from teaching, the meetings kept us in touch with what was happening in our country and the rest of the world.

NOTES

1. The large glyph block that introduces the inscription in Figure 12.1 indicates that the five glyph blocks that follow it refer to an initial series date. The first three glyph blocks in the initial series date have bar-and-dot numbers above them (one bar representing "5" and one dot representing "1"). The bar-and-dot number above the first block is "9" (one bar and four dots). The number above the second block is composed of three bars and one dot, representing "16" (3 x 5 = 15 + 1). The number above the third block has a single bar representing "5." The fourth and fifth blocks are surmounted by signs for "zero." Therefore, the full expression can be transcribed as 9.16.5.0.0. It is paired with the calendar-round date, 8 Ahau 8 Zodz, the two sets of expressions corresponding to 10 April AD 756 in our Gregorian calendar.

   The main signs in the glyph blocks represent temporal periods that, for the most part, increase in size by a factor of 20. The fifth block refers to the number of days, which is zero, and the fourth block refers to the number of 20-day "months," which is also zero. The third block refers to five 360-day years or 1800 days. The second block refers to sixteen 20-year periods or 115,200 days. And the first block represents nine 400-year periods or 25,920,000 days.

Both the initial series date and the two parts of the calendar round are legible in this inscription. In others, one or both parts of the calendar round may be damaged and therefore illegible. The damaged parts can be restored by reducing the initial series notation to a cumulative total of days and extracting multiples of the 260-day *tzolkin* or the 365-day *haab* and analyzing the remainders. Such calculations can be done more accurately by an electronic calculator than by hand.

2. After he left Tulane, Thom expanded the scope of his programs, incorporating routines for calculating Moon ages and additional constants for correlating the Maya with the Western calendar.

3. Victoria R. Bricker and Harvey M. Bricker, "A Method for Cross-Dating Almanacs with Tables in the Dresden Codex," in *The Sky in Mayan Literature,* ed. Anthony F. Aveni (New York: Oxford University Press, 1992), 43–86.

4. Harvey M. Bricker and Victoria R. Bricker, "Zodiacal References in the Maya Codices" in *The Sky in Mayan Literature,* ed. Anthony F. Aveni (New York: Oxford University Press, 1992), 148–83.

5. Floyd C. Lounsbury, "Astronomical Knowledge and Its Uses at Bonampak, Mexico" in *Archaeoastronomy in the New World*, ed. Anthony F. Aveni (Cambridge, UK: Cambridge University Press, 1982), 166–67.

6. In advocating the cross-dating method for placing almanacs in historical time, I was challenging the long-held view that all almanacs had a divinatory function and therefore could be recycled indefinitely. If almanacs contain historically specific references, then they cannot be used over and over again. However, other

almanacs were undoubtedly used and reused for divinatory purposes.

7. Victoria R. Bricker and Gabrielle Vail, eds., *Papers on the Madrid Codex* Publication 64 (New Orleans, LA: Tulane University, Middle American Research Institute, 1997).

Subsequently, Gaby teamed up with Anthony Aveni in co-editing a second volume on the Madrid Codex: Gabrielle Vail and Anthony Aveni, eds., *The Madrid Codex: New Approaches to Understanding an Ancient Maya Manuscript* (Boulder: University of Colorado Press, 1997).

And in 2013, she published a commentary on the Madrid Codex [Gabrielle Vail, *Códice de Madrid: Descripción de los folios* (Guatemala City: Universidad Mesoamericana, 2013)], as well as another volume on the Maya codices, co-authored with Christine Hernández, one of the students who had participated in the second Codex seminar: Gabrielle Vail and Christine Hernández, *Re-Creating Primordial Time: Foundation Rituals and Mythology in the Postclassic Maya Codices* (Boulder: University of Colorado Press, 2013).

8. *Ibid.*, p. 25.

9. Anthony F. Aveni, "Possible Astronomical Orientations in Ancient Mesoamerica," in *Archaeoastronomy in Pre-Columbian America*, ed. Anthony F. Aveni (Austin: University of Texas Press, 1975), 182–85.

10. Harvey M. Bricker and Victoria R. Bricker, "Astronomical References in the Throne Inscription of the Palace of the Governor at Uxmal," *Cambridge Archaeological Journal* 6, no. 2 (1996): 191–229.

11. Another such experience had taken place a few days earlier, when the three of us visited Ebtun. It was Sunday, and when we arrived at the plaza on foot, the door of the church opened suddenly, and some men came out in a group. I recognized two of them and introduced them to Harvey and his mother. One of them grabbed her, kissed her on both cheeks, and called her *Mamacita*. She was startled, but evidently not offended, because she signed the Christmas card that she sent us at the end of the year as "Mamacita."

12. Harvey M. Bricker and Victoria R. Bricker, "Astronomical Orientation of the Skyband Bench at Copán," *Journal of Field Archaeology* 26, no. 4 (1999): 435–42.

13. William A. Saturno, David Stuart, Anthony F. Aveni, and Franco Rossi, "Ancient Maya Astronomical Tables from Xultun, Guatemala," *Science* 336 no. 6082 (2012): 714–17.

14. Victoria R. Bricker, Anthony F. Aveni, and Harvey M. Bricker, "Deciphering the Handwriting on the Wall: Some Astronomical Interpretations of the Recent Discoveries at Xultun, Guatemala," *Latin American Antiquity* 25, no. 2 (2014): 152–69.

15. A somewhat ironic development (and certainly one of the oddities of my career) is that I was holding a grant from the National Endowment for the *Humanities* at that time.

16. From the Mission Statement of the American Philosophical Society, page v of the Yearbook for 2006 (Philadelphia: American Philosophical Society, 2006).

13

KATRINA:
AFTERMATH OF A DISASTER

During the last week of August in 2005, the storm brewing in the Gulf was heading for New Orleans. My sister Anne completed a five-day visit with us near the end of that week and left to fly to Seattle, with a change of planes in Salt Lake City, before going on to her home in Anchorage. Classes were scheduled to begin on Monday, and I was making last-minute preparations for my courses. Late on Friday afternoon, I attended a meeting of the President's Faculty Advisory Committee in Scott Cowen's office. His last words to us were: "I do hope that this storm misses New Orleans."

That evening it became apparent that the storm that would become Hurricane Katrina was not going to miss New Orleans. As it approached the coast, it was wobbling, and it was not yet clear whether it would veer to the east or to the west when it made landfall. Harvey and I had decided that we would evacuate New Orleans the next morning, but we did not know which way to go. If the storm veered to the east, we should go toward Houston. But if it veered to the west, we should head for Atlanta. This uncertainty meant that we could not make a hotel reservation in one of those cities before we went to bed that night.

By the time we woke up early on Saturday morning, it was clear that the storm would move east after it reached the coast. We called the hotel near the airport in Houston where we liked to stay and discovered to our amazement that it still had a room available for four nights. In packing, we benefited from our experience during our evacuation ahead of Hurricane Ivan the previous September (see Chapter 14). This time we packed the car in an hour and a half, taking along a notebook containing the chapters of our book that we had already written, as well as some books and other materials we would need for later chapters. We left our house fifteen minutes before mandatory evacuation orders were issued for the entire region, but in our haste we forgot to close and secure the shutters on one bedroom window, which later imploded from the force of the storm.

Our drive from New Orleans to Houston was uneventful and was completed in the normal seven hours. After checking into the hotel, we settled down for what we initially thought was a stay of three or four days before returning to New Orleans after the storm had passed.

The next morning (Sunday), we woke up to the grim news that the storm would indeed pass directly over New Orleans. An announcement on the Tulane website said that the school would shut down at noon. At that point, I called Gaby Vail and asked her to serve as a clearinghouse for colleagues and friends who might contact her for news about our whereabouts. She agreed to do this and suggested that we establish an e-mail account at yahoo.com. We followed her advice and sent her our new e-mail address. I also telephoned my mother and asked her to inform the rest of the family that we were out of harm's way in Texas.

Katrina made landfall at the Mississippi/Louisiana border on the morning of August 29 (Monday). Although there was considerable wind damage in New Orleans from the 80-mile-per-hour winds as the hurricane came ashore, it was not, at first, the catastrophe that had been predicted. However, later that day, those who had remained in the city gradually became aware that the levees in several parts of the city had failed, and that flood waters were pouring in from Lake Pontchartrain north of the city, eventually covering 80 percent of the urban area.

We sat with our eyes glued to the television set in our room or in a large common area on the first floor of the hotel for the rest of the day, as report after report of the devastation in New Orleans rolled in. In the meantime, relief workers from all over the country had moved into our hotel and other hotels in the vicinity in preparation for a call from the governor of Louisiana to move into the state to help with the crisis there (a call that never came!). Pallets of supplies were stacked against the walls of the hallways, as planes brought more and more volunteers to the staging area that the hotel had become.

At one point, the governor appeared on television and urged the people who had left the New Orleans area not to come back. We should stay where we were, she said soothingly, where we could be safe and have access to food and shelter. We realized then that we would not be going home soon, if ever. Our reservation was limited to two more nights at the hotel. It was time for us to look for somewhere else to go.

It was then that Harvey remembered our friends Don and Barbara Parrish, who owned a ranch in the hill country of Texas, about a day's drive northwest of Houston. They were often away, but Harvey thought it was worth calling them to see whether they were at home. Don answered the phone, and when he learned of our plight, he said: "You-all come right over here!"

We decided to stay in Houston for one more day (Tuesday) in order to take care of some financial matters. On Wednesday, we drove over to the Parrish ranch, a few miles outside Fredericksburg in a region that had been settled by German immigrants during the nineteenth century. The differences in climate and ethnicity between the hill country of Texas and southeastern Louisiana could not have been starker. In New Orleans, we were accustomed to a humid climate and a cuisine and culture that blended Caribbean and French elements, whereas it was very dry in the region around Fredericksburg, the streets in the city had German names instead of French, and the local cuisine had both German and Mexican roots. I was disoriented by these changes for days afterwards.

The Parrishes welcomed us with open arms. That evening they took us along to a dinner party at the home of two of their friends, where we were asked to explain what was going on in New Orleans. People could not have been nicer to us.

There were several unoccupied houses on the Parrish ranch, one of which had been recently renovated and placed on the market. They decided to take it off the market and made it available to us for, as Don said, "as long as we needed it." Don also arranged for the installation of a telephone line to the house so that we could have Internet service while we were living there.

Harvey and I decided that, with all the uncertainty that had come into our lives, the best way of weathering this situation would be to focus on the research for our book. Accordingly, we purchased some folding tables and chairs, lamps, a heavy-duty printer for our laptop computer, and a small bookcase, which we set up at one end of the large living room in the house. This became our office for the remainder of our stay on the Parrish ranch.

Through Gaby, some of our friends and colleagues found us, as did graduate students who were writing theses and dissertations under our direction. An acquaintance of ours Randa Marhenke, whom I had originally met at one of Linda Schele's Maya workshops in Austin and who had been a passenger on the Easter cruise for which we had lectured in 1988, contacted us and asked whether we would like to have a copy of her digital library of Mesoamerican books and articles. Of course, we accepted her kind offer. The seven DVDs she sent us were a veritable treasure trove of relevant materials for our research, including some sources of which we were previously unaware that otherwise would never have been mentioned in our book.

During the weeks leading up to Hurricane Katrina at the end of August, it had become apparent that Harvey's mother's health was declining. His sister reported that the family had decided not to schedule a party for her 94th birthday on August 17, but only to visit her briefly on that day. Her health continued to decline in September while we were in Texas. In one of the daily telephone conversations Harvey had with her during that month, she said that she wished that she could see him again, but that she understood why that was not possible for him at that time. Nevertheless, it came as a shock to us one morning when she said goodbye to him. At that time, it was impossible for him to leave Texas because Hurricane Rita was bearing down on Houston, and four million Houstonians were stuck in traffic fleeing the city. All the roads between Fredericksburg and major cities with airports were clogged with the evacuation traffic. The evacuees who had succeeded in getting out of Houston had cleaned the shelves of food and bottled water in the grocery stores in Fredericksburg.

The eye of the storm made landfall well east of Houston on September 24, and that city was spared (although much of western Louisiana was damaged). But it took a few days before all the residents could return home. In contrast with the chaos that accompanied the attempted evacuation of Houston, the much-criticized evacuation of New Orleans and its hinterland one month earlier was a model of careful planning and cooperation.

Harvey's mother died on September 27, and her funeral was scheduled for Saturday, October 1, 2005. By then, the roads had cleared, and we were able to fly out of San Antonio to Philadelphia, where we rented a car and drove to her retirement home in Ephrata, where the funeral service was held. Harvey's family gathered from all directions to honor this kind and generous woman, who had meant so much to them while she was alive. She was buried beside his father in St. John's cemetery outside Shiremanstown, where she was born.

In the meantime, our tenant had been able to visit our house in New Orleans and check on its condition. He found that the National Guard had set up a command post in front of our house, which happened to be in one of the few parts of the city that did not flood. This meant that our house was protected from the looting that took place in a few homes elsewhere in our neighborhood.

Our tenant was called back to work in New Orleans and stayed for a time with his friends in the suburbs. He eventually returned to his apartment on the other side of our duplex, where he was able to keep us informed of what was happening in our city. We asked him to let us know when water, electricity, and gas had been restored in our neighborhood, when it was possible to refuel cars at neighborhood gas stations, and when grocery stores had re-opened and were well stocked. We stayed in our borrowed house on the Parrish ranch for another two weeks, during which we made plans for our return to New Orleans.

By then, cold weather had come to the hill country of Texas. There was frost on the ground in the mornings. It was time for us to get flu shots, but the local doctors were hoarding their supplies of vaccine for their regular patients and were not helpful to the refugees from Hurricane Katrina. We were told to inquire at the Good Samaritan Center in Fredericksburg, which was willing to give us tetanus shots, but not flu shots. Their supply of flu vaccine was provided by the federal government and was earmarked for indigent residents of the region, not people like us.

Our solution to this problem was to suggest a barter arrangement with the Good Samaritan Center, whereby we offered to donate the office furniture we had purchased for our stay in Texas, but would no longer need after returning to New Orleans, in exchange for flu shots. The Center needed the lamps, bookcase, and folding chairs and tables that we offered and gladly agreed to this proposal. We did, however, pay for the flu shots anyway.

About the time we were making these arrangements, I received an e-mail requesting my presence at a meeting of President Cowen's Faculty Advisory Committee in Houston on October 19. That obligation set the timetable for our return to New Orleans; it made sense to carry on to our home in Louisiana the day after the meeting.

The committee meeting took place in what had become the command center for Tulane's administration in exile on the outskirts of Houston. Options discussed at that meeting focused on the economic survival of the university. Harvey and I drove back to New Orleans the next day.

After leaving Houston on Thursday morning, we headed to Beaumont. On the way, we gradually saw evidence of Hurricane Rita's destruction in East Texas. I-10 runs some miles north of the area near the coast where the most serious damage occurred. We saw signs along the highway that had been bent into weird shapes, some of which resembled modern sculptures on display in art museums. Some houses had been blown off their foundations and collapsed. Others had serious roof damage. Still others had blue tarps spread over their roofs (about which more later). In some areas, pine trees whose trunks had snapped littered the side of the road.

The western part of Louisiana had evidence of similar damage, particularly in the region around Lake Charles. As we continued eastward, the scenery gradually returned to normal. Then, as we approached New Orleans, we began to see evidence of Katrina's mighty winds. Many trees were down on both sides of the highway, there were houses with only their walls standing, and collapsed buildings could be seen here and there.

The marshes along the western edge of Lake Pontchartrain were flooded. When we reached the south shore, we could see evidence of wind damage and some flooding. Looking over the city from an overpass of I-10, we saw a sea of blue roofs. In some areas, virtually every roof was damaged, and the damage was covered with blue tarps, neatly held down with strips of wood that had been nailed to the decking below. We later learned that FEMA had asked the Army Corps of Engineers to help residents protect their damaged roofs, and this work was well underway. When we reached our house at 911 Cherokee Street, there was a piece of paper taped beside our mailbox, informing us that we were not eligible for a blue roof because there was no visible damage to our roof (true). We also discovered that a cousin of Harvey's, who is a civil engineer who was working with FEMA in New Orleans, was one of the people involved in certifying houses for blue roofs. Apparently, members of the Corps had checked the roof of every residence in the city, identifying those whose roofs were damaged, but not completely destroyed, and therefore qualified for blue roofing.

As we drove south through Lakeview, a wealthy district near Lake Pontchartrain, toward Uptown, the district where we lived, we passed block after block of homes that had been flooded, whose yards and bushes were dead and brown. We could tell from the high-water marks on the houses how high the waters rose. Some of the marks reached to the top of front doors. The high-water line gradually dropped as we moved from north to south. The streets of Lakeview were deserted, but on some blocks there were signs of activity, namely, the piles of soggy drywall that had been ripped out from the interiors of houses and placed on the curbs, indicating that the owners intended to refurbish them. On Broadway, the area between Claiborne and Willow Street not far from Tulane, showed evidence of flooding; many of the magnolia trees on that street had died because their roots had been standing in water. By the time we reached Freret a few blocks from our house, the only signs of Katrina were some fallen trees and damaged roofs.

We came home to a house that was structurally intact except for a broken window in our bedroom and the loss of "hats" on our chimneys, blown off by Katrina's winds. A tree in an adjacent yard brought down most of our fences, giving our property an unkempt air. On the other hand, some purple impatiens that were planted before we left, were in full bloom when we returned, a bright spot of color in an otherwise messy landscape.

Virtually everyone returning to New Orleans had to cope with a refrigerator containing rotten food and a house full of small insects because the electricity had been off for almost two months, and we were no exception. (Our next-door neighbor, who remained in her house through the hurricane and five days afterward until the water was shut off, had the foresight to remove everything from her refrigerator before she drove away; she must have been one of the few exceptions.) The first order of business for many returnees was to wind tape around the refrigerator so that it would stay closed and haul it out of the house to the curb. The odor of our refrigerator was indescribably awful, and I was very happy when some friends, who had a dolly, got it out of our house. After that, I could breathe more easily, both literally and figuratively.

In the vocabulary of post-Katrina New Orleans, refrigerators were called *white goods* (even though many of them were not white). So also were washing machines and dryers that were ruined by the flood. They were removed by teams of entrepreneurs who sold the items to representatives of the Environmental Protection Agency. The refrigerators contained freon and the switches of the other appliances had other kinds of environmentally harmful substances that had to be disposed of properly. Our refrigerator remained on the curb for only 24 hours. The next afternoon, Harvey spotted a man using a "Bobcat" to move abandoned refrigerators to a collection point around the corner, where they were being lifted into a truck, and persuaded him to include ours in his haul. We saw the truck drive off with it with mixed feelings. Our brown Amana refrigerator had served us well for 33 years, but after Katrina, its electrical system was dead.

While we were in "exile" in Texas, about 65 miles northwest of San Antonio, we saw a headline in the San Antonio newspaper urging Tom Benson, the owner of the Saints, New Orleans's NFL football team, to move the team permanently to San Antonio. After the Superdome was wrecked by Katrina, where 20,000 to 30,000 people had been locked up without food or water, Benson moved his team to San Antonio. Half the home games were to be played in San Antonio and the other

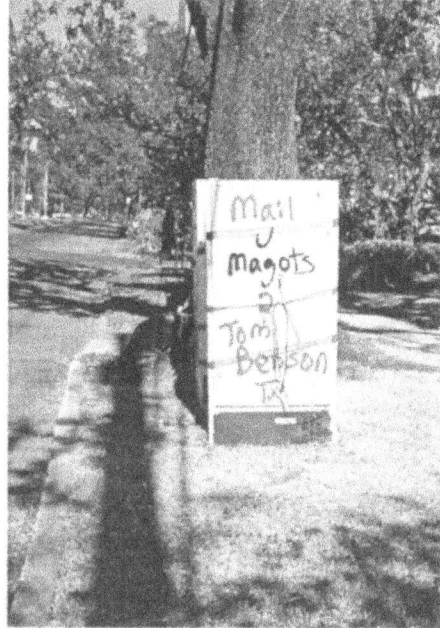

a

b

FIGURE 13.1. Refrigerator graffiti.
Photos by Harvey M. Bricker.

half in Baton Rouge. Now Benson was being pressured to keep the team in San Antonio, so that it would become the San Antonio Saints.

Tom Benson is a wealthy businessman whose fortune came from a string of automobile dealerships in San Antonio and New Orleans. Now he was threatening to deprive New Orleans of its NFL team. The people of Louisiana were outraged that he would even consider such a possibility, and those returning to New Orleans expressed their ire in refrigerator graffiti. As we drove around town, we saw the doors of many refrigerators covered in Tom Benson graffiti (Figure 13.1). One graffito said: "Benson inside. No open" (Figure 13.1a). Another proclaimed: "Mail magots 2 Tom Benson Tx" (Figure 13.1b). Thus, the burning question in New Orleans became: "Will the Saints go marching OUT?" Our mayor was quoted as saying: "Keep the Saints! Fire the owner!"

What in other cities are called *median strips* are called *neutral grounds* in New Orleans. They are the grassy dividers that separate lanes of traffic going in opposite directions along major thoroughfares of the city. In the days leading up to an election, they are covered with electioneering signs. Much to our surprise, we discovered that the neutral grounds in New Orleans were covered with such signs after the hurricane, but they were not about an election. It turns out that this was the method chosen by restaurants, grocery stores, florists, clinics, hospitals, and other businesses to announce that they were open. However, the majority of the signs we saw advertised the services of roofers, sheetrock removers, de-molders and de-mildewers who had descended on the city to assist with the rehabilitation of houses damaged by wind and water. Their brightly colored signs littered the neutral grounds, giving them a festive air.

Not all neutral grounds were so appealing. The broad neutral ground of West End Boulevard in the suburbs, which covers the space formerly occupied by a wide canal, had a grimmer purpose. It was one of the places to which the post-Katrina debris had been hauled, and it was a veritable mountain of fallen trees, ripped-out drywall, and wood from collapsed houses and roofs. FEMA was responsible for clearing the streets of debris. Thus, there were three categories of "stuff" on the street waiting to be hauled away: "white goods," debris, and household garbage. Those responsible for removing items in the first two categories refused to touch what they call *domestic refuse*. Residents had been told that garbage would be picked up once a week, but no garbage trucks collected it from our block during the first week after our return.

Life in post-Katrina New Orleans reminded me of the years when I lived in San Cristobal Las Casas in Mexico. One never knew what the day would bring. For example, on the day when our broken windows were being replaced, a garbage truck suddenly appeared on our block. Harvey rushed into the house, saying that the men on the truck would take anything that was bagged or in a garbage can. We rushed around the house emptying wastebaskets and bagging every bit of trash we could find, not knowing when another garbage truck would wander down our street. Then, about an hour later, a mailman suddenly showed up with some mail for us. Apparently, he had noticed that we had returned and came back with our mail. He brought us some more mail the next day as well. But the service was irregular.

People were visible in Uptown: on the streets, in restaurants and grocery stores, and in Audubon Park. The two grocery stores where we habitually shopped on Saturday morning—Langenstein's on Arabella Street and Dorignac's on Veterans Memorial Boulevard in the suburbs—were open and well stocked. At Langenstein's some days after our return, we were standing behind Peggy Wilson, our former city councilwoman, who told Harvey that Langenstein's was like a village square. And indeed it was! We had been there three times since our return, and each time it was full of people who were comparing notes on the condition of their homes and where they had spent the last two months. Uptown was alive and, if not well, it was certainly on the mend. People were subdued but going about their business with determination.

The streets of Uptown looked kind of frowzy, like a woman with uncombed hair. This was because the vegetation around people's homes had not been cared for during the previous two months, there was litter left by downed trees, and the dried leaves on broken branches hung down from trees that were still standing, not to mention the piles of debris left by roofers, the occasional refrigerator put out on the curb to be hauled away, and sidewalks broken by uprooted trees. Nevertheless, there was a clear sense that things were getting better here. People were scurrying around taking care of their affairs.

In contrast, Audubon Park, across St. Charles Avenue from Tulane, was an oasis whose serenity contrasted with the blighted neighborhoods in other parts of the city. Apparently, the soldiers of the National Guard camped there for some days after they were permitted to enter the city, and before they moved elsewhere, they cleaned up all the debris in the park, leaving it as neat as a pin. The grass on the golf course had been maintained, and a few golfers were in sight when we took a walk there one afternoon. It was rather comforting to have this park as a reminder of what much of the city was like in better days.

In the immediate aftermath of Katrina, our favorite restaurant in the suburbs set up a stand on a major thoroughfare and handed out food to everyone who walked by. Since then, Red Cross units from various states were distributing meals from vans in parking lots in many places. One of them was in the parking lot of our grocery store in the suburbs. We saw hot food in styrofoam clamshell containers being handed out at that location every Saturday at noon, even though it was by then almost three months after the storm. Such vans could be found parked in vacant lots in the city as well, where workmen and other people who came by were given hot food.

A few days after our return to New Orleans, I was allowed to visit the Anthropology building at Tulane to retrieve some books from my office. Our building was one of the few in New Orleans with a basement, which flooded with four feet of rainwater after the power went down and the sump pumps stopped working. During the hurricane, a large branch from the pecan tree next to our building fell on the roof and made a hole in it, the water bringing down the false ceiling in the faculty office below it. Work on cleaning up the mess in our building began on the weekend before our return. In order to enter it, I had to put on a white HAZMAT suit. Cold dry air was being pumped into the building in large plastic pipes to remediate the mold in some of the offices. The books in my office and Harvey's seemed to be in good condition, but other offices sustained serious damage to their contents; the building was never re-occupied and was eventually torn down.

The gradual repopulating of a city is an interesting phenomenon. The day we returned, only one family was living on our block. Two days later, someone moved back into the apartment building next to us. The next day, we saw the woman who lived across the street. A few days later, almost all the houses on our side of the street had people living in them. There was a concomitant daily increase in the number of people on the streets and cars on the roads. As more people returned,

FIGURE 13.2.   A house in the Lower Ninth Ward that had floated off its foundations
and come to rest on an overturned truck.
Photo taken by Harvey M. Bricker in January 2006, three months after the storm.

the debris was picked up at a faster rate. Next, we saw a truck on
Broadway cleaning out manholes and catch basins and crews cutting
the grass on the neutral ground. The pace of life was picking up palpably.
The city was losing its disheveled air.

One month after we returned to New Orleans some patterns had
begun to emerge. For example, it had been clear for weeks that people
who returned to the city and the surrounding region must have a place
to live and a source of income. It had also been clear for some time
that many people had one or the other, but not both. There were people
whose homes were not flooded and experienced little or no roof damage
who had lost their jobs. On the other hand, jobs in some sectors were
plentiful, but prospective employees could not return because they had
nowhere to live: Their homes had been severely damaged by the storm
or had floated off their foundations and collapsed (e.g., Figure 13.2).

It was a dynamic situation, with some employers shedding workers while others were trying to attract them. But the jobs people were leaving were very different from the ones that were opening up, and so also were the salaries. The problem of trying to match jobs with housing proved intractable, and this was making it impossible to predict what the eventual effect of Katrina on the region would be. This was one of the factors that delayed the return of people to southern Louisiana.

There were several stumbling blocks to restoring housing in the New Orleans area. One was insurance. The magnitude of Katrina's devastation was so great that there were not enough insurance adjusters to evaluate the properties in a timely fashion so that the owners could have the funds to make major repairs. The second was uncertainty over what needed to be done to the homes that were flooded to make them eligible for insurance again. Only FEMA could make this decision, and at that date it hadn't.

To be fair, FEMA had a number of different responsibilities, most of which it carried out well. Without FEMA, there would have been an army of refrigerators festering on the curbs and many more piles of debris in front of houses. FEMA protected the roofs of thousands of homes with blue tarps, even before their owners returned, and FEMA arranged for regular pickup of domestic refuse.

In some of the more devastated parts of town, FEMA would require owners to raise their houses above the flood plain and would pay part or all of the cost of this structural change. However, so soon after the hurricane, no one knew which houses needed to be raised and how much of that cost would be subsidized. This meant that owners could not move ahead with repairing their houses, because they did not know what kinds of repairs would be necessary. They remained paralyzed until these questions could be answered. This was a major factor that was slowing down the recovery effort.

Nevertheless, there were signs of life in the Lakeview area. We did not see many people there, but the number of piles of moldy plaster and sheetrock on the streets there was growing, indicating that some people had returned and had stripped their homes down to the studs, which was a necessary first step before their homes could be made habitable again. One month before, Lakeview looked like it had been hit by a neutron bomb that removed the people but left their homes standing in neat brown yards. A month later, the messy piles on the streets were a sign that there might be life in Lakeview after Katrina after all.

There was a new category of people in the city: "upstairs dwellers." There were many two-story homes in the city where the floodwaters affected only the first floor. In those cases, it was possible to limit the removal of sheetrock and plaster to the first floor, which had been stripped down to the studs, and the owners could live in the upper story. However, this was only possible where utilities had been restored, and there were still large parts of the city where there was neither electricity nor gas. Our energy company—Entergy—was very slow to provide power, which was the fourth factor that was preventing people from repopulating the city.

All this made me question the federal government's wisdom in insisting on evacuating the city so completely and for so long. If the people whose houses were damaged but not destroyed had been able to remain in their homes, instead of being prevented from returning for weeks, they could have protected their belongings from mold and theft, and the damage would not have been as great. The homes of many people were also damaged during Hurricane Betsey, but people placed tarps on their damaged roofs, protected many of their possessions in plastic, and dried out their homes right away, as did the people in the French Quarter who refused to leave this time. Much of the damage to people's homes was an unnecessary by-product of the mandatory evacuations and increased the cost of recovery dramatically.

Employment and housing, however, were not the only factors affecting people's decision of when or whether to return. Schools were equally important. Families began to return to Uptown and the surrounding parishes only when schools began to reopen. The Catholic schools in the region led the way, and almost overnight children became highly visible in Uptown. The officials of St. Bernard Parish, where virtually every home and business was flooded and many were completely destroyed, made reopening schools a high priority. They brought in trailers for this purpose, and as soon as it was announced that they would reopen, 250 students and their parents showed up for registration. The Catholic Church opened the first school in the French Quarter very soon after Katrina struck, and it filled very quickly. They gradually brought other schools on line, and as they filled, still others were opened. Those schools played an important role in bringing people back.

Unfortunately, the school board of Orleans Parish did not act so quickly, and the state had to take over most of the school system, which was all to the good. Several public schools became charter schools under the sponsorship of local universities, which realized that their employees would not return unless there were schools for their children to attend. This was a positive development, perhaps the only benefit of Katrina, giving the city an opportunity to build a new school system from the ground up.

Perhaps the most impressive response to Katrina we saw was how people categorized their misfortune. A woman whose roof was damaged said that she was lucky because her house was not flooded. A home with 18 inches of water was better than one with three feet of water. And so it went. One had only to look at a neighbor, friend, or acquaintance whose losses were greater than one's own to realize that it could have been worse. People rarely complained about their misfortune or invited pity. The response of the people we met to what Katrina did to them bears witness to the resilience of the human spirit.

14

RETIREMENT:
NO, IT WAS NOT THE END
OF THE WORLD

It was during the fall of 2004, the second year of my two-year term as chairman of the Anthropology Department, that Harvey first broached the question of retirement with me. He explained that his teaching obligations were heavier than most because, as the only Old World archaeologist in the department, he was responsible for the archaeology of most of the world, excluding only the Americas, courses for which were offered by three members of the faculty. Keeping up with the archaeology of so many regions and all time periods was particularly burdensome because the field changes rapidly, sometimes from week to week, in contrast to some of the other subdisciplines of anthropology (including my own), where new information appears less frequently. Furthermore, he wanted to retire while he was still professionally competent, still able to do his job the way it ought to be done. He did not want to hang on with declining abilities to the point when he became an embarrassment to himself and everyone else.

Harvey wanted me to retire at the same time as he did. If I continued teaching after he retired, our lives would still be governed by an academic schedule, and we could not take advantage of opportunities that might arise during the academic year.

Had I not been chairing the department, I probably would have been reluctant to retire at that time. But I was finding the chairmanship much more demanding than I anticipated, and I no longer had the stamina to handle the workload without wearing myself out. I had had the same thoughts about retiring while I was still effective in my job. There was also the book on Maya astronomy that we were anxious to finish before long. That project would move along faster if we were no longer teaching.

Therefore, shortly before the end of 2004, we informed the other members of the department and the dean of our intention to retire one year later, on December 31, 2005. In hindsight, our decision could not have been better timed, as later events were to prove.

My mentor, Evon Vogt, had died during the spring of 2004, and I had accepted an invitation to speak at his memorial service at Harvard during the third week of September in the same year. But some days before we had to fly up to Boston for that event, it became apparent that a storm then forming in the Gulf of Mexico might hit New Orleans. If that happened, the airport might be closed on the day of our scheduled departure. And if it made landfall further east, as was possible, the airport in Atlanta, where we had to change planes, might be closed. Either way, the chances of our arriving in time for the memorial service looked dicey. Therefore, we decided that it would be better to change our reservations to fly to Boston from Houston, even though to do so would increase the cost of our trip and mean driving to Houston and back, before and after our flights. This decision paid off, because Ivan veered east of New Orleans when it approached the coast, and the airport in Atlanta was closed on the day of our originally scheduled departure.

We left New Orleans well before the storm in the Gulf became the monster hurricane Ivan. We decided to take with us the necessary materials for our book and all our financial records, which we arranged to store at the home of a former student of Harvey's in Houston while we were in Massachusetts, in case Ivan did hit New Orleans and we were unable to return afterwards.

This was our first experience with packing our car for an evacuation ahead of a storm. By then, we had lived in New Orleans for 35 years, and not once had it been necessary to leave town for such a reason. Ironically, had it not been for the memorial service at Harvard, we would have stayed in New Orleans through Ivan. Our preparations for evacuation ahead of Ivan served as a dress rehearsal for what we would have to do in advance of Hurricane Katrina less than a year later (see Chapter 13).

But first I had to get through the second year of chairing my department and my last year of teaching. We had been given permission to make two faculty hires that year: a North American archaeologist to replace T. R. Kidder, who had moved on to a position at Washington University in Saint Louis, and a new position in Asian cultural anthropology. In addition, new space was being prepared in another building for the Center for Archaeology, and the basement of the Anthropology building was being renovated with a new teaching lab for archaeology. I had my hands full that year.

A year or so earlier, Joel Sherzer at the University of Texas in Austin had contacted me about archiving my tape recordings on his new website, the Archive of the Indigenous Languages of Latin America (AILLA), hosted by the Sid Richardson Library at his university. I thought it was a good idea, but was reluctant to commit myself then, because I knew that the task of preparing the meta-documentation for the recordings would be very time-consuming. Joel contacted me again at the end of April in 2005, with another invitation to participate in his project, for which he was writing a grant proposal. With my term as chairman ending in two months and the prospect of retirement six months later, I was more receptive to his invitation this time and agreed to offer my collection of Maya language tapes for inclusion in his grant proposal. Joel and I were in correspondence on this matter in the days leading up to Hurricane Katrina in late August.

My tape recordings were left behind in my study on the second floor of our house when Harvey and I evacuated from New Orleans in advance of Hurricane Katrina. Our house was spared from the wrath of the storm, but its severity emphasized the need for me to move my tapes into a more secure environment outside Louisiana as soon as possible. Therefore, Harvey and I decided to take advantage of our presence in Texas after the hurricane and make a visit to Austin, where we could meet with Joel and Heidi Johnson, the project manager of the website, to arrange for their receipt of my tapes and to discuss the nature of the meta-documentation I would have to prepare. In this way, the archiving of my tapes on the AILLA website became the first project I undertook after I retired from teaching at Tulane.

Harvey and I had originally planned to remain in our house in New Orleans after we retired. But the devastation wrought by Katrina and the forced evacuation of people from the city for so many weeks afterward made us realize that we needed to have somewhere to go outside Louisiana during hurricane season. We had no children who could take us in in an emergency, and we were reluctant to impose on friends like the Parrishes on a regular basis. Evacuations are stressful enough for young people and would become even more difficult as we aged. It was time for us to leave New Orleans or to establish a second home outside Louisiana to which we could repair during hurricane season. The money Harvey inherited from his mother after her death while we were in Texas made the second option feasible.

Because we intended to continue doing research and writing after retirement, we decided that we wanted our second home to be in a place with a university whose library was relevant for our needs. We also wanted it to be in the South, within one or two days driving distance from New Orleans. The two southern universities that fulfilled our criteria were in Austin, Texas, and Gainesville, Florida, both of which had collections that were comparable to those in the Latin American Library at Tulane (the Nettie Benson Library at the University of Texas and the Latin American Collection of the Smathers Library at the University of Florida). I had visited Austin many times over the years, but neither of us had ever been to Gainesville. In February 2006, we visited Gainesville for several days on our way back to New Orleans from a conference in Boca Raton. Our friend Susan Milbrath gave us a tour of the campus and the city, pointing out residential areas where we might live. We also met with Ken Sassaman, the chairman of the Anthropology Department at the University of Florida, who told us that, if we chose Gainesville for our second home, it would be possible to arrange courtesy appointments in his department that would give us access to the university's libraries and digital resources. Before leaving Gainesville, we consulted with a real estate company about the kind of housing available and its cost.

We returned to Austin for the same purpose during the first week of April, bringing along the tapes for the AILLA website.[1] We were equally well received by the chairman of the Department of Anthropology at the University of Texas, who told us that we could have courtesy appointments that would give us access to the University's library resources. However, the rental apartments and condos were considerably more expensive in Austin than in Gainesville, and property taxes were also higher. For these reasons, we decided on Gainesville as the place for our second home.

Sandwiched among our trips to Gainesville and Austin were two wonderful celebrations in honor of our retirement, hosted by our colleagues and former students in the Department of Anthropology and the Center for Latin American Studies. The retirement dinner in February fell on one of the weekends before Mardi Gras. It took place at a hotel in the French Quarter. Unbeknownst to the organizers of the dinner, they had chosen the night when the Krewe de Vieux was scheduled to parade in the French Quarter. While one of the organizers was at the microphone, there was a sudden burst of music outside the hotel, and the parade could be seen through the windows on one side of the dining room. Almost everyone rushed to the windows to see what was going on and then went outside to watch the parade. After it had passed, our friends drifted back in, and the program resumed where it had left off before the parade had come into view. For me, that Mardi Gras parade interrupting our retirement dinner was the perfect capstone to my career at Tulane in New Orleans!

The other event was organized by three of our former and then current students: Gaby Vail, Tim Knowlton, and Markus Eberl. It was a conference that took place during the second half of March in 2006, with presentations by a number of faculty colleagues and current and former students. In the same year, the proceedings were published as a Festschrift by *Human Mosaic*, the journal of the graduate students at Tulane.

Preparing for the move to Gainesville occupied most of the time we spent in New Orleans that spring. Many of the books in my faculty office were duplicates of ones I had at home. Instead of giving them to students as I had originally intended, we packed them in cartons to be shipped to our second home in Gainesville. Some pieces of furniture and household equipment that had accumulated during the years we had lived in New Orleans went along with the books in the moving van.

Once we were settled in our apartment in Gainesville, we went back to our book on Maya astronomy that we had last worked on during our exile in Texas after Hurricane Katrina. We gradually adjusted to the new rhythm of our lives, with the months from mid-June to mid-October in Gainesville and the rest of the year in New Orleans.

When our friends and acquaintances learned that we planned to retire at the end of 2005, some of them asked us whether we would use the time freed up from teaching to travel. We said no, that we had already traveled a great deal during our lives, and we intended to spend our time on research and writing. However, we did a considerable amount of traveling during the first seven years of our retirement. We had not anticipated that we might be in demand as lecturers, and most of our travels abroad involved professional meetings that facilitated our examination of original manuscripts relevant to our book, *Astronomy in the Maya Codices*.

In 2007, I was invited to participate in two conferences in Europe, one in Munich in November and the other five weeks later in Paris. The conference in Munich would place us within striking distance of Dresden, where the original Dresden Codex was curated in the Saxon State and University Library. And the one in Paris, if arranged well in advance, could give us access to the Paris Codex.

Harvey and I had thought for some time that we should make every effort to see all three Maya codices curated in Europe before completing our book, in order to resolve any questions that we might have about them. The conferences in Munich and Paris represented a golden opportunity to accomplish this goal by allowing us to see two of them in one year.

I asked Daniel Graña-Behrens, one of the organizers of the conference in Munich, for advice on how to get permission to see the Dresden Codex. He wanted to see it, too, and offered to accompany us to Dresden and to make the necessary arrangements in advance. Markus Eberl, then a graduate student at Tulane and a participant in the conference, joined us, and we set off on the train from Munich to Dresden together.

Dresden is in the eastern part of Germany near the Polish border. To get there meant traveling through much of the former German Democratic Republic, where we saw mile after mile of deserted factories and overgrown fields that were abandoned after reunification. In Dresden, we were welcomed by Dr. Thomas Bürger, the director of the Saxon State and University Library, who was eager to show us the Codex. In spite of its great age and the damage that it had suffered during the Second World War, it is still an exquisitely beautiful object, its colors still vibrant and the hieroglyphs in it drawn with a fine pen. And, as we hoped, inspecting the original Codex, even through the glass case in which it is housed, allowed us to resolve questions that even the best facsimile could not.

The Paris Codex is housed in the Bibliothèque Nationale de France in central Paris, and permission to see it was more difficult to obtain. My colleague Aurore Monod-Bequelin, the organizer of the conference in Paris, went to great lengths on our behalf, and we are truly grateful to her for her efforts to make it possible. The Paris Codex is also a beautiful object. We could not understand why only the center of each page had pictures and writing on it until we examined the original Codex and saw evidence that it had once been in water, loosening the original plaster around the edges of the page. In this case, we were actually able to handle it. We turned the pages carefully so that no more bits of plaster would flake off.

The third Codex we wanted to see is in Madrid, and for this we requested help from our friend and colleague Alfonso Lacadena. Our trip to Madrid, in October 2009, was combined with a visit with our friends Paul and Anny Mellars in Cambridge, England, where we gave a talk on our astronomical research. We went to Madrid first and were there for one week. Alfonso took us to the Museo de las Américas and joined us in the vault, where we were able to view the original Codex in a glass case. It was normally possible to rotate the case to bring the reverse side of the Codex into view, but because the case was being worked on at that time, it was not locked and could not be rotated without endangering the contents. Not to worry! Harvey asked whether we could lie down on the floor and inspect the other side of the Codex with flashlights from below. Yes, that was possible. The staff went off to get flashlights and pillows for us to lie on, and the three of us took turns lying on the floor as we examined the other side of the Codex.[2]

Thus, each of the visits to see the codices was an adventure in its own way. They were some of the most exciting days of my life.

Astronomy in the Maya Codices was published by the American Philosophical Society, to which I had been elected a member in 2002 (as explained in Chapter 12). The book appeared during the summer of 2011 and received the Society's John Frederick Lewis Award for the best book published that year. In 2013, it received the Donald S. Osterbrock Book Prize for Historical Astronomy from the Historical Astronomy Division of the American Astronomical Association.

The timing of the publication of our book may have had something to do with the amount of traveling we did in 2012, as did the fact that the 5,125-year Maya era was scheduled to end on the winter solstice that year. For some people worldwide, but not for the Maya themselves, the end of the Maya era meant that the world would end on December 21, 2012. The media were full of reports of people preparing for the Apocalypse. Museums arranged exhibitions to explain the Maya calendar to the public, various organizations sponsored conferences, some scholarly, others not, and many tours of the Maya area were scheduled for the last two weeks of December. Books, some predicting, others debunking, the end of the world appeared in bookstores in the United States and Europe.[3]

Harvey and I were invited to participate in six conferences or workshops and a Wilderness Travels tour that year, most of them having to do with the Maya calendar.[4] The tour brought us to Mexico and Guatemala for sixteen days during the last two weeks of December. It began at Uxmal, where I gave a talk on the Maya calendar in the afternoon of the day of the winter solstice. The solstice itself had taken place without incident during the wee hours of the morning, and most or all of us slept through it. Two days later, our group set off for the visits to archaeological sites in Chiapas, followed by two days at Tikal and one day at Kaminaljuyu in Guatemala. We returned to New Orleans on New Year's Eve.

I had wanted to visit Yaxchilan in Chiapas for many years, but the logistics of getting there were daunting. The site sits on a bluff overlooking the Usumacinta River and was accessible only by a long boat ride down the river. In recent years, however, the development of the corridor for tourism along the west side of the river had made it feasible to contemplate such a visit, and the Wilderness Travels tour provided the means.

The nineteen members on our tour stayed at a hotel called *Escudo Jaguar* about fifty feet from the river. We boarded two small launches early the next morning and pulled up at the small landing below the site after an hour. At that hour, we were the only tourists at the site, it was still cool, and the surroundings were magical. It was easy to imagine what life at the site must have been like during the heyday of Maya civilization. For me this visit was a dream come true. I had cut my teeth on the inscriptions of Yaxchilan in the 1970s, and they were the centerpiece of the course I began teaching in 1981. In this way, a circle in my life had closed.

But there was another sense in which my life had come full circle on that journey along the Usumacinta River in eastern Chiapas. To explain that requires some knowledge of the prior history of the region. At the time of the Conquest, this area was inhabited by people who spoke an ancestral form of the Chol language. They resisted Spanish rule by raiding Christianized settlements in the highlands to the east and west of the region and were so bellicose that, over time, the Spaniards gradually moved them away from their original location into towns where they could be more closely monitored.

One group of these people, who were known as the *Chol Lacandons*, were resettled in the towns of Tila, Tumbala, and Palenque, in what is today the northern part of the state of Chiapas. Harvey and I had driven through this region on several visits to Chiapas, and I was aware that Chol was the language of Palenque.

The original homeland of the Chol Lacandons in what is today eastern Chiapas was gradually repopulated by another group of Maya, who spoke a dialect of Yucatecan Maya, and they, as well as their language, also became known as *Lacandon*. The original Lacandons who spoke Chol remained in the northern part of the state, and their replacements from the southern parts of the Yucatan peninsula spoke the Yucatecan dialect that is now known as *Lacandon*.[5]

Trudi Blom, in whose home I lived for four months in 1968 and 1969, was a close friend of the Lacandons who lived in the settlement of Naha in eastern Chiapas. One of the rooms in her house was available for their use whenever they came to San Cristobal, and they came and went during the time I was living there. The men wore their hair long and loose on their shoulders, and their clothing consisted of a *huipil* or dress-like garment and leather sandals. The women wore a shorter version of that garment over skirts. Their hair was arranged in a single long braid ending in a stuffed bird with bright feathers. They were the only Maya whose traditional religion had not been influenced by Christianity.

One of my students, Dale Davis, and her husband, Michael Rees, whose dissertation was being directed by Ed Edmonson, decided to carry out their dissertation research among this group of Lacandons, she on their music and he on their kinship terms. I put them in touch with Trudi, and she assisted them with their arrangements to work in Naha. They had been there for some time in 1974, when Harvey and I planned to be in Chiapas after the visit we made to Guatemala on a mission for Tulane's Center for Latin American Studies (see Chapter 7). They suggested that we visit them for a few days while they were in Naha, an invitation we were happy to accept.

In those days, the Selva Lacandona where the Lacandons lived was accessible only by a small plane, on foot, or on the back of a horse or a mule. Mike and Dale went back and forth between Naha and San Cristobal in small planes, and they suggested that we do the same. A pilot named Captain Luna was making regular flights into the jungle, and we made arrangements with him to take us to Naha. At the last minute, Trudi and Angel Robles, the head of Indian Affairs in Chiapas, hitched a ride in our plane as far as one of the Tzeltal towns in the region, to broker a dispute that had arisen there. Also on the plane were provisions that Mike and Dale had asked us to bring along. There had not been room for them on the plane on which they had flown to Naha a day or so before us.

As we flew over the mountains into eastern Chiapas, I was amazed at how much the landscape had changed in that region since I had last flown over the area in the mid-1960s. Where before, the slopes of the mountains had been completely covered with trees, there were now cornfields almost everywhere. Speakers of Tzeltal were on the move, colonizing their way into the eastern jungle, encroaching on lands claimed by the Lacandons and coming into conflict with each other, as evidenced by the mission of the other passengers on our plane, who had been dropped off earlier in a Tzeltal town.

Eventually, we came to a small lake in the middle of the jungle, and our pilot began his descent. We landed in a small clearing near the lake, unloaded our gear from the plane, and shook hands with the pilot, who promised to return in three days time to take us back to San Cristobal. Then he took off in his plane, and we were left alone in the middle of the jungle.

After ten minutes or so, we heard the sound of "slurp, slurp, slurp" coming from the lake, and shortly thereafter, we heard voices. Mike and Dale were coming to pick us up from the airstrip in a large mahogany dugout poled by a Lacandon. We got into the dugout with our gear and were poled across the lake to the settlement of Naha, where we would spend the next days getting acquainted with the people and life in Naha.

Mike and Dale had planned to take us into the jungle to visit another Lacandon settlement not far away. But there were rumors that guerrillas were in the area that summer (1974), and they decided that we would be safer if we stayed near the settlement of Naha. This was, after all, only a few years after the student uprising and massacre in Mexico City; some of the survivors had fled into the jungle and were causing trouble there.

The head of Naha was an old man named Chan Kin Viejo, who lived in a long house divided into separate rooms for his multiple wives. He remembered when, as a boy, he saw the anthropologist Alfred Tozzer making the first ethnographic study of his community and its language in 1904.[6]

We arrived when the first maize crop was ready for harvest and watched as two of his wives prepared green corn tamales for the ceremony in honor of the first fruits of the season. The settlement had a large god house (*ku na* in Lacandon), where all ceremonies took place. It was a long structure with a thatched roof that reached almost to the ground, leaving space for light to come in and for people sitting on the ground outside to see what was going on within. Mike and Harvey could enter the god house; Dale and I could not because we were women. Nevertheless, I was able to see the rows of god pots, into the open mouths of which lumps of incense were ladled from an incense board, a prototype of which can be seen in the Dresden Codex. Outside the god house was an old dugout, in which the mead called *balche* was fermenting.

The Lacandons made bows and arrows to sell to tourists at Palenque and other places. Harvey was interested in comparing their techniques for making arrows from chunks of flint with the ones used for making flint tools during Palaeolithic times. Mike had arranged with one of the Lacandon flint knappers to show Harvey how he made his arrows, and Harvey reciprocated by demonstrating how he made Palaeolithic stone artifacts.

I was, of course, interested in the culture of Naha, but I had a more burning question: Were Yucatecan Maya and Lacandon mutually intelligible languages? I found it possible to communicate with the men in Naha, but this may have been because they had had some experience conversing with speakers of Yucatecan Maya in the course of their travels to other places in search of customers for their bows and arrows. On the other hand, I had no success in conversing with Lacandon women, but they may have had their own way of speaking that differed from the men, as is sometimes the case in such communities.

Chan Kin Viejo was a gifted storyteller, and one evening he sat in his hammock and recounted a myth, parts of which I could understand, if only from his striking gestures and voice modulations, as he mimicked the different creatures in the myth. It was a treat to listen to such a talented raconteur.

Our days in Naha passed quickly. Happily, Captain Luna did arrive on the appointed day, circling over the settlement three times to announce his arrival and give us time to get across the lake to the airstrip to meet his plane.

A few years later, a dirt road was built from Palenque into eastern Chiapas, and the Lacandons of Naha moved away from the lake to a new location next to the road. Learning of their impending move, Mike Rees returned to Chiapas with two filmmakers to record the move and its effect on the community.[7] At a later date, in an effort to keep an eye on the Zapatista rebels who were operating in the jungle and to exert some control over the flood of refugees coming from western Guatemala during their civil war, the Mexican Army built a road along the Usumacinta River, which forms the boundary between Chiapas and Guatemala. I hoped to travel on that road some day in order to understand what had happened to the Lacandons I had visited in 1974.

That opportunity came in 2012, when Harvey and I were invited to serve as guest lecturers on a Wilderness Travels tour in connection with the end of the previous Maya era on the winter solstice of that year (as explained earlier). I suggested that the tour include a visit to four sites in Chiapas: Palenque, Tonina, Bonampak, and Yaxchilan. I was particularly interested in visiting Yaxchilan, whose inscriptions I had lectured on for so many years. That involved a boat trip on the Usumacinta River that I was anxious to make.

However, it was the bus ride along the border that made the greatest impression on me. Unbeknownst to me before then, the road from Palenque to Naha had made it possible for the Chols to return to their original homeland from which they had been forcibly removed during the Colonial period! They were highly visible all along the road, having established towns and even the tourist hotel where we spent two nights. As sophisticated townspeople, they have become, once again, the dominant ethnic group in eastern Chiapas, competing with the Tzeltals for land once regarded by the Lacandons as entirely their own and hemming them in on all sides.

NOTES

1. Joel and Heidi received the grant for digitizing my tapes and placing them on the AILLA website, and I spent much of 2007 preparing the metadata for the individual recordings. I returned to Austin for a week at the end of February in 2008 to show the graduate student

who had digitized my tapes where one text ended and another began, so that they could be separated and called up individually on the website. The original tapes are now archived in the Library of the American Philosophical Society in Philadelphia.

2. Alfonso insisted that I take advantage of our presence in Madrid to examine the original version of Diego de Landa's *Relación de las Cosas de Yucatán* in the Royal Academy of History, and he sat beside me commenting on it as I looked at every page. He also took us to Cifuentes, Landa's birthplace, and we visited the church where his body is interred in the wall of a side chapel. It was there that we saw the copy of the painting of Landa that hangs in the church in Izamal in Yucatan.

    Knowing of Harvey's interest in Palaeolithic archaeology, Alfonso and his wife, Laura, took us on an excursion over the weekend that included a visit at the site of Atapuerca. Also included in our itinerary that weekend was a visit to the Moorish fortress of Castillo de Gormaz.

3. For example, Anthony F. Aveni, *The End of Time: The Maya Mystery of 2012* (Boulder: University Press of Colorado, 2009); David Stuart, *The Order of Days: The Maya World and the Truth about 2012* (New York: Harmony Books, 2011).

4. We had speaking engagements in Memphis (Tennessee) in March, Providence (Rhode Island) in June, Miami (Florida) in July, Dresden (Germany) in September, and in Washington, DC, and Leiden (Netherlands) in October. With such a schedule, most of our free time was spent preparing our presentations for the next trip. I had accepted Katie Sampeck's invitation to participate in an ethnohistory conference at the John Carter Brown Library in Providence because of the opportunity it would provide for me to examine the original manuscript of the *Calepino de Motul* that was curated there. I was, at that time, in the process of familiarizing myself with a facsimile edition of the manuscript in preparation for writing a historical grammar of Yucatecan Maya, the project that followed our work on the Maya codices.

5. A more circumstantial historical treatment appears on pages 46–50 of my book, *The Indian Christ, the Indian King: The Historical Substrate of Maya Myth and Ritual* (Austin: University of Texas Press, 1981).

6. Alfred M. Tozzer, *A Comparative Study of the Mayas and the Lacandones* (New York: Macmillan, 1907).

7. Brian Huberman (producer), Ed Hugetz (producer), and Mike Rees (anthropologist), *To Put Away the Gods: Two Ways to Palenque* (film, 1989).

15

LOOKING BACK

In retrospect, I now see that my life has been punctuated by a series of journeys, beginning two weeks after my birth in 1940, when my mother and I evacuated to Shanghai ahead of the Japanese occupation of Hong Kong. Although I was then too young for that first journey to be construed as "transformational," the location of my birth in Hong Kong was itself an outcome of my parents' transformational journeys to China, my father from Vienna in 1932 and my mother from London in 1935.

My interest in language may have been stimulated by some of my early experiences in Shanghai, where I was exposed on a daily basis to multiple kinds of English: the British dialect of my mother, her parents, and her sisters; the heavily accented English of my German-speaking father and his sister; and the pidgin English of our amahs. Having to cope with so much variation in a single language, not to mention the background chatter in Chinese, may have sensitized me to variation in pronunciation and vocabulary.

My second journey, from China to the United States in 1947, resulted in my transformation from a speaker of British English to a speaker of the Northwest Coast dialect of American English that I retained for the rest of my life, except for a few locutions borrowed from the southern dialect of American English, such as "you-all." My Americanization was completed officially in 1953, when I was naturalized along with my parents and my brother and sister who had been born in Shanghai.

My next transformational journey took me from Seattle to Stanford University in California and from there to Germany in 1960, where I found my calling as an ethnologist in what was then a peasant village twelve kilometers south of Stuttgart. There I learned that, above all, I enjoyed the experience of being immersed in an unfamiliar culture and gradually learning how to navigate in it. Although my professional training in anthropology did not begin until after I graduated from Stanford, the six months I spent in Germany during my sophomore year sowed the seeds for what eventually became my life's work.

It was also at Stanford that I began to form an opinion of what constitutes effective teaching. The lecture courses I found most interesting were those that had a pedagogical directionality—a beginning, middle, and an end—demonstrating the cumulation of knowledge. They contrasted with survey courses that catalogued the strengths and weaknesses of different approaches, without considering how the differences might be reconciled. Whenever possible in my own teaching in later years, I structured my courses in terms of the first model.

My next journey took me to Harvard University in Massachusetts, where I spent some of the best years of my life. It was there that I met my husband, Harvey Bricker, whom I married in 1964. Harvard served as the springboard for my next journey, this time to Chiapas in southern Mexico, where I conducted my first fieldwork between 1963 and 1969 in a Maya peasant community. It was also during the time I was affiliated with Harvard that I first accompanied Harvey to France, where I lived in a peasant village for a total of three years. These experiences in Chiapas and southern France, when compared with the ones I had had in southern Germany, gave me a sense of what might be universal in the peasant way of life.

My first teaching experiences took place at Harvard, giving me multiple opportunities to teach Tzotzil to college students with the assistance of a native speaker and presaging one of the paths that my future teaching would take. My involvement as a teaching assistant in undergraduate courses in biological evolution, primitive religion, and summer fieldwork emphasized my interdisciplinary training at Harvard, which would later be reflected in my own teaching and research.

From Chiapas I moved on to Tulane University in New Orleans, Louisiana, where Harvey and I were offered positions for one year. That journey involved the teaching of an entirely new Mayan language from scratch. With the help of a native speaker of Yucatecan Maya, I was able to keep one lesson ahead of the class. At the end of that year, Harvey and I were able to negotiate contracts that ultimately resulted in New Orleans becoming our home and Tulane the center of our professional lives for the next 35 years.

The wonderful resources in the Latin American Library and the Middle American Research Institute at Tulane and the opportunity to co-teach the Spoken Yucatecan Maya course with Elut on a biennial basis produced a significant transformation in my research agenda from the anthropology of Tzotzil-speaking communities in highland Chiapas to Maya-speaking ones in the state of Yucatan. And that, in turn, was partly responsible for my moving back in time, first to the nineteenth century and eventually into the sixteenth century in search of documents written by literate Mayas that would help me reconstruct the history of grammatical change in their language. Along the way, I developed an interest in the impact of Spanish colonialism on Maya culture and language, followed by a preoccupation with the hieroglyphic writing system that first came into use more than a millennium earlier. Harvey's assistance with computer programming once I fell under the spell of epigraphy led him into research on the pre-Columbian astronomy of the Maya and a thirty-year collaboration with me on that endeavor. That in turn, led to short journeys to archaeological sites in Mexico, Guatemala, and Honduras to examine astronomical texts and cosmograms in murals and on the façades and benches of buildings and to Dresden, Paris, and Madrid to verify our interpretations of astronomical passages in the surviving Maya codices. Each of these journeys informed the others and ultimately figured in our teaching of several generations of Tulane students.

The teaching opportunities offered by a research university like Tulane, with its variety of related disciplines, had a major impact on my scholarship. The spontaneity and infectious curiosity of undergraduates, combined with the budding professional interests of graduate students, created such a synergy with my research that I found that I was more productive during the semesters when I was teaching than during those when I was on leave. Accordingly, I limited my sabbaticals to one semester, instead of two, and occasionally took an additional one-semester leave at other times when a project required my full attention (and funding for this purpose was available). The contact with students in lecture courses and seminars and as research assistants was especially important in moving my ethnohistorical, epigraphic, and linguistic research forward in ways that I could not have done alone.

All that was brought to an end somewhat prematurely by our evacuation from New Orleans ahead of Hurricane Katrina, which harked back to my first journey to Shanghai ahead of the Japanese occupation of Hong Kong two weeks after my birth, where my family and I weathered the rest of World War II, and to my second journey to Seattle ahead of the Communist occupation of Shanghai seven years later. Evacuations seem to have bracketed the course of my life. The most recent journey brought us to Gainesville, Florida, where we pre-evacuate each year at the beginning of the hurricane season.

All of these journeys have resulted in experiences that enriched my life, and most of them have led to twists and turns in my scholarly path. They placed me in contact with new groups of people, who expanded my personal and professional horizons. Given this trajectory, it seems that life as an ethnologist was the most meaningful one I could have had.

INDEX

A

Abreu Sierra, Xavier (Mayor of
     Merida), 177
Abri Pataud (France), 97–99, 103,
     130, 153
Acapulco (Mexico), 206
achiote (annatto pigment), 196
agriculture, 258, 267
Aguilar de Marrufo, Alba Isela, 175
Ah Canul, 217
air raids, 22–23
Ake (Yucatan), 197
American Anthropological
     Association, 155, 158n12
American Oriental Society, 25
American Philosophical Society, 34,
     268, 299, 305–306n1
Andrews, E. Wyllys V, 176–177,
     196
Andrews, Joann, 196, 220n11
Anthropology, Department of
     (Tulane), 142–143, 286, 293,
     297
Antigua (Guatemala), 152
archaeology, xiii, 85, 94, 97, 153–
     154, 177, 239–240, 251,
     293–294
Archive of the Indigenous
     Languages of Latin America
     (AILLA), 295–296, 305
Archivo General de Indias (Seville,
     Spain), 131
Archivo Nacional de Centroamérica
     (Guatemala City), 152
astrology, 267
astronomical syntax, 244
astronomy, historical, xiii, 246, 252,
     255, 260–261, 265–266, 293,
     297, 299–300, 313

Atapuerca (Spain), 306n2
Athens (Greece), 59–61
Atlanta (Georgia), 275, 294
Aurora University (Shanghai),
     24–25
Austin (Texas), 295–296, 305
Aveni, Anthony F. xv, 255, 262,
     265

B

balche (mead), 304
Barrera Vásquez, Alfredo, 146, 162,
     185, 217
barrio (ward of town), 206
Becal (Campeche), 217
Behrman, Suzan, 48, 50, 53–54, 57–
     58, 64, 66, 68–69
Belize, 151, 154
Berlin (Germany), 6, 8, 53, 61,
     230–231
     East Berlin, 62–65, 74–75n4, 231
     West Berlin, 62–65
Beutelsbach (Germany), 50–53, 65–
     66, 75nn5–7, 104
     changes in, 75nn5–6, 109n7
Bey, George, 220n8
"Big Foot," 243–244
Bill, Cassandra R., 261
Bischofsheim (Germany), 53
"Blackmen," 130
Blair, Barbara, 47
Blom, Frans, 114, 135, 143
Blom, Gertrude "Trudi" Duby, 114,
     131, 135–136, 301–302
Boerner, Peter, 51
bomb shelter, 23
Bonampak (Chiapas), 208, 262,
     305
Boone, Elizabeth H., 265

Bordeaux (France), 99

Bordes, François, 99–100

Borgia Codex, 265

Boston (Massachusetts), 105, 113, 294

Bouyssou, Paulette, 93, 95–96, 100

"Boy," 19, 21

Bradburn, Anne S., xv, 167, 169–171, 174, 186, 262

Bradburn, Donald, 262

Breeden, Jane, 48, 50, 69, 83

Bricker, Florence Miller, 100, 102–103, 264, 267, 270n11, 278–279

Bricker, George Harry, 100, 103, 279

Bricker, Harvey M., xiv, 83, 91, 95, 101, 103–106, 123, 127, 129–131, 135, 141–142, 145, 147–148, 167, 170, 174, 192, 195, 197–198, 202–203, 205, 211, 219, 228, 230–231, 239–240, 245–246, 247n5, 251, 267, 275, 277–278, 280, 282, 286, 295, 302–303, 305, 306n2, 312–313
  archaeological research in France, 92–93, 97–100, 107, 153–154
  collaboration with, 252–266, 298–300
  marriage to, 85–87

British Honduras, 151, 153

Brno (Moravia), 230

Brown, Annie Horowitz, 4, 13, 16

Brown, Mendel, 3, 4, 10n1, 13, 16, 18, 22–23

Brown, Lilly, 4–5, 13, 16, 22, 26n2

Brown, Millicent "Peter," 4, 5, 13, 16, 22

bull–impersonators, dance of, 122

Bürger, Thomas, 298

Burton, Jane, 70

C

calendar, Maya, 251–254, 268–269n1, 300
  haab, 252, 258
  initial series, 251–252
  long count date, 255, 257–258
  tzolkin, 251–252, 255, 257–258, 265

Calkini (Campeche), 216–217

Calnek, Edward E., 151

Cambridge (England), 299

Cambridge, University of, 106

Campeche (Campeche), 125

Canché Yah, Valerio, 175

Cancuc (Chiapas), 151–152

Cancun (Quintana Roo), 190, 205–207, 209, 219

Cárdenas, Venustiano (President of Mexico), 149

Carnaval, fiesta of, 128, 130–133, 137n7, 143–145, 152, 192, 195, 197, 199, 203

Carrillo Puerto (Quintana Roo), 147–150

Caste War of Yucatan, 136, 147–151, 185, 197, 219n2, 225–226, 229
  Maya letters of, 146–147, 185, 197, 225–226, 229

Castillo de Gormaz (Spain), 306n2

Cazéres (France), 154

cenote (sinkhole), 205

Center for Latin American Studies (Tulane), 142, 157n9, 166–167, 176, 297, 302

Chamula (Chiapas), 114, 131–132, 134, 136, 144, 151, 157n3, 243

Chamula Center, 132–134

Chancah (Quintana Roo), 150

Chan Kin Viejo, 303–304

Chan Kom (Yucatan), 187, 190–191, 199, 202, 206, 212, 218

Chan Kom bus, 190–191

Chan Santa Cruz (Quintana Roo), 147, 154; *see also* Carrillo Puerto

Chenalho (Chiapas), 131–132, 137n7, 151–152, 157n3

Chiaotung University (Shanghai), 8

Chiapas (Mexico), xiv, 71, 84, 106, 114–115, 118, 120, 123, 126, 129–131, 143–146, 151, 156n3, 200, 208, 216, 300–302, 305, 312–313

Chicago, University of, 225

Chichen Itza (Yucatan), 83, 126, 187, 189–190, 204, 212, 262

China, xiii, xv, 311

Chinese News Agency (Berlin), 6, 8, 53

Chol (language), 301

Chol Lacandons, 301

Chols, 305

Christensen, Mark Z., 228

Chuchiak, John F., IV, 228

Chumayel, Book of Chilam Balam of, 227

Chunhuhub (Quintana Roo), 226, 229

Chunyaxche (Quintana Roo), 219

Cifuentes (Spain), 220n5, 306n2

Cilley, Ann, 48, 50, 53–54, 57–58, 64, 66, 69

cinco calles (intersection of five streets), 194–195, 211, 219

Civil Assembly Centre, 14–15, 17, 20, 24, 28, 29n12

Clay, Berle, 97, 99, 135, 141

Cline, Patricia, 50, 69

Clottes, Jean, 153

Coba (Quintana Roo), 201, 219

codices, Maya, 243–245, 260–261, 265
  divinatory, 265
  grammar of, 244
  reading order of, 244

Coe, Michael D., 239

cofradía (sodality), 226, 228–229

Cohuo Po'ot, Francisca, 187–188, 191–192, 195–196, 200, 203–208, 210–212, 214–215, 218–219

Collier, George A., 87, 113–115, 117, 134–135, 156–157n3, 162–163

Collier, Jane Fishburne, 115, 117, 134

colonia (new quarter of a town), 208, 216

color classification, 39, 43n2, 173–174

comisario (head of small town), 186, 201–202

commensuration, 266

compadre (co-father), 209

computer science, 87, 252

concordances, 227–229, 234n4

constellations, 255–257, 262–263
  Gemini, 262, 264

Libra, 257
Orion, 257, 265
Pleiades, 257, 262
Sagittarius, 262, 264
Scorpius, 257, 262
Copan (Honduras), 264–265
Corozal (Belize), 151
Couch, Arthur, 87
Cowen, Scott, 275, 280
cross–dating, 255, 257–258,
    269–270n6
cultural astronomy, 267
Cuncunul (Yucatan), 191, 214–215
curing ceremonies, 119–120,
    133–134

D
dance–drama, 192, 205
Davis, Virginia Dale, 302–304
debt peonage, 212
decipherment, 239
    phonetic, 254
Diebold, Richard, 89
Dresden (Germany), 298, 313
Dresden Codex, 245, 254, 260,
    298–299
    eclipse table in, 254–255, 257
    Mars table in, 266
    seasonal tables in, 260, 266
    Venus almanac in, 257, 259
    Venus table in, 255, 257–259
Du Bois, Cora, 82, 85, 87–90,
    108nn3–4
Durbin, Marshall, 135, 147,
    161–164
Dzitnup (Yucatan), 191–192, 194,
    203, 205, 209, 214–215,
    220n3
Dzul, Domingo, 217

Dzul de Po'ot, Ofelia, 166–168,
    170–173, 175, 198, 203–204,
    215

E
Eberl, Markus, 297–298
Ebtun (Yucatan), 185–196, 203,
    205–206, 209, 211–212, 214–
    215, 218–220, 225, 229
    church in, 170n11, 188–189, 195
    crosses in, 193
    dialect of, 233
    map of, 194–196, 211, 219
Ebtun, Titles of, 185, 187, 189, 194,
    211–212, 214, 228
editorships, 153, 155–156
    American Anthropologist, Book
        Review Editor of, 153
    American Ethnologist, Editor of,
        155
    *Supplement to the Handbook of
        Middle American Indians*,
        General Editor of, 156
Edmonson, Barbara, 141, 143, 170,
    195, 203
Edmonson, Munro S., 123, 129,
    135, 141, 143, 152–153, 161,
    170, 195, 197, 201–203, 302
Ek Balam (Yucatan), 201, 220n8
Elmendorf, Mary, 187, 190, 204
Elut, *see* Po'ot Yah, Eleuterio
emblem glyphs (at Yaxchilan), 242
Ephrata (Pennsylvania), 279
epigraphy, Maya, 244, 251, 267,
    313
ethnobotany, Maya, xv, 167–171,
    203–204, 267
    in Dresden Codex, 246
    in Hocaba, 167–171

ethnohistory, xiii, 146, 151–154,
    157–158n9, 239, 267, 313
  courses in, 152
ethnology, xiii, 239, 251, 314
etiquette (in Zinacantan), 122–123
evil eye, 133–134

F
Far East, 85
Fasching, 54–56, 130, 143
FEMA (Federal Emergency
    Management Agency), 281,
    284, 286
fiestas, 99, 117–118, 121–122, 127–
    129, 131–134, 137n7, 144–
    145, 157n3, 192, 195, 199,
    197, 203, 212
  in Chamula, 131–134, 144
  in Chenalho, 131–132, 137n7
  in Ebtun, 212
  in Hocaba, 144–145, 197
  in Merida, 192, 195, 199
  in Spain, 99
  in Telchaquillo, 213, 220n11
  in Tizimin, 203
  in Zinacantan, 117–118, 121–122,
    127–129, 131, 157n3
Fischer, Ann, 154–155
Fischer, Jack, 154–155
Florida, University of (Gainesville),
    296
folklore, 132, 267
food technology, 40
football, 282–284
formal eliciting, 115–116
France, 251, 312
Fredericksburg (Texas), 277–278
  German and Mexican roots of
    cuisine, 277

Good Samaritan Center, 279
French (language), 95–96
Fullington, Mary, 35
Furbee, Louanna, 216–217

G
Gainesville (Florida), 296–297, 314
Gamboa, Góngora, María Teresa,
    175–176
Gates, William, 143
General Inquirer, 87, 107n2
Germany, xiv, 49–56, 61–66, 227,
    311
Gossen, Eleanor "Elli" Adam, 132
Gossen, Gary, 132, 137n7
Governor's Palace (Uxmal), 257,
    262–264
Graff, Donald H., 261
Graham, Ian, 239
Graña–Behrens, Daniel, 298
Grandfather impersonators
    (Zinacantan), 127, 131,
    180–181n7
Grandmother impersonators
    (Zinacantan), 127, 131
Greenleaf, Richard E., 157–158n9
gremio (sodality), 215
Guadalupe, fiesta of, 121–122
Guadalupe, Virgin of, 210
Guatemala, 146, 300, 302, 305, 313
Guggenheim, John Simon, 242

H
Hamburg (Germany), 230–231
Hamburg, University of, 225
Hanks, William F., 228, 233–234n1,
    234n2
Hansen, Craig A., 228
Harden, Robert Lee, 69

Harvard Chiapas Project, 118–119,
    131, 232
Harvard University (Massachusetts),
    25, 71, 81–82, 83–103
    passim, 105, 113, 123, 126,
    129, 219, 240, 293–294, 312
    experience of women at, 87–90
    student unrest at, 105–106
    Tozzer Library at, 185, 228
Haviland, John B., 103
henequen, 162, 197
Hernández, Christine, 170n7
"He–Sheba Contest," *see* Mardi
    Gras
hieroglyphs, Mayan, xiv, 239–240,
    242
history, 146
Hocaba (Yucatan), 142, 144–145,
    147, 161, 167, 169–170, 172,
    186, 197, 203, 213, 218,
    220–221n12, 228, 233, 246,
    262
    cofradía book from, 228
Hoesch, Herbert, 52, 96
Honduras, 313
Hong Kong (China), 3–4, 8, 10,
    311, 314
Honouliuli Internment Camp
    (Hawaii), 26n3
Houston (Texas), 275–278, 280,
    294
Howells, William, 81, 85, 89
Huastec (language), 195
humor, xiii, 114–115, 117–118, 123,
    128, 130, 239
    ritual humor, 94, 96, 127, 130,
    133, 136, 145
hurricanes
    Betsey, 289
        Ivan, 275, 294
        Katrina, 275–276, 280–281, 286,
            288–290, 294–295, 297, 314
        Rita, 278, 280

I
Ibero–Amerikanisches Institut
    Preussischer Kulturbesitz
    (Berlin), 230–231
interviewing, xiii
Ivan, *see* hurricanes
Izamal (Yucatan), 197

J
Jacobsen, Marcey, 137n7
Johnson, Heidi, 295, 305
Justeson, John S., 240, 265–266

K
Kabah (Yucatan), 126
Kalin, Jesse, 69
Kaminaljuyu (Guatemala), 300
Kaqchikel (language), 240
Katrina, *see* hurricanes
Kaua (Yucatan), 192, 220n3, 229
Kaua, Book of Chilam Balam of,
    229–231
Kelley, David H., 251
Kidder, Tristram R., 294
K'iche' (language), 240
kinship, 121
Knowlton, Timothy W., 297
Köngas Maranda, Elli, 87
Koufas, Anna, 56–57, 60
Kuluba (Yucatan), 219
Kurjack, Edward, 195–196, 211
Kwakiutl Indians, 70

L
Labna (Yucatan), 126
Lacadena, Alfonso, 299, 306n2

Lacandon (language), 301, 304
Lacandons, 301–305
La Gravette (France), 100
Lake Charles (Louisiana), 280
Lake Pontchartrain (Louisiana), 280–281
Lamb, Weldon, 217
Lamphere, Louise, 83
Landa, Diego de, 145, 197, 228, 306n2
Latin (language), 38
Latin American Library (Tulane), 142, 156n3, 185, 225, 227–228, 296, 312
Laughlin, Robert M., 103, 113, 115, 129–130
Les Eyzies (Dordogne, France), 93–94, 97, 99, 106
Lespinasse (Dordogne, France), 93, 94
Li, Fang–Kuei, 84
libélula (dragonfly), 199
liberation, 23–24
linguistics, xiii, 239, 267, 313
literacy, Maya, 146
Lockhart, James, 157–158n9
London (England), 3–4, 23, 66–68, 76n11, 95–96, 104, 153, 157, 311
Louisiana, 107
Lounsbury, Floyd G., 239, 255
Ludlow, Florence, 35
lunar eclipse, 265
Lyon (France), 99

M
machine translation, 42
MacLeod, Barbara, 242
Madrid (Spain), 299, 306n2, 313

Madrid Codex, 260–261, 270n7, 299
maestro cantor (lay assistant to Catholic priest), 211
Maler, Teobert, 230
Manzanar Internment Camp (California), 26n4
Maranda, Pierre, 87
Mardi Gras, 56, 143–145, 195, 199, 297
Marhenke, Randa, 277–278
MARI, *see* Middle American Research Institute (Tulane)
Marín Mendoza, Ermilo, 142, 144–145, 161
Marren, Janet, 137n7
Martínez Hernández, Juan, 225
Maxwell, Judith M., 176–177
May Day, 63–65
May, Francisco, General, 148–149
May May, Miguel Angel, 177
Mayacal (calendrical programs), 252
Mayapan (Yucatan), 200n11
Mayordomo Rey, 117
McQuown, Norman A., 217, 225
meaning in life, 73–74
Mellars, Anny 106, 299
Mellars, Paul, 106, 299
Merida (Yucatan), 123, 126–127, 145–147, 151, 162–164, 166, 169, 175–178, 186–187, 192, 195–197, 203–204, 215–216, 218–219, 226–228
Mesoamerica, 141–142, 254
metate (grinding stone), 220
meteorology, 267
Metzger, Duane, 71, 115

Mexican Revolution of 1910–1917, 189

Mexico, 34, 81, 84–85, 92–93, 98–99, 105, 113, 123, 144, 151, 205–206, 208, 251, 300, 313

Mexico City, 113–114, 123, 131

Middle American Research Institute (Tulane), 135–136, 142–143, 254, 312

Milbrath, Susan, xv, 296

Miram, Helga–Maria "Pauline," 229–231

Miram, Wolfgang, 229, 231

modular arithmetic, 258, 260

Monod–Becquelin, Aurore, 299

Moors and Christians, 130

morphology, 242

Motul (Yucatan), 197

Motul, Calepino de, 225, 257, 306n4
authenticity of, 225, 233–234n1

Movius, Hallam, 83, 99, 101, 103, 105, 130

Munich (Germany), 298

Museo de las Américas (Madrid), 299

music, 36–37, 52, 54, 61, 63, 117–118, 127

myths, 70, 146
myth and history, relationship between, 146, 151

N

naabal (layered thick tortillas), 214

Nabenchauc (Zinacantan), 121, 129, 136n3

Na Bolom, 114, 131, 135

Nagy, Christopher L. von, 261

Naha (Chiapas), 301–305
god house in, 303

Nanney, Herbert, 52, 54

National Academy of Sciences, 267, 271n15

National Endowment for the Humanities, 230

National Guard, 279

New Orleans (Lousiana), 107, 135, 141, 143–145, 147, 151, 154, 199, 205, 229–230, 275–277, 280–284, 294–296, 300, 314
Audubon Park in, 285–286
Caribbean and French elements of cuisine, 277
French Quarter in, 289–290, 297
Lakeview (district), 281, 288–289
Orleans Parish, 290
repopulation of, 286–287
Saints football team, 282–284
Uptown (district), 281, 285, 289

New Year's ceremonies, 242–243

novena, 210, 212, 220n10

Nunkini (Campeche), 217

O

Oliver, Douglas L., 82, 85

oral tradition, xiii, 70

Orie, Olanike "Nike," 233

Osuna, David, 37

P

Palenque (Chiapas), 215–216, 242–243, 254, 301, 304

Palenque Round Tables, 243, 247n8, 251, 255

Palmer, Betty, 19

papadzules (soft tacos filled with chopped hard–boiled eggs), 170

Paris (France), 66, 95, 100, 106–107, 298

Paris Codex, 255, 261–262, 298–299, 313
  zodiacal almanac in, 255–256, 262, 264

Parrish, Barbara, 276, 295

Parrish, Donald, 276–277, 295

Parrish ranch (Texas), 276–277, 279

participant–observation, xiii, 116, 121

Patchakan (Belize), 151

Paxton, Merideth, 261

Peabody Museum (Harvard), 81, 89–90, 114

Pelzel, John, 85

Périgueux (Dordogne, France), 107

Pichucalco (Chiapas), 124–125

Piedras Negras (Guatemala), 254

Pig's Head, Dance of, 212–213, 220n11
  in Ebtun, 212
  in Telchaquillo, 213, 220n11

Po'ot, Crescencio, 149, 157n5

Po'ot Yah, Eleuterio "Elut," 146–150, 157n4, 160–181, 185, 190, 192, 197–198, 203–205, 215–216, 218, 226, 233, 239, 262, 313

Prague (Czech Republic), 230, 234n6

print shop, 37

prioste (steward of sodality), 210

procreation, 267

Proskouriakoff, Tatiana, 82–83, 107n1

psychiatric technician, 71–73

Public Record Office (London), 153, 157

Pyrénées, 153–154, 251

R

rainmaking ceremonies, 213–214
  in Dresden Codex, 245
  in Ebtun, 213–214
  in Hocaba, 213–214, 245
  offerings made during, 245–246

ramillete (bouquet), 212

rebellions, Maya Indian, 145, 147, 151–152

Redfield, Robert, 219n1

Reed, Nelson, 136, 146, 150

Rees, Michael J., 302–305

Reese, Thomas, 176

refresco (soft drink), 197, 205

refugees, 63, 65

Reifler, Anne Irene Millicent, 23, 42, 91, 94, 267–268, 275

Reifler, Bernhard, 6–7

Reifler, Consuela Margaret, 35–36, 42, 91

Reifler, Dorothea, 6, 8, 13, 16–17, 25, 28n7, 33, 35

Reifler, Erwin, 5–7, 8–9, 13, 16–17, 41–42, 83, 84, 90–91, 204

Reifler, Frank, xv, 14–16, 18–19, 22, 24, 41–42, 91, 104, 108n5, 267

Reifler, Henrietta Brown, 3–5, 9, 13, 15, 40, 69, 83–84, 91, 96, 108n5, 267, 276

Reifler, Joschia, 5–6

Reifler, Michaela Thea, 36, 42, 91, 108n5

Reifler, Viktoria Zentner, 3, 6, 8

relleno negro (stuffing made of chopped egg whites and

burnt chile wrapped around whole egg yolks), 198–199, 213, 220n6
reparations, 28n11
Ringle, William M., 220n8, 227–229, 234n4
ritual, 146
ritual humor, *see* humor
ritual kinship, 121
Robertson, Merle Greene, 243
Robles, Angel, 302
Rome, 53–54, 93–94
Rosenmontag, 54–56, 130; *see also* Mardi Gras and San Sebastian, fiesta of
Rottweil (Germany), 55, 130, 143
Roys, Ralph L., 185, 219–220n3, 228

S
Saint Bernard Parish, 289–290
saint exchange, 214–215, 221n14
Salonika (Greece), 57–61
Sampeck, Katie, 306n4
San Antonio de Padua, fiesta of in Ebtun, 212–213
San Bartolomé, patron saint of Ebtun, 212, 214
San Cristobal las Casas (Mexico), 84, 113–114, 119–120, 123, 126–127, 132–134, 136, 137n7, 156n3, 200, 243, 284, 301–303
San Lorenzo, fiesta of (Zinacantan), 117, 221n14
San Sebastian, fiesta of (Zinacantan), 56, 128, 130–133; *see also* Mardi Gras
Santa Rita (Yucatan), 201

Sassaman, Kenneth E., 296
Satayoshi, Mrs., 19, 23
Sayil (Yucatan), 126
Schele, Linda, 239, 243, 278
Schwäbisch (dialect of German), 53
science, 38–39, 47–48, 266
Scott, David, 39
Seattle (Washington), 25, 33–43, 68, 81, 90–92
Shanghai (China), 3–4, 8, 13–26, 27–28n5, 33–34, 41–42, 67, 204, 311, 314
Sherzer, Joel F., 295, 305
Shiremanstown (Pennsylvania), 279
Smailus, Ortwin, 225–227, 234n2
Smith, Helen Bricker, 267, 278
Smith, Jeffrey, 77n13
Smith, Mary Elizabeth "Betsy," 260–261, 265
Smith–Stark, Thomas C., 252, 254, 269n2
solar zenith passage, 264
Southeast Asia, 84, 87–90
Spain, 97–99, 154
    fiestas in, 99
Spanish (language), 36–38, 42, 43n3, 114–116, 123, 210, 216
Spindler, George D., 52, 54, 69
Stanford University (California), 47–77 *passim*, 311–312
Stephens, John Lloyd, 201
Stilo, Mary Jane, 34
Stockton State Mental Hospital (California), 71–73
Stone, Philip, 87
Stucky, Philip, 39
summer solstice, 258–259
syntax, 242

T

Tabi, Documentos de, 228
Tahmek (Yucatan), 228
tamarindito (tamarind sweet), 206
Tambourets, Les (France), 153–154
Tarshis, Lorie, 61, 69
Taylor, George E., 25, 33
Taylor, Walter, 97–99
teaching, 141–142, 254, 260–261,
   265, 275, 295, 311–313
Tekanto (Yucatan), 153
   Maya documents from, 228–229
Tekom (Yucatan), 214–215
Telchaquillo (Yucatan), 213,
   220n11
Temozon (Yucatan), 201
Tenney, Cece, 34
Texas, University of (Austin), 243,
   295–296
Thompson, J. Eric S., 239, 244–245
Thompson, Philip C., 152, 226,
   228
Tikal (Guatemala), 300
Tila (Chiapas), 301
Timm, Arley, 47, 69
Tixcacalcupul (Yucatan), 214–215
Tizimin (Yucatan), 203
Tizimin, Book of Chilam Balam of,
   227
Tojolabal (language), 216
Tonina (Chiapas), 305
Totonicapan (Guatemala), 152
Totonicapan revolt of 1820, 152
Toulouse (France), 153
Tozzer, Alfred M., 303
"triangulation," 258
trigonometry, 39, 41, 260
Tulane University, xiv, 107, 134–
   136, 141–145, 161–163, 176–

177, 239, 265–266, 269n2,
   276, 281, 285–286, 297–298,
   312–313
Herbarium at, 167, 169–170,
   180n3
student unrest at, 144–145
students of, 178, 243, 260, 313
tulix (dragonfly), 199
Tulum (Quintana Roo), 208
Tumbala (Chiapas), 301
Tuxtla Gutierrez (Chiapas),
   127–128
Tzeltal (language), 216
Tzeltal rebellion of 1712, 151
Tzeltals, 302, 305
Tzotzil (language), 84–85, 92–93,
   95, 102–103, 113–117, 119,
   127, 129–131, 133, 135, 142,
   145, 161, 188, 216, 232–233,
   239–240, 312–313
   tape recordings of, 117–118, 123,
   127–129, 295

U

Uayma (Yucatan), 214–215
Uitti, Carol, 38
unrest, student, 105–106, 144–145
   at Harvard, 105–106
   at Tulane, 144–145
Usumacinta River (Chiapas), 300–
   301, 305
Uxmal (Yucatan), 126, 257, 262,
   264, 300

V

Vail, Gabrielle "Gaby," 261, 276–
   277, 297
Valencia (Spain), 97

Valladolid (Yucatan), 185–187, 190, 192, 195, 199–200, 202–204, 207, 215, 219–220n3

Venus, 257–259, 262, 264–265

Vienna (Austria), 5–8, 60, 68

Villa Rojas, Alfonso, 187, 190, 219n1

Villahermosa (Tabasco), 125, 127, 251

visita (tour of inspection), 226

Vogt, Catherine Christine "Nan" Hiller, 130, 267

Vogt, Eric, 103

Vogt, Evon Z. "Vogtie," 81, 89, 101–102, 105–106, 113–114, 117–118, 120, 129–130, 267, 293

W

Ward, James, 164, 166

Washington, University of (Seattle), 25, 38, 41, 84, 108n5

Wauchope, Robert, 143, 156

Webster, David, 264

Welden, Arthur L., 167

Whittaker, Virgil, 61, 70

Wilder, Laura Ingalls, 35

Wilderness Travels, 300–301, 305

Willey, Gordon R., 84, 89

Williams, Stephen, 85, 89

Wong, Anna May, 53, 74n2

X

Xcalacoop (Yucatan), 212

Xcaret (Quintana Roo), 219

Xlapak (Yucatan), 126

Xultun (Guatemala), 265

Y

Yajalon (Chiapas), 216

Yap, Lorene, 83

Yaxcaba (Yucatan), 189

Yaxchilan (Chiapas), 208, 242, 254, 300–301, 305

Yucatan (Mexico), 142, 145, 150–151, 186–187, 195, 262, 264

Inquisition in, 145

Yucatan peninsula, 146

Yucatecan Maya (language), 135, 142, 145–147, 161, 178, 185–186, 191, 200–201, 225, 312–313

alphabet for, 174, 200–201, 232, 239, 304

conversation in, 218–219

dictionary of, 164, 166, 173–175, 186, 200, 203, 211, 215, 229, 233, 262

grammar of, 173–174, 185, 229, 233, 239, 306n4, 313

"real" Maya, 188

spelling variation, 231–233, 234n7, 234–235n9

tape–recordings of, 146–147, 149–151, 191, 203, 218–219, 295

Yugoslavia, 57

Yu Yuen Road (Shanghai), 14, 15, 20, 29n12

Z

Zimbalist, Michelle "Shelley," 113

Zinacantan (Chiapas), 99, 101, 109n6, 114–115, 117–119, 121–122, 132–134, 137n7, 157n3, 188, 221n14, 232–233

Zinacantan Center, 117, 120, 122, 127–129, 131

Zinacantec Indians, 84, 114, 116, 118–120, 123, 133, 232, 239

www.ingramcontent.com/pod-product-compliance
Lightning Source LLC
Chambersburg PA
CBHW061754260326
41914CB00006B/1106